Constitutional Law

Sixth Edition

2021 Supplement

2021 Supplement

Constitutional Law

Sixth Edition

Erwin Chemerinsky
Dean and Jesse H. Choper Distinguished Professor of Law
University of California, Berkeley School of Law

Published by Wolters Kluwer in New York.

Wolters Kluwer Legal & Regulatory U.S. serves customers worldwide with CCH, Aspen Publishers, and Kluwer Law International products. (www.WKLegaledu.com)

To contact Customer Service, e-mail customer.service@wolterskluwer.com, call 1-800-234-1660, fax 1-800-901-9075, or mail correspondence to:

Wolters Kluwer
Attn: Order Department
PO Box 990
Frederick, MD 21705

Printed in the United States of America.

1 2 3 4 5 6 7 8 9 0

ISBN 978-1-5438-4627-0

About Wolters Kluwer Legal & Regulatory U.S.

Wolters Kluwer Legal & Regulatory U.S. delivers expert content and solutions in the areas of law, corporate compliance, health compliance, reimbursement, and legal education. Its practical solutions help customers successfully navigate the demands of a changing environment to drive their daily activities, enhance decision quality and inspire confident outcomes.

Serving customers worldwide, its legal and regulatory portfolio includes products under the Aspen Publishers, CCH Incorporated, Kluwer Law International, ftwilliam.com and MediRegs names. They are regarded as exceptional and trusted resources for general legal and practice-specific knowledge, compliance and risk management, dynamic workflow solutions, and expert commentary.

Contents

Preface

The Sixth Edition of *Constitutional Law* was published in early 2020 and is current through the end of October Term 2018 and includes the decisions through June 2019. This Supplement focuses on the two terms since then: October Term 2019 and October Term 2020.

There have been many major constitutional rulings in these two terms. *Chapter 1* includes a discussion of three important cases concerning the constitutional requirements for standing: *Uzuegbunam v. Preczewski, California v. Texas,* and *Transunion v. Ramirez.* It also includes the discussion of third-party standing from the abortion case, *June Medical Services L.L.C. v. Russo.* Finally as to mootness it includes the Supreme Court dismissing as moot a challenge to the New York City gun law in *New York Rifle & Pistol Association, Inc. v. City of New York.*

Chapter 3, on executive power, includes the two major cases concerning subpoenas of financial institutions doing business with President Trump, *Trump v. Vance* and *Trump v. Mazars USA.* It includes an important case concerning the appointments power, *United States v. Arthrex.* It also includes a major case limiting Congress's power to restrict presidential removal of agency heads, *Seila Law LLC v. Consumer Financial Protection Bureau* and a subsequent case applying it, *Collins v. Yellen.* This chapter also includes the case that states can require that electors vote a particular way in the Electoral College, *Chiafalo v. Washington.*

Chapter 5 includes *Ramos v. Louisiana*, where the Court held that the Sixth Amendment's unanimous jury requirement applies to the states.

Chapter 6 includes a case on the Takings Clause, *Cedar Point Nursery v. Hassim.*

Chapter 8 presents *June Medical Services L.L.C. v. Russo*, where the Court struck down a Louisiana law requiring doctors to have admitting privileges at a hospital within 30 miles in order to perform an abortion.

Chapter 9 presents three new cases about freedom of speech: *Barr v. American Association of Political Consultants*, which struck down a part of the law limiting "robocalls" as a content-based restriction on speech; *Mahanoy Area School Dist. v. B.L.*, concerning First Amendment protection for student speech over social media; and *Americans for Prosperity v. Bonta*, which invalidated a requirement for non-profits in California to disclose their donors.

Finally, *Chapter 10*, which focuses on religion, includes the many cases from the last two years concerning the Free Exercise Clause. In *Fulton v. City of Philadelphia*, the Court clarified and applied the test used for this constitutional provision. In *Our Lady of Guadalupe School v. Morrissey-Berru,* the Court said that religious schools cannot be sued under employment discrimination laws for the choices it makes as to their teachers. There also are two rulings from the Court invalidating restrictions on religious gatherings, imposed to stop the spread of COVID-19. Also, *Espinoza v. Montana Department of Revenue* overruled a decision of the Montana Supreme Court, striking down a state law which would have provided tax credits to parents who sent their children to religious schools.

I, of course, will prepare annual Supplements every year and always appreciate comments and suggestions from users of the book.

Erwin Chemerinsky
Berkeley, California
July 2021

Constitutional Law

Sixth Edition

2021 Supplement

Chapter 1

The Federal Judicial Power

B. Limits on the Federal Judicial Power

3. Justiciability Limits

b. Standing

i. Constitutional Standing Requirements

In October Term 2020, the Supreme Court decided three major cases concerning the constitutional requirements for standing.[1] First, is a claim for nominal damages enough to support standing. The Court said yes.

UZUEGBUNAM v. PRECZEWSKI
141 S. Ct. 792 (2021)

Justice THOMAS delivered the opinion of the Court.

At all stages of litigation, a plaintiff must maintain a personal interest in the dispute. The doctrine of standing generally assesses whether that interest exists at the outset, while the doctrine of mootness considers whether it exists throughout the proceedings. To demonstrate standing, the plaintiff must not only establish an injury that is fairly traceable to the challenged conduct but must also seek a remedy that redresses that injury. And if in

---

1. In addition to the cases discussed in this chapter, the Court also dismissed two other cases for lack of standing. In *Trump v. New York*, 141. S. Ct. 530 (2020), the Court, 6-3, held that the plaintiffs lacked standing to challenge the constitutionality of the President's memorandum directing exclusion of undocumented citizens from apportionment bases for congressional apportionment from the census. The Court said that any injury to the plaintiff was too speculative. In *Carney v. Adams*, 141 S. Ct. 493 (2020), the Court dismissed for lack of standing a challenge to a Delaware law that required political balance on the courts. The Supreme Court said that the plaintiff lacked standing because Adams did not show that he was "able and ready" to apply for a judicial vacancy in the imminent future, and therefore failed to show a personal concrete and imminent injury necessary for Article III standing.

the course of litigation a court finds that it can no longer provide a plaintiff with any effectual relief, the case generally is moot. This case asks whether an award of nominal damages by itself can redress a past injury. We hold that it can.

I

According to the complaint, Chike Uzuegbunam is an evangelical Christian who believes that an important part of exercising his religion includes sharing his faith. In 2016, Uzuegbunam decided to share his faith at Georgia Gwinnett College, a public college where he was enrolled as a student. At an outdoor plaza on campus near the library where students often gather, Uzuegbunam engaged in conversations with interested students and handed out religious literature.

A campus police officer soon informed Uzuegbunam that campus policy prohibited distributing written religious materials in that area and told him to stop. Uzuegbunam complied with the officer's order. To learn more about this policy, he then visited the college's Director of the Office of Student Integrity, who was directly responsible for promulgating and enforcing the policy. When asked if Uzuegbunam could continue speaking about his religion if he stopped distributing materials, the official said no. The official explained that Uzuegbunam could speak about his religion or distribute materials only in two designated "free speech expression areas," which together make up just 0.0015 percent of campus. And he could do so only after securing the necessary permit. Uzuegbunam then applied for and received a permit to use the free speech zone.

Twenty minutes after Uzuegbunam began speaking on the day allowed by his permit, another campus police officer again told him to stop, this time saying that people had complained about his speech. Campus policy prohibited using the free speech zone to say anything that "disturbs the peace and/or comfort of person(s)." The officer told Uzuegbunam that his speech violated this policy because it had led to complaints. The officer threatened Uzuegbunam with disciplinary action if he continued. Uzuegbunam again complied with the order to stop speaking. Another student who shares Uzuegbunam's faith, Joseph Bradford, decided not to speak about religion because of these events.

Both students sued a number of college officials in charge of enforcing the college's speech policies, arguing that those policies violated the First Amendment. As relevant here, they sought nominal damages and injunctive relief. Respondents initially attempted to defend the policy, stating that Uzuegbunam's discussion of his religion "arguably rose to the level of 'fighting words.'" But the college officials quickly abandoned that strategy and instead decided to get rid of the challenged policies. They then moved to dismiss, arguing that the suit was moot, because of the policy change. The students agreed that injunctive relief was no longer available, but they disagreed that the case was moot. They contended that their case was still live because they had also sought nominal damages. The District Court dismissed the case, holding that the students' claim for nominal damages was insufficient by itself to establish standing.

The Eleventh Circuit affirmed.

II

To satisfy the " 'irreducible constitutional minimum' " of Article III standing, a plaintiff must not only establish (1) an injury in fact (2) that is fairly traceable to the challenged conduct, but he must also seek (3) a remedy that is likely to redress that injury. There is no dispute that Uzuegbunam has established the first two elements. The only question is whether the remedy he sought—nominal damages—can redress the constitutional violation that Uzuegbunam alleges occurred when campus officials enforced the speech policies against him.

In determining whether nominal damages can redress a past injury, we look to the forms of relief awarded at common law. "Article III's restriction of the judicial power to 'Cases' and 'Controversies' is properly understood to mean 'cases and controversies of the sort traditionally amenable to, and resolved by, the judicial process.'" The parties here agree that courts at common law routinely awarded nominal damages. They, instead, dispute what kinds of harms those damages could redress.

Both sides agree that nominal damages historically could provide prospective relief. The award of nominal damages was one way for plaintiffs at common law to "obtain a form of declaratory relief in a legal system with no general declaratory judgment act." For example, a trespass to land or water rights might raise a prospective threat to a property right by creating the foundation for a future claim of adverse possession or prescriptive easement. By obtaining a declaration of trespass, a property owner could "vindicate his right by action" and protect against those future threats. Courts at common law would not declare property boundaries in the abstract, "but the suit for nominal damages allowed them to do so indirectly."

The parties disagree, however, about whether nominal damages alone could provide retrospective relief. Stressing the declaratory function, respondents argue that nominal damages by themselves redressed only continuing or threatened injury, not past injury.

But cases at common law paint a different picture. Early courts required the plaintiff to prove actual monetary damages in every case. Later courts, however, reasoned that *every* legal injury necessarily causes damage, so they awarded nominal damages absent evidence of other damages (such as compensatory, statutory, or punitive damages), and they did so where there was no apparent continuing or threatened injury for nominal damages to redress. Admittedly, the rule allowing nominal damages for a violation of any legal right, though "decisively settled," was not universally followed — as is true for most common-law doctrines. And some courts only followed the rule in part, recognizing the availability of nominal damages but holding that the improper denial of nominal damages could be harmless error. Yet, even among these courts, many adopted the rule in full whenever a person proved that there was a violation of an "important right."

That this rule developed at common law is unsurprising in the light of the noneconomic rights that individuals had at that time. A contrary rule would have meant, in many cases, that there was no remedy at all for those rights, such as due process or voting rights, that were not readily reducible to monetary valuation. By permitting plaintiffs to pursue nominal damages whenever they suffered a personal legal injury, the common law avoided the oddity of privileging small-dollar economic rights over important, but not easily quantifiable, nonpecuniary rights.

The next difficulty faced by respondents and the dissent is their inability to square their argument with established principles of standing. Because redressability is an " 'irreducible' " component of standing, no federal court has jurisdiction to enter a judgment unless it provides a remedy that can redress the plaintiff's injury. Yet early courts routinely awarded nominal damages alone. Certainly, no one seems to think that those judgments were without legal effect. Those nominal damages necessarily must have provided redress.

Because nominal damages were available at common law in analogous circumstances, we conclude that a request for nominal damages satisfies the redressability element of standing where a plaintiff's claim is based on a completed violation of a legal right.

This is not to say that a request for nominal damages guarantees entry to court. Our holding concerns only redressability. It remains for the plaintiff to establish the other elements of standing (such as a particularized injury); plead a cognizable cause of action,; and meet all other relevant requirements. We hold only that, for the purpose of Article III standing, nominal damages provide the necessary redress for a completed violation of a legal right.

Applying this principle here is straightforward. For purposes of this appeal, it is undisputed that Uzuegbunam experienced a completed violation of his constitutional rights when respondents enforced their speech policies against him. Because "every violation [of a right] imports damage," nominal damages can redress Uzuegbunam's injury even if he cannot or chooses not to quantify that harm in economic terms.[*]

Chief Justice ROBERTS, dissenting.

Petitioners Chike Uzuegbunam and Joseph Bradford want to challenge the constitutionality of speech restrictions at Georgia Gwinnett College. There are just a few problems: Uzuegbunam and Bradford are no longer students at the college. The challenged restrictions no longer exist. And the petitioners have not alleged actual damages. The case is therefore moot because a federal court cannot grant Uzuegbunam and Bradford "any effectual relief whatever."

The Court resists this conclusion, holding that the petitioners can keep pressing their claims because they have asked for "nominal damages." In the Court's view, nominal damages can save a case from mootness because any amount of money—no matter how trivial—"can redress a past injury." But an award of nominal damages does not alleviate the harms suffered by a plaintiff, and is not intended to. If nominal damages can preserve a live controversy, then federal courts will be required to give advisory opinions whenever a plaintiff tacks on a request for a dollar. Because I would place a higher value on Article III, I respectfully dissent.

The Court sees no problem with turning judges into advice columnists. In its view, the common law and (to a lesser extent) our cases require that federal courts open their doors to any plaintiff who asks for a dollar. I part ways with the Court regarding both the framework it applies and the result it reaches.

Begin with the framework. The Court's initial premise is that we must "look to the forms of relief awarded at common law" in order to decide "whether nominal damages can redress a past injury." Because the Court finds that "nominal damages were available at common law in analogous circumstances" to the ones before us, it "conclude[s] that a request for nominal damages satisfies the redressability element of standing where a plaintiff's claim is based on a completed violation of a legal right."

Any lessons that we learn from the common law, however, must be tempered by differences in constitutional design. The structure and function of 18th-century English courts were in many respects irreconcilable with "the role assigned to the judiciary in a tripartite allocation of power." Perhaps most saliently, in England "all jurisdictions of courts [were] either

mediately or immediately derived from the crown,",", an organizational
principle the Framers explicitly rejected by separating the Executive from
the Judiciary. This difference in organization yielded a difference in operation. To give just one example, "English judicial practice with which
early Americans were familiar had long permitted the Crown to solicit
advisory opinions from judges."

It is in any event entirely unclear whether common law courts would
have awarded nominal damages in a case like the one before us. There is
no dispute that "nominal damages historically could provide *prospective*
relief," because such awards allowed "plaintiffs at common law to obtain
a form of declaratory relief in a legal system with no general declaratory
judgment act." Yet the petitioners in this case no longer seek prospective relief. Although they initially asked for a declaratory judgment and
a preliminary injunction, they abandoned those requests once the college
rescinded the challenged policies.

The Court is correct to note that plaintiffs at common law often received
nominal damages for past violations of their rights. Those awards, however, were generally limited to situations in which prevailing plaintiffs
tried and failed to prove actual damages. Notwithstanding the Court's pro-
testations to the contrary, nominal damages in such cases were in fact a
"consolation prize," awarded as a hook to allow prevailing plaintiffs to at
least recover attorney's fees and costs.

At bottom, the Court relies on a handful of indeterminate sources to
justify a radical expansion of the judicial power. The Court acknowledges that "the rule allowing nominal damages for a violation of any legal
right . . . was not universally followed," but even this concession under-
states the equivocal nature of the historical record. I would require more
before bursting the bounds of Article III.

Today's decision risks a major expansion of the judicial role. Until now,
we have said that federal courts can review the legality of policies and
actions only as a necessary incident to resolving real disputes. Going forward, the Judiciary will be required to perform this function whenever a
plaintiff asks for a dollar. For those who want to know if their rights have
been violated, the least dangerous branch will become the least expensive
source of legal advice.

In an effort to downplay these consequences, the Court argues that plaintiffs who seek nominal damages will often be able to seek actual damages
as well. In this case, for example, the Court notes that Uzuegbunam and
Bradford "would have satisfied redressability if instead of one dollar in
nominal damages they sought one dollar in compensation for a wasted
bus fare to travel to the free speech zone." *Ante,* at 802. Maybe they would

have, and maybe they should have. The Court is mistaken, however, to equate a small amount of actual damages with the token award of nominal damages. The former redresses a compensable harm and satisfies Article III, while the latter is a legal fiction with "no existence in point of quantity."

The best that can be said for the Court's sweeping exception to the case-or-controversy requirement is that it may itself admit of a sweeping exception: Where a plaintiff asks only for a dollar, the defendant should be able to end the case by giving him a dollar, without the court needing to pass on the merits of the plaintiff's claims.

Perhaps defendants will wise up and moot such claims by paying a dollar, but it is difficult to see that outcome as a victory for Article III. Rather than encourage litigants to fight over farthings, I would affirm the judgment of the Court of Appeals.

***

In *California v. Texas*, the Court dismissed, for lack of standing, a constitutional challenge to the Patient Protection and Affordable Care Act. The case is important because 21 million people receive health care through the Act.

CALIFORNIA v. TEXAS
141 S. Ct. 2104 (2021)

Justice BREYER delivered the opinion of the Court.

As originally enacted in 2010, the Patient Protection and Affordable Care Act required most Americans to obtain minimum essential health insurance coverage. The Act also imposed a monetary penalty, scaled according to income, upon individuals who failed to do so. In 2017, Congress effectively nullified the penalty by setting its amount at $0.

Texas and 17 other States brought this lawsuit against the United States and federal officials. They were later joined by two individuals (Neill Hurley and John Nantz). The plaintiffs claim that without the penalty the Act's minimum essential coverage requirement is unconstitutional. Specifically, they say neither the Commerce Clause nor the Tax Clause (nor any other enumerated power) grants Congress the power to enact it. They also argue that the minimum essential coverage requirement is not severable from the rest of the Act. Hence, they believe the Act as a whole is invalid. We do not reach these questions of the Act's validity, however, for Texas and the other plaintiffs in this suit lack the standing necessary to raise them.

I

We begin by describing the provision of the Act that the plaintiffs attack as unconstitutional. The Act says in relevant part:

"(a) **Requirement to maintain minimum essential coverage**
"An applicable individual shall . . . ensure that the individual, and any dependent . . . who is an applicable individual, is covered under minimum essential coverage . . . .
"(b) **Shared responsibility payment**
"(1) **In general**
"If a taxpayer who is an applicable individual . . . fails to meet the requirement of subsection (a) . . . there is hereby imposed on the taxpayer a penalty . . . in the amount determined under subsection (c).
"(2) **Inclusion with return**
"Any penalty imposed by this section . . . shall be included with a taxpayer's return . . . for the taxable year . . . ."

As first enacted, the Act set forth a schedule of penalties applicable to those who failed to meet its minimum essential coverage requirement. The penalties varied with a taxpayer's income and exempted, among others, persons whose annual incomes fell below the federal income tax filing threshold. And the Act required that those subject to a penalty include it with their annual tax return. In 2017, Congress amended the Act by setting the amount of the penalty in each category in § 5000A(c) to "$0," effective beginning tax year 2019.

Before Congress amended the Act, the Internal Revenue Service (IRS) had implemented § 5000A(b) by requiring individual taxpayers to report with their federal income tax return whether they carried minimum essential coverage (or could claim an exemption). After Congress amended the Act, the IRS made clear that the statute no longer requires taxpayers to report whether they do, or do not, maintain that coverage.

In 2018, Texas and more than a dozen other States (state plaintiffs) brought this lawsuit against the Secretary of Health and Human Services and the Commissioner of Internal Revenue, among others. They sought a declaration that § 5000A(a)'s minimum essential coverage provision is unconstitutional, a finding that the rest of the Act is not severable from § 5000A(a), and an injunction against the rest of the Act's enforcement. Hurley and Nantz (individual plaintiffs) soon joined them. Although nominally defendants to the suit, the United States took the side of the plaintiffs. Therefore California, along with 15 other States and the District of Columbia (state intervenors), intervened in order to defend the Act's constitutionality, as did the U. S. House of Representatives at the appellate stage.

II

We proceed no further than standing. The Constitution gives federal courts the power to adjudicate only genuine "Cases" and "Controversies." Art. III, § 2. That power includes the requirement that litigants have standing. A plaintiff has standing only if he can "allege personal injury fairly traceable to the defendant's allegedly unlawful conduct and likely to be redressed by the requested relief." Neither the individual nor the state plaintiffs have shown that the injury they will suffer or have suffered is "fairly traceable" to the "allegedly unlawful conduct" of which they complain.

A

We begin with the two individual plaintiffs. They claim a particularized individual harm in the form of payments they have made and will make each month to carry the minimum essential coverage that § 5000A(a) requires. The individual plaintiffs point to the statutory language, which, they say, commands them to buy health insurance. But even if we assume that this pocketbook injury satisfies the injury element of Article III standing, the plaintiffs nevertheless fail to satisfy the traceability requirement.

Their problem lies in the fact that the statutory provision, while it tells them to obtain that coverage, has no means of enforcement. With the penalty zeroed out, the IRS can no longer seek a penalty from those who fail to comply. Because of this, there is no possible Government action that is causally connected to the plaintiffs' injury—the costs of purchasing health insurance. Or to put the matter conversely, that injury is not "fairly traceable" to any "allegedly unlawful conduct" of which the plaintiffs complain. They have not pointed to any way in which the defendants, the Commissioner of Internal Revenue and the Secretary of Health and Human Services, will act to enforce § 5000A(a). They have not shown how any other federal employees could do so either. In a word, they have not shown that any kind of Government action or conduct has caused or will cause the injury they attribute to § 5000A(a).

The matter is not simply technical. To find standing here to attack an unenforceable statutory provision would allow a federal court to issue what would amount to "an advisory opinion without the possibility of any judicial relief." It would threaten to grant unelected judges a general authority to conduct oversight of decisions of the elected branches of Government. Article III guards against federal courts assuming this kind of jurisdiction.

B

Next, we turn to the state plaintiffs. We conclude that Texas and the other state plaintiffs have similarly failed to show that they have alleged an "injury fairly traceable to the defendant's allegedly *unlawful* conduct." They claim two kinds of pocketbook injuries. First, they allege an indirect injury in the form of the increased use of (and therefore cost to) state-operated medical insurance programs. Second, they claim a direct injury resulting from a variety of increased administrative and related expenses required, they say, by the minimum essential coverage provision, along with other provisions of the Act that, they add, are inextricably "'interwoven'" with it.

First, the state plaintiffs claim that the minimum essential coverage provision has led state residents subject to it to enroll in state-operated or state-sponsored insurance programs such as Medicaid, the Children's Health Insurance Program (CHIP), see § 1397aa, and health insurance programs for state employees. The state plaintiffs say they must pay a share of the costs of serving those new enrollees. As with the individual plaintiffs, the States also have failed to show how this injury is directly traceable to any actual or possible unlawful Government conduct in enforcing § 5000A(a). That alone is enough to show that they, like the individual plaintiffs, lack Article III standing.

But setting aside that pure issue of law, we need only examine the initial factual premise of their claim to uncover another fatal weakness: The state plaintiffs have failed to show that the challenged minimum essential coverage provision, without any prospect of penalty, will harm them by leading more individuals to enroll in these programs.

We have said that, where a causal relation between injury and challenged action depends upon the decision of an independent third party (here an individual's decision to enroll in, say, Medicaid), "standing is not precluded, but it is ordinarily 'substantially more difficult' to establish " To satisfy that burden, the plaintiff must show at the least "that third parties will likely react in predictable ways." And, "at the summary judgment stage, such a party can no longer rest on . . . mere allegations, but must set forth . . . specific facts" that adequately support their contention. The state plaintiffs have not done so.

The programs to which the state plaintiffs point offer their recipients many benefits that have nothing to do with the minimum essential coverage provision of § 5000A(a). Given these benefits, neither logic nor intuition suggests that the presence of the minimum essential coverage requirement would lead an individual to enroll in one of those programs that its absence would lead them to ignore. A penalty might have led some inertia-bound individuals to enroll. But without a penalty, what incentive could the provision provide?

Unsurprisingly, the States have not demonstrated that an unenforceable mandate will cause their residents to enroll in valuable benefits programs that they would otherwise forgo. It would require far stronger evidence than the States have offered here to support their counterintuitive theory of standing, which rests on a "highly attenuated chain of possibilities."

The state plaintiffs add that § 5000A(a)'s minimum essential coverage provision also causes them to incur additional costs directly. They point to the costs of providing beneficiaries of state health plans with information about their health insurance coverage, as well as the cost of furnishing the IRS with that related information.

The problem with these claims, however, is that other provisions of Act, not the minimum essential coverage provision, impose these other requirements. Nothing in the text of these form provisions suggests that they would not operate without § 5000A(a). To show that the minimum essential coverage requirement is unconstitutional would not show that enforcement of any of these other provisions violates the Constitution. The state plaintiffs do not claim the contrary. The Government's conduct in question is therefore not "fairly traceable" to enforcement of the "allegedly unlawful" provision of which the plaintiffs complain — § 5000A(a).

For these reasons, we conclude that the plaintiffs in this suit failed to show a concrete, particularized injury fairly traceable to the defendants' conduct in enforcing the specific statutory provision they attack as unconstitutional. They have failed to show that they have standing to attack as unconstitutional the Act's minimum essential coverage provision.

Justice THOMAS, concurring.

There is much to commend Justice Alito's account of "our epic Affordable Care Act trilogy." This Court has gone to great lengths to rescue the Act from its own text. So have the Act's defenders, who argued in first instance that the individual coverage mandate is the Act's linchpin, yet now, in an about-face, contend that it is just a throwaway sentence.

But, whatever the Act's dubious history in this Court, we must assess the current suit on its own terms. And, here, there is a fundamental problem with the arguments advanced by the plaintiffs in attacking the Act—they have not identified any unlawful action that has injured them. Today's result is thus not the consequence of the Court once again rescuing the Act, but rather of us adjudicating the particular claims the plaintiffs chose to bring.

The plaintiffs failed to demonstrate that the harm they suffered is traceable to unlawful conduct. Although this Court has erred twice before in cases involving the Affordable Care Act, it does not err today.

Justice ALITO, with whom Justice GORSUCH joins, dissenting.

Today's decision is the third installment in our epic Affordable Care Act trilogy, and it follows the same pattern as installments one and two. In all three episodes, with the Affordable Care Act facing a serious threat, the Court has pulled off an improbable rescue.

In this suit, as I will explain, Texas and the other state plaintiffs have standing, and now that the "tax" imposed by the individual mandate is set at $0, the mandate cannot be sustained under the taxing power. As a result, it is clearly unconstitutional, and to the extent that the provisions of the ACA that burden the States are inextricably linked to the individual mandate, they too are unenforceable.

We may consider the merits of this appeal if even one plaintiff has standing, but the majority concludes that no plaintiff—neither the States that originally brought suit nor the individual plaintiffs who later joined them—has standing under Article III of the Constitution. That is a remarkable holding. While the individual plaintiffs' claim to standing raises a novel question, the States have standing for reasons that are straightforward and meritorious. The Court's contrary holding is based on a fundamental distortion of our standing jurisprudence.

The governing rules are well-settled. To establish Article III standing, a plaintiff must show: (1) "an injury in fact"; (2) that this injury "is fairly traceable to the challenged conduct of the defendant"; and (3) that the injury "is likely to be redressed by a favorable judicial decision."

In the present suit, there is no material dispute that the States have satisfied two of these requirements. First, there is no question that the States have demonstrated an injury in fact. An injury in fact is "an invasion of a legally protected interest that is concrete and particularized and actual or imminent, not conjectural or hypothetical." A financial or so-called "pocketbook" injury constitutes injury in fact, and even a small pocketbook injury—like the loss of $1—is enough. Here, the States have offered plenty of evidence that they incur substantial expenses in order to comply with obligations imposed by the ACA.

There is likewise no material dispute that these financial injuries could be redressed by a favorable judgment. The District Court declared the entire ACA unenforceable, and that judgment, if sustained, would spare the States from the costs of complying with the ACA's provisions. So too would a more modest judgment limited to only those ACA provisions that directly burden the States.

The standing dispute in this suit thus turns on traceability. But once this requirement is properly understood, it is apparent that it too is met. Our cases explain that traceability requires "a causal connection between the injury and *the conduct complained of*."

The States have clearly shown that they suffer concrete and particularized financial injuries that are traceable to conduct of the Federal Government. The ACA saddles them with expensive and burdensome obligations, and those obligations are enforced by the Federal Government. That is sufficient to establish standing. As the Court observed in *Lujan*, when a party is "an object of the action . . . at issue," "there is ordinarily little question that the action . . . has caused [that party] injury"—*i.e.*, that the injury is traceable to that action—"and that a judgment preventing . . . the action will redress it." That is precisely the situation here. The state plaintiffs have shown that they are the object of potential federal enforcement actions if they do not comply with costly and burdensome obligations that the ACA imposes.

The state plaintiffs have similarly demonstrated standing to seek relief from ACA provisions requiring them to offer expensive health insurance coverage for their employees. Consider the ACA's requirement that group health plans and health insurance offerings extend coverage to adult children until they reach the age of 26. Texas has spent more than $80 million complying with that rule. Missouri has spent more than $10 million. These obligations, too, are backed by substantial enforcement mechanisms.

While I have outlined two examples of concrete, traceable, and redressable injuries demonstrated by the state plaintiffs, these examples are not exhaustive. The ACA is an enormously complex statute, and the States have offered evidence of ongoing financial injuries relating to compliance with many other different (and enforceable) ACA provisions.

I would hold that the States have demonstrated standing to seek relief from the ACA provisions that burden them and that they claim are inseparable from the individual mandate.

Because the state plaintiffs have standing, I proceed to consider the merits of this lawsuit. That requires assessing whether the individual mandate is unlawful and whether it is inseverable from the provisions that burden the States. [Justice Alito then argued that the individual mandate was unconstitutional and that this provision is not severable from the rest of the law, thus in his view making the entire Affordable Care Act unconstitutional.]

***

In *Transunion v. Ramirez*, the Court limited to have standing based on Congress creating a right, the infringement of which is the injury for standing purposes. The case is important in restricting the ability to find standing based on injury to rights created by statutes.

TRANSUNION v. RAMIREZ
141 S.Ct. ___ (2021)

Justice KAVANAUGH delivered the opinion of the Court.

To have Article III standing to sue in federal court, plaintiffs must demonstrate, among other things, that they suffered a concrete harm. No concrete harm, no standing. Central to assessing concreteness is whether the asserted harm has a "close relationship" to a harm traditionally recognized as providing a basis for a lawsuit in American courts — such as physical harm, monetary harm, or various intangible harms including (as relevant here) reputational harm. *Spokeo, Inc. v. Robins* (2016).

In this case, a class of 8,185 individuals sued TransUnion, a credit reporting agency, in federal court under the Fair Credit Reporting Act. The plaintiffs claimed that TransUnion failed to use reasonable procedures to ensure the accuracy of their credit files, as maintained internally by TransUnion. For 1,853 of the class members, TransUnion provided misleading credit reports to third-party businesses. We conclude that those 1,853 class members have demonstrated concrete reputational harm and thus have Article III standing to sue on the reasonable-procedures claim. The internal credit files of the other 6,332 class members were *not* provided to third-party businesses during the relevant time period. We conclude that those 6,332 class members have not demonstrated concrete harm and thus lack Article III standing to sue on the reasonable-procedures claim.

In two other claims, all 8,185 class members complained about formatting defects in certain mailings sent to them by TransUnion. But the class members other than the named plaintiff Sergio Ramirez have not demonstrated that the alleged formatting errors caused them any concrete harm.

Therefore, except for Ramirez, the class members do not have standing as to those two claims.

I

In 1970, Congress passed and President Nixon signed the Fair Credit Reporting Act. The Act seeks to promote "fair and accurate credit reporting" and to protect consumer privacy. To achieve those goals, the Act regulates the consumer reporting agencies that compile and disseminate personal information about consumers.

The Act "imposes a host of requirements concerning the creation and use of consumer reports." Three of the Act's requirements are relevant to this case. *First*, the Act requires consumer reporting agencies to "follow reasonable procedures to assure maximum possible accuracy" in consumer reports. *Second*, the Act provides that consumer reporting agencies must, upon request, disclose to the consumer "[a]ll information in the consumer's file at the time of the request." *Third*, the Act compels consumer reporting agencies to "provide to a consumer, with each written disclosure by the agency to the consumer," a "summary of rights" prepared by the Consumer Financial Protection Bureau.

The Act creates a cause of action for consumers to sue and recover damages for certain violations. The Act provides: "Any person who willfully fails to comply with any requirement imposed under this subchapter with respect to any consumer is liable to that consumer" for actual damages or for statutory damages not less than $100 and not more than $1,000, as well as for punitive damages and attorney's fees.

TransUnion is one of the "Big Three" credit reporting agencies, along with Equifax and Experian. As a credit reporting agency, TransUnion compiles personal and financial information about individual consumers to create consumer reports. TransUnion then sells those consumer reports for use by entities such as banks, landlords, and car dealerships that request information about the creditworthiness of individual consumers.

Beginning in 2002, TransUnion introduced an add-on product called OFAC Name Screen Alert. OFAC is the U. S. Treasury Department's Office of Foreign Assets Control. OFAC maintains a list of "specially designated nationals" who threaten America's national security. Individuals on the OFAC list are terrorists, drug traffickers, or other serious criminals. It is generally unlawful to transact business with any person on the list. TransUnion created the OFAC Name Screen Alert to help businesses avoid transacting with individuals on OFAC's list.

When this litigation arose, Name Screen worked in the following way: When a business opted into the Name Screen service, TransUnion would conduct its ordinary credit check of the consumer, and it would also use third-party software to compare the consumer's name against the OFAC list. If the consumer's first and last name matched the first and last name of an individual on OFAC's list, then TransUnion would place an alert on the credit report indicating that the consumer's name was a "potential match" to a name on the OFAC list. TransUnion did not compare any data other than first and last names. Unsurprisingly, TransUnion's Name Screen product generated many false positives. Thousands of law-abiding Americans happen to share a first and last name with one of the terrorists, drug traffickers, or serious criminals on OFAC's list of specially designated nationals.

Sergio Ramirez learned the hard way that he is one such individual. On February 27, 2011, Ramirez visited a Nissan dealership in Dublin, California, seeking to buy a Nissan Maxima. Ramirez was accompanied by his wife and his father-in-law. After Ramirez and his wife selected a color and negotiated a price, the dealership ran a credit check on both Ramirez and his wife. Ramirez's credit report, produced by TransUnion, contained the following alert: "***OFAC ADVISOR ALERT - INPUT NAME MATCHES NAME ON THE OFAC DATABASE." A Nissan salesman told Ramirez that Nissan would not sell the car to him because his name was on a "terrorist list.'" Ramirez's wife had to purchase the car in her own name.

The next day, Ramirez called TransUnion and requested a copy of his credit file. TransUnion sent Ramirez a mailing that same day that included his credit file and the statutorily required summary of rights prepared by the CFPB. The mailing did not mention the OFAC alert in Ramirez's file. The following day, TransUnion sent Ramirez a second mailing—a letter alerting him that his name was considered a potential match to names on the OFAC list. The second mailing did not include an additional copy of the summary of rights. Concerned about the mailings, Ramirez consulted a lawyer and ultimately canceled a planned trip to Mexico. TransUnion eventually removed the OFAC alert from Ramirez's file.

In February 2012, Ramirez sued TransUnion and alleged three violations of the Fair Credit Reporting Act. *First*, he alleged that TransUnion, by using the Name Screen product, failed to follow reasonable procedures to ensure the accuracy of information in his credit file. *Second*, he claimed that TransUnion failed to provide him with *all* the information in his credit file upon his request. In particular, TransUnion's first mailing did not include the fact that Ramirez's name was a potential match for a name on the OFAC list. *Third*, Ramirez asserted that TransUnion violated its obligation to provide him with a summary of his rights "with each written disclosure," because TransUnion's second mailing did not contain a summary of Ramirez's rights. Ramirez requested statutory and punitive damages.

Ramirez also sought to certify a class of all people in the United States to whom TransUnion sent a mailing during the period from January 1, 2011, to July 26, 2011, that was similar in form to the second mailing that Ramirez received. TransUnion opposed certification. The U. S. District Court for the Northern District of California rejected TransUnion's argument and certified the class.

Before trial, the parties stipulated that the class contained 8,185 members, including Ramirez. The parties also stipulated that only 1,853 members of the class (including Ramirez) had their credit reports disseminated by TransUnion to potential creditors during the period from January 1, 2011, to July 26, 2011. The District Court ruled that all 8,185 class members had Article III standing.

After six days of trial, the jury returned a verdict for the plaintiffs. The jury awarded each class member $984.22 in statutory damages and $6,353.08 in punitive damages for a total award of more than $60 million. The U. S. Court of Appeals for the Ninth Circuit affirmed in relevant part.

II

The question in this case is whether the 8,185 class members have Article III standing as to their three claims. In Part II, we summarize the requirements of Article III standing—in particular, the requirement that plaintiffs demonstrate a "concrete harm." In Part III, we then apply the concrete-harm requirement to the plaintiffs' lawsuit against TransUnion.

The "law of Art. III standing is built on a single basic idea—the idea of separation of powers." To answer that question in a way sufficient to establish standing, a plaintiff must show (i) that he suffered an injury in fact that is concrete, particularized, and actual or imminent; (ii) that the injury was likely caused by the defendant; and (iii) that the injury would likely be redressed by judicial relief.

Requiring a plaintiff to demonstrate a concrete and particularized injury caused by the defendant and redressable by the court ensures that federal courts decide only "the rights of individuals," and that federal courts exercise "their proper function in a limited and separated government," Under Article III, federal courts do not adjudicate hypothetical or abstract disputes. Federal courts do not possess a roving commission to publicly opine on every legal question. Federal courts do not exercise general legal oversight of the Legislative and Executive Branches, or of private entities. And federal courts do not issue advisory opinions.

In sum, under Article III, a federal court may resolve only "a real controversy with real impact on real persons." The question in this case focuses on the Article III requirement that the plaintiff's injury in fact be "concrete" — that is, "real, and not abstract." *Spokeo, Inc. v. Robins* (2016).

What makes a harm concrete for purposes of Article III? As a general matter, the Court has explained that "history and tradition offer a meaningful guide to the types of cases that Article III empowers federal courts to consider." And with respect to the concrete-harm requirement in particular, this Court's opinion in *Spokeo* v. *Robins* indicated that courts should assess whether the alleged injury to the plaintiff has a "close relationship" to a harm "traditionally" recognized as providing a basis for a lawsuit in American courts. That inquiry asks whether plaintiffs have identified a close historical or common-law analogue for their asserted injury. *Spokeo* does not require an exact duplicate in American history and tradition. But *Spokeo* is not an open-ended invitation for federal courts to loosen Article III based on contemporary, evolving beliefs about what kinds of suits should be heard in federal courts.

As *Spokeo* explained, certain harms readily qualify as concrete injuries under Article III. The most obvious are traditional tangible harms, such as physical harms and monetary harms. If a defendant has caused physical or monetary injury to the plaintiff, the plaintiff has suffered a concrete injury in fact under Article III.

Various intangible harms can also be concrete. Chief among them are injuries with a close relationship to harms traditionally recognized as providing a basis for lawsuits in American courts. Those include, for example, reputational harms, disclosure of private information, and intrusion upon seclusion.

In determining whether a harm is sufficiently concrete to qualify as an injury in fact, the Court in *Spokeo* said that Congress's views may be "instructive." Courts must afford due respect to Congress's decision to impose a statutory prohibition or obligation on a defendant, and to grant a plaintiff a cause of action to sue over the defendant's violation of that statutory prohibition or obligation. In that way, Congress may "elevate to the status of legally cognizable injuries concrete, *de facto* injuries that were previously inadequate in law." But even though "Congress may 'elevate' harms that 'exist' in the real world before Congress recognized them to actionable legal status, it may not simply enact an injury into existence, using its lawmaking power to transform something that is not remotely harmful into something that is."

Importantly, this Court has rejected the proposition that "a plaintiff automatically satisfies the injury-in-fact requirement whenever a statute grants a person a statutory right and purports to authorize that person to sue to vindicate that right." As the Court emphasized in *Spokeo*, "Article III standing requires a concrete injury even in the context of a statutory violation."

Congress's creation of a statutory prohibition or obligation and a cause of action does not relieve courts of their responsibility to independently decide whether a plaintiff has suffered a concrete harm under Article III any more than, for example, Congress's enactment of a law regulating speech relieves courts of their responsibility to independently decide whether the law violates the First Amendment.

For standing purposes, therefore, an important difference exists between (i) a plaintiff's statutory cause of action to sue a defendant over the defendant's violation of federal law, and (ii) a plaintiff's suffering concrete harm because of the defendant's violation of federal law. Congress may enact legal prohibitions and obligations. And Congress may create causes of action for plaintiffs to sue defendants who violate those legal prohibitions or obligations. But under Article III, an injury in law is not an injury in fact. Only those plaintiffs who have been *concretely harmed* by a defendant's statutory violation may sue that private defendant over that violation in federal court.

To appreciate how the Article III "concrete harm" principle operates in practice, consider two different hypothetical plaintiffs. Suppose first that a Maine citizen's land is polluted by a nearby factory. She sues the company, alleging that it violated a federal environmental law and damaged her property. Suppose also that a second plaintiff in Hawaii files a federal lawsuit alleging that the same company in Maine violated that same environmental law by polluting land in Maine. The violation did not personally harm the plaintiff in Hawaii.

Even if Congress affords both hypothetical plaintiffs a cause of action (with statutory damages available) to sue over the defendant's legal violation, Article III standing doctrine sharply distinguishes between those two scenarios. The first lawsuit may of course proceed in federal court because the plaintiff has suffered concrete harm to her property. But the second lawsuit may not proceed because that plaintiff has not suffered any physical, monetary, or cognizable intangible harm traditionally recognized as providing a basis for a lawsuit in American courts. An uninjured plaintiff who sues in those circumstances is, by definition, not seeking to remedy any harm to herself but instead is merely seeking to ensure a defendant's "compliance with regulatory law." Those are not grounds for Article III standing.

As those examples illustrate, if the law of Article III did not require plaintiffs to demonstrate a "concrete harm," Congress could authorize virtually any citizen to bring a statutory damages suit against virtually any defendant who violated virtually any federal law. Such an expansive understanding of Article III would flout constitutional text, history, and precedent. In our view, the public interest that private entities comply with the law cannot "be converted into an individual right by a statute that denominates it as such, and that permits all citizens (or, for that matter, a subclass of citizens who suffer no distinctive concrete harm) to sue."

A regime where Congress could freely authorize *unharmed* plaintiffs to sue defendants who violate federal law not only would violate Article III but also would infringe on the Executive Branch's Article II authority. We accept the "displacement of the democratically elected branches when necessary to decide an actual case." But otherwise, the choice of how to prioritize and how aggressively to pursue legal actions against defendants who violate the law falls within the discretion of the Executive Branch, not within the purview of private plaintiffs (and their attorneys). Private plaintiffs are not accountable to the people and are not charged with pursuing the public interest in enforcing a defendant's general compliance with regulatory law.

In sum, the concrete-harm requirement is essential to the Constitution's separation of powers. To be sure, the concrete-harm requirement can be difficult to apply in some cases. Some advocate that the concrete-harm requirement be ditched altogether, on the theory that it would be more efficient or convenient to simply say that a statutory violation and a cause of action suffice to afford a plaintiff standing. But as the Court has often stated, "the fact that a given law or procedure is efficient, convenient, and useful in facilitating functions of government, standing alone, will not save it if it is contrary to the Constitution." So it is here.

III

We now apply those fundamental standing principles to this lawsuit. We must determine whether the 8,185 class members have standing to sue TransUnion for its alleged violations of the Fair Credit Reporting Act. The plaintiffs argue that TransUnion failed to comply with statutory obligations (i) to follow reasonable procedures to ensure the accuracy of credit files so that the files would not include OFAC alerts labeling the plaintiffs as potential terrorists; and (ii) to provide a consumer, upon request, with his or her complete credit file, including a summary of rights.

We first address the plaintiffs' claim that TransUnion failed to "follow reasonable procedures to assure maximum possible accuracy" of the plaintiffs' credit files maintained by TransUnion. In particular, the plaintiffs argue that TransUnion did not do enough to ensure that OFAC alerts labeling them as potential terrorists were not included in their credit files.

Start with the 1,853 class members (including the named plaintiff Ramirez) whose reports were disseminated to third-party businesses. The plaintiffs argue that the publication to a third party of a credit report bearing a misleading OFAC alert injures the subject of the report. The plaintiffs contend that this injury bears a "close relationship" to a harm traditionally recognized as providing a basis for a lawsuit in American courts — namely, the reputational harm associated with the tort of defamation.

We agree with the plaintiffs. Under longstanding American law, a person is injured when a defamatory statement "that would subject him to hatred, contempt, or ridicule" is published to a third party. TransUnion provided third parties with credit reports containing OFAC alerts that labeled the class members as potential terrorists, drug traffickers, or serious criminals. The 1,853 class members therefore suffered a harm with a "close relationship" to the harm associated with the tort of defamation. We have no trouble concluding that the 1,853 class members suffered a concrete harm that qualifies as an injury in fact.In short, the 1,853 class members whose reports were disseminated to third parties suffered a concrete injury in fact under Article III.

The remaining 6,332 class members are a different story. To be sure, their credit files, which were maintained by TransUnion, contained misleading OFAC alerts. But the parties stipulated that TransUnion did not provide those plaintiffs' credit information to any potential creditors during the class period from January 2011 to July 2011. Given the absence of dissemination, we must determine whether the 6,332 class members suffered some other concrete harm for purposes of Article III.

The initial question is whether the mere existence of a misleading OFAC alert in a consumer's internal credit file at TransUnion constitutes a concrete injury. The standing inquiry in this case thus distinguishes between (i) credit files that consumer reporting agencies maintain internally and (ii) the consumer credit reports that consumer reporting agencies disseminate to third-party creditors. The mere presence of an inaccuracy in an internal credit file, if it is not disclosed to a third party, causes no concrete harm. In cases such as these where allegedly inaccurate or misleading information sits in a company database, the plaintiffs' harm is roughly the same, legally speaking, as if someone wrote a defamatory letter and then stored it in her desk drawer. A letter that is not sent does not harm anyone, no matter how insulting the letter is. So too here.

Because the plaintiffs cannot demonstrate that the misleading information in the internal credit files itself constitutes a concrete harm, the plaintiffs advance a separate argument based on an asserted *risk of future harm*. They say that the 6,332 class members suffered a concrete injury for Article III purposes because the existence of misleading OFAC alerts in their internal credit files exposed them to a material risk that the information would be disseminated in the future to third parties and thereby cause them harm.

TransUnion advances a persuasive argument that in a suit for damages, the mere risk of future harm, standing alone, cannot qualify as a concrete harm — at least unless the exposure to the risk of future harm itself causes a *separate* concrete harm. TransUnion contends that if an individual is exposed to a risk of future harm, time will eventually reveal whether the risk materializes in the form of actual harm. If the risk of future harm materializes and the individual suffers a concrete harm, then the harm itself, and not the pre-existing risk, will constitute a basis for the person's injury and for damages. If the risk of future harm does *not* materialize, then the individual cannot establish a concrete harm sufficient for standing, according to TransUnion.

Here, the 6,332 plaintiffs did not demonstrate that the risk of future harm materialized — that is, that the inaccurate OFAC alerts in their internal TransUnion credit files were ever provided to third parties or caused a denial of credit. Nor did those plaintiffs present evidence that the class members were independently harmed by their exposure to the risk itself — that is, that they suffered some other injury (such as an emotional injury) from the mere risk that their credit reports would be provided to third-party businesses. Therefore, the 6,332 plaintiffs' argument for standing for their damages claims based on an asserted risk of future harm is unavailing.

No concrete harm, no standing. The 1,853 class members whose credit reports were provided to third-party businesses suffered a concrete harm and thus have standing as to the reasonable-procedures claim. The 6,332 class members whose credit reports were not provided to third-party businesses did not suffer a concrete harm and thus do not have standing as to the reasonable-procedures claim. As for the claims pertaining to the format of TransUnion's mailings, none of the 8,185 class members other than the named plaintiff Ramirez suffered a concrete harm.

Justice THOMAS, with whom Justice BREYER, Justice SOTOMAYOR, and Justice KAGAN join, dissenting.

TransUnion generated credit reports that erroneously flagged many law-abiding people as potential terrorists and drug traffickers. In doing so, TransUnion violated several provisions of the Fair Credit Reporting Act (FCRA) that entitle consumers to accuracy in credit-reporting procedures; to receive information in their credit files; and to receive a summary of their rights. Yet despite Congress' judgment that such misdeeds deserve redress, the majority decides that TransUnion's actions are so insignificant that the Constitution prohibits consumers from vindicating their rights in federal court. The Constitution does no such thing.

Key to the scope of the judicial power, then, is whether an individual asserts his or her own rights. At the time of the founding, whether a court possessed judicial power over an action with no showing of actual damages depended on whether the plaintiff sought to enforce a right held privately by an individual or a duty owed broadly to the community. But where an individual sued based on the violation of a duty owed broadly to the whole community, such as the overgrazing of public lands, courts required "not only *injuria* [legal injury] but also *damnum* [damage]."

This distinction mattered not only for traditional common-law rights, but also for newly created statutory ones. The First Congress enacted a law defining copyrights and gave copyright holders the right to sue infringing persons in order to recover statutory damages, even if the holder "could not show monetary loss." In the patent context, a defendant challenged an infringement suit brought under a similar law.

The principle that the violation of an individual right gives rise to an actionable harm was widespread at the founding, in early American history, and in many modern cases. And this understanding accords proper respect for the power of Congress and other legislatures to define legal rights. No one could seriously dispute, for example, that a violation of property rights is actionable, but as a general matter, "[p]roperty rights are created by the State." In light of this history, tradition, and common practice, our test should be clear: So long as a "statute fixes a minimum of recovery . . . , there would seem to be no doubt of the right of one who establishes a technical ground of action to recover this minimum sum without any specific showing of loss." While the Court today discusses the supposed failure to show "injury in fact," courts for centuries held that injury in law to a private right was enough to create a case or controversy.

Here, each class member established a violation of his or her private rights. The jury found that TransUnion violated three separate duties created by statute. All three of those duties are owed to individuals, not to the community writ large. Take § 1681e(b), which requires a consumer reporting agency to "follow reasonable procedures to assure maximum possible accuracy of the information concerning the individual about whom the report relates." This statute creates a duty: to use reasonable procedures to assure maximum possible accuracy. And that duty is particularized to an individual: the subject of the report. Section 1681g does the same. It requires an agency to "clearly and accurately disclose" to a consumer, upon his request, "[a]ll information in the consumer's file at the time of the request" and to include a written "summary of rights" with that "written disclosure." Those directives likewise create duties: provide all information in the consumer's file and accompany the disclosure with a summary of rights. And these too are owed to a single person: the consumer who requests the information.

Were there any doubt that consumer reporting agencies owe these duties to specific individuals — and not to the larger community — Congress created a cause of action providing that "[a]ny person who willfully fails to comply" with an FCRA requirement "with respect to any *consumer* is liable to *that consumer*." If a consumer reporting agency breaches any FCRA duty owed to a specific consumer, then that individual (not all consumers) may sue the agency. No one disputes that each class member possesses this cause of action. And no one disputes that the jury found that TransUnion violated each class member's individual rights. The plaintiffs thus have a sufficient injury to sue in federal court.

Even assuming that this Court should be in the business of second-guessing private rights, this is a rather odd case to say that Congress went too far. TransUnion's misconduct here is exactly the sort of thing that has long merited legal redress. As an initial matter, this Court has recognized that the unlawful withholding of requested information causes "a sufficiently distinct injury to provide standing to sue." Here, TransUnion unlawfully withheld from each class member the OFAC version of his or her credit report that the class member requested. And TransUnion unlawfully failed to send a summary of rights.

But even setting aside everything already mentioned — the Constitution's text, history, precedent, financial harm, libel, the risk of publication, and actual disclosure to a third party — one need only tap into common sense to know that receiving a letter identifying you as a potential drug trafficker or terrorist is harmful. All the more so when the information comes in the context of a credit report, the entire purpose of which is to demonstrate that a person can be trusted.

And if this sort of confusing and frustrating communication is insufficient to establish a real injury, one wonders what could rise to that level. If, instead of falsely identifying Ramirez as a potential drug trafficker or terrorist, TransUnion had flagged him as a "potential" child molester, would that alone still be insufficient to open the courthouse doors? What about falsely labeling a person a racist? Including a slur on the report? Or what about openly reducing a person's credit score by several points because of his race? If none of these constitutes an injury in fact, how can that possibly square with our past cases indicating that the inability to "observe an animal species, even for purely esthetic purposes, . . . undeniably" is?

Ultimately, the majority seems to pose to the reader a single rhetorical question: Who could possibly think that a person is harmed when he requests and is sent an incomplete credit report, or is sent a suspicious notice informing him that he may be a designated drug trafficker or terrorist, or is *not* sent anything informing him of how to remove this inaccurate red flag? The answer is, of course, legion: Congress, the President, the jury, the District Court, the Ninth Circuit, and four Members of this Court.

Justice KAGAN, with whom Justice BREYER and Justice SOTOMAYOR join, dissenting.

The Court here transforms standing law from a doctrine of judicial modesty into a tool of judicial aggrandizement. It holds, for the first time, that a specific class of plaintiffs whom Congress allowed to bring a lawsuit cannot do so under Article III. [O]ur Article III precedents teach that Congress has broad "power to create and define rights." And Congress may protect those rights by authorizing suits not only for past harms but also for the material risk of future ones. Under those precedents, this case should be easy. In the Fair Credit Reporting Act, Congress determined to protect consumers' reputations from inaccurate credit reporting. TransUnion willfully violated that statute's provisions by preparing credit files that falsely called the plaintiffs potential terrorists, and by obscuring that fact when the plaintiffs requested copies of their files. To say, as the majority does, that the resulting injuries did not "'exist' in the real world" is to inhabit a world I don't know. And to make that claim in the face of Congress's contrary judgment is to exceed the judiciary's "proper—and properly limited—role."

I add a few words about the majority's view of the risks of harm to the plaintiffs. In addressing the claim that TransUnion failed to maintain accurate credit files, the majority argues that the "risk of dissemination" of the plaintiffs' credit information to third parties is "too speculative." But why is it so speculative that a company in the business of selling credit reports to third parties will in fact sell a credit report to a third party?

ii.   Prudential Standing Requirements (casebook p. 66)

In *Singleton v. Wulff* (casebook p. 67), the Court held that doctors and health professionals have third-party standing to present the claims of their women patients in challenging laws restricting abortions. In *June Medical Services L.L.C. v. Russo*, the Court reaffirmed this.

JUNE MEDICAL SERVICES L.L.C. v. RUSSO

140 S. Ct. 2103 (2020)

[The Louisiana law provided that in order for a doctor to perform an abortion, the doctor must have admitting privileges within 30 miles. The Court declared this unconstitutional as an impermissible undue burden on a woman's right to abortion. This part of the opinion is found in Chapter 8 of this Supplement. There also was the issue of whether the health care providers had standing to challenge this law on behalf of their patients.]

Justice BREYER wrote the opinion joined by Justices GINSBURG, SOTOMAYOR and KAGAN.

We initially consider a procedural argument that the State raised for the first time in its cross-petition for certiorari. As we have explained, the plaintiff abortion providers and clinics in this case have challenged Act 620 on the ground that it infringes their patients' rights to access an abortion. The State contends that the proper parties to assert these rights are the patients themselves. We think that the State has waived that argument.

The State's argument rests on the rule that a party cannot ordinarily "'rest his claim to relief on the legal rights or interests of third parties.'" This rule is "prudential." It does not involve the Constitution's "case-or-controversy requirement." And so, we have explained, it can be forfeited or waived.

[T]he State's memorandum opposing the plaintiffs' TRO request urged the District Court to proceed swiftly to the merits of the plaintiffs' undue-burden claim. It argued that there was "no question that the physicians had standing to contest" Act 620. And it told the District Court that the Fifth Circuit had found that doctors challenging Texas' "identical" law "had third-party standing to assert their patients' rights." Noting that the Texas law had "already been upheld," the State asserted that it had "a keen interest in removing any cloud upon the validity of its law." It insisted that this suit was "the proper vehicle to do so." The State did not mention its current objection until it filed its cross-petition—more than five years after it argued that the plaintiffs' standing was beyond question.

The State's unmistakable concession of standing as part of its effort to obtain a quick decision from the District Court on the merits of the plaintiffs' undue-burden claims bars our consideration of it here.

In any event, the rule the State invokes is hardly absolute. We have long permitted abortion providers to invoke the rights of their actual or potential patients in challenges to abortion-related regulations. And we have generally permitted plaintiffs to assert third-party rights in cases where the "'enforcement of the challenged restriction *against the litigant* would result indirectly in the violation of third parties' rights.'"

The case before us lies at the intersection of these two lines of precedent. The plaintiffs are abortion providers challenging a law that regulates their conduct. The "threatened imposition of governmental sanctions" for noncompliance eliminates any risk that their claims are abstract or hypothetical. That threat also assures us that the plaintiffs have every incentive to "resist efforts at restricting their operations by acting as advocates of the rights of third parties who seek access to their market or function." And, as the parties who must actually go through the process of applying for and maintaining admitting privileges, they are far better positioned than their patients to address the burdens of compliance. They are, in other words, "the least awkward" and most "obvious" claimants here.

Our dissenting colleagues suggest that this case is different because the plaintiffs have challenged a law ostensibly enacted to protect the women whose rights they are asserting. But that is a common feature of cases in which we have found third-party standing. The restriction on sales of 3.2% beer to young men challenged by a drive-through convenience store in *Craig* was defended on "public health and safety grounds," including the premise that young men were particularly susceptible to driving while intoxicated. Nor is this the first abortion case to address provider standing to challenge regulations said to protect women.

In short, the State's strategic waiver and a long line of well-established precedents foreclose its belated challenge to the plaintiffs' standing. We consequently proceed to consider the merits of the plaintiffs' claims.

Justice THOMAS, dissenting.

Today a majority of the Court perpetuates its ill-founded abortion jurisprudence by enjoining a perfectly legitimate state law and doing so without jurisdiction. As is often the case with legal challenges to abortion regulations, this suit was brought by abortionists and abortion clinics. Their sole claim before this Court is that Louisiana's law violates the purported substantive due process right of a woman to abort her unborn child. But they concede that this right does not belong to them, and they seek to vindicate no private rights of their own. Under a proper understanding of Article III, these plaintiffs lack standing to invoke our jurisdiction.

Despite the fact that we granted Louisiana's petition specifically to address whether "abortion providers [can] be presumed to have third-party standing to challenge health and safety regulations on behalf of their patients," a majority of the Court all but ignores the question.

For most of its history, this Court maintained that private parties could not bring suit to vindicate the constitutional rights of individuals who are not before the Court. But in the 20th century, the Court began to deviate from this traditional rule against third-party standing. From these deviations emerged our prudential third-party standing doctrine, which allows litigants to vicariously assert the constitutional rights of others when "the party asserting the right has a 'close' relationship with the person who possesses the right" and "there is a 'hindrance' to the possessor's ability to protect his own interests."

The plurality feints toward this doctrine, claiming that third-party standing for abortionists is well settled by our precedents. But, ultimately, it dodges the question, claiming that Louisiana's standing challenge was waived below. Both assertions are erroneous. First, there is no controlling precedent that sets forth the blanket rule advocated for by plaintiffs here — i.e., abortionists may challenge health and safety regulations based solely on their role in the abortion process. Second, that Louisiana did not waive its standing challenge below.

But even if there were a waiver, it would not be relevant. Louisiana argues that the abortionists and abortion clinics lack standing under Article III to assert the putative rights of their potential clients. No waiver, however explicit, could relieve us of our independent obligation to ensure that we have jurisdiction before addressing the merits of a case. And under a proper understanding of Article III's case-or-controversy requirement, plaintiffs lack standing to invoke our jurisdiction because they assert no private rights of their own, seeking only to vindicate the putative constitutional rights of individuals not before the Court.

The Court has previously asserted that the traditional rule against third-party standing is "not constitutionally mandated, but rather stem[s] from a salutary 'rule of self-restraint'" motivated by "prudential" concerns. The plurality repeats this well-rehearsed claim, accepting its validity without question. But support for this assertion is shallow, to say the least, and it is inconsistent with our more recent standing precedents.

As an initial matter, this Court has never provided a coherent explanation for why the rule against third-party standing is properly characterized as prudential. Many cases reciting this claim rely on the Court's decision in *Barrows*, which stated that the rule against third-party standing is a "rule of self-restraint" "[a]part from the jurisdictional requirement" of Article III, But *Barrows* provides no reasoning to support that distinction and even admits that the rule against third-party standing is "not always clearly distinguished from the constitutional limitation[s]" on standing. The sole authority *Barrows* cites in support of the rule's "prudential" label is a single-Justice concurrence in *Ashwander v. TVA* (1936) (opinion of Brandeis, J.).

Justice Brandeis' concurrence, however, raises more questions than it answers. The opinion does not directly reference third-party standing. It only obliquely refers to the concept by invoking the broader requirement that a plaintiff must "show that he is injured by [the law's] operation." Justice Brandeis claims that this requirement was adopted by the Court "for its own governance in cases confessedly within its jurisdiction." But most of the cases he cites frame the matter in terms of the Court's jurisdiction and authority; none of them invoke prudential justifications. Thus, the "prudential" label for the rule against third-party standing remains a bit of a mystery.

The Court's previous statements on the rule against third-party standing have long suggested that the "proper place" for that rule is in Article III's case-or-controversy requirement. The Court has acknowledged that the traditional rule against third-party standing is "closely related to Art[icle] III concerns." It has repeatedly noted that the rule "is not completely separable from Art[icle] III's requirement that a plaintiff have a sufficiently concrete interest in the outcome of [the] suit to make it a case or controversy." Moreover, the Court has even expressly stated that the rule against third-party standing is "grounded in Art[icle] III limits on the jurisdiction of federal courts to actual cases and controversies."

A brief historical examination of Article III's case-or-controversy requirement confirms what our recent decisions suggest: The rule against third-party standing is constitutional, not prudential. An examination of these limitations reveals that a plaintiff could not establish a case or controversy by asserting the constitutional rights of others.

When a private plaintiff seeks to vindicate someone else's legal injury, he has no private right of his own genuinely at stake in the litigation. Even if the plaintiff has suffered damages as a result of another's legal injury, he has no standing to challenge a law that does not violate his own private rights.

Applying these principles to the case at hand, plaintiffs lack standing under Article III and we, in turn, lack jurisdiction to decide these cases. Thus, "[i]n light of th[e] 'overriding and time-honored concern about keeping the Judiciary's power within its proper constitutional sphere, we must put aside the natural urge to proceed directly to the merits of [an] important dispute and to "settle" it for the sake of convenience and efficiency.'"

Contrary to the plurality's assertion otherwise, *ante*, at 16, abortionists' standing to assert the putative rights of their clients has not been settled by our precedents. It is true that this Court has reflexively allowed abortionists and abortion clinics to vicariously assert a woman's putative right to abortion. But oftentimes the Court has not so much as addressed standing in those cases. And questions "merely lurk[ing] in the record, neither brought to the attention of the court nor ruled upon," are not "considered as having been so decided as to constitute precedents."

The first — and only — time the Court squarely addressed this question with a reasoned decision was in *Singleton v. Wulff* (1976). In that case, a fractured Court concluded that two abortionists had standing to challenge a State's refusal to provide Medicaid reimbursements for abortions. Perfunctorily applying this Court's requirements for third-party standing, Justice Blackmun, joined by three other Justices, asserted that abortionists generally had standing to litigate their clients' rights. Justice Stevens concurred on considerably narrower grounds, reasoning that the abortionists had standing because they had a financial stake in the outcome of the litigation and sought to vindicate their own constitutional rights as well. Notably, Justice Stevens declined to join the plurality's discussion of third-party standing, explaining that he was "not sure whether [that analysis] would, or should, sustain the doctors' standing, apart from" their own legal rights and financial interests being at stake in that specific case. The four remaining Justices dissented in part, concluding that the abortionists lacked standing to litigate the rights of their clients. Because Justice Stevens' opinion "concurred in the judgmen[t] on the narrowest grounds," it is the controlling opinion regarding abortionists' third-party standing.

To the extent Justice Stevens' opinion could be read as concluding that abortionists have standing to vicariously assert their clients' rights so long as the abortionists establish standing on their own legal claims, his position has been abrogated by this Court's more recent decisions, which have "confirm[ed] that a plaintiff must demonstrate standing for each claim he seeks to press." But more importantly, Justice Stevens' opinion does not support the abortionists in these cases, because his opinion rested on case-specific facts not implicated here—namely, the fact that the abortionists would directly receive Medicaid payments from the defendant agency if they prevailed and that they asserted violations of *their own* constitutional rights. In these cases, there is no dispute that the abortionists' sole claim before this Court is that Louisiana's law violates the purported substantive due process rights *of their clients.*

Under a proper understanding of Article III, plaintiffs lack standing. As explained above, in suits seeking to vindicate private rights, the owners of those rights can establish a sufficient injury simply by asserting that their rights have been violated. Constitutional rights are generally considered "private rights" to the extent they "'belon[g] to individuals, considered as individuals.'" And the purported substantive due process right to abort an unborn child is no exception—it is an individual right that is inherently personal. After all, the Court "creat[ed the] right" based on the notion that abortion "'involv[es] the most intimate and personal choices a person may make in a lifetime, choices central to personal dignity and autonomy.'"

Thus, under a proper understanding of Article III, plaintiffs lack standing and, consequently, this Court lacks jurisdiction.

d.   *Mootness*

In *New York State Rifle & Pistol Association, Inc. v. City of New York*, the Court dismissed as moot a major case concerning the Second Amendment because the government repealed the challenged law while the matter was pending in the Supreme Court.

NEW YORK STATE RIFLE & PISTOL ASSOCIATION, INC.
v. CITY OF NEW YORK
140 S. Ct. 1525 (2020)

PER CURIAM.

In the District Court, petitioners challenged a New York City rule regarding the transport of firearms. Petitioners claimed that the rule violated the Second Amendment. Petitioners sought declaratory and injunctive relief against enforcement of the rule insofar as the rule prevented their transport of firearms to a second home or shooting range outside of the city. The District Court and the Court of Appeals rejected petitioners' claim.

After we granted certiorari, the State of New York amended its firearm licensing statute, and the City amended the rule so that petitioners may now transport firearms to a second home or shooting range outside of the city, which is the precise relief that petitioners requested in the prayer for relief in their complaint. Petitioners' claim for declaratory and injunctive relief with respect to the City's old rule is therefore moot. Petitioners now argue, however, that the new rule may still infringe their rights. In particular, petitioners claim that they may not be allowed to stop for coffee, gas, food, or restroom breaks on the way to their second homes or shooting ranges outside of the city. The City responds that those routine stops are entirely permissible under the new rule. We do not here decide that dispute about the new rule. "Our ordinary practice in disposing of a case that has become moot on appeal is to vacate the judgment with directions to dismiss."

However, in instances where the mootness is attributable to a change in the legal framework governing the case, and where the plaintiff may have some residual claim under the new framework that was understandably not asserted previously, our practice is to vacate the judgment and remand for further proceedings in which the parties may, if necessary, amend their pleadings or develop the record more fully.

Petitioners also argue that, even though they have not previously asked for damages with respect to the City's old rule, they still could do so in this lawsuit. Petitioners did not seek damages in their complaint; indeed, the possibility of a damages claim was not raised until well into the litigation in this Court. The City argues that it is too late for petitioners to now add a claim for damages. On remand, the Court of Appeals and the District Court may consider whether petitioners may still add a claim for damages in this lawsuit with respect to New York City's old rule.

Justice ALITO, with whom Justice GORSUCH joins, and with whom Justice THOMAS joins except for Part IV-B, dissenting.

By incorrectly dismissing this case as moot, the Court permits our docket to be manipulated in a way that should not be countenanced. Twelve years ago in *District of Columbia v. Heller* (2008), we held that the Second Amendment protects the right of ordinary Americans to keep and bear arms. Two years later, our decision in *McDonald v. Chicago* (2010), established that this right is fully applicable to the States. Since then, the lower courts have decided numerous cases involving Second Amendment challenges to a variety of federal, state, and local laws. Most have failed. We have been asked to review many of these decisions, but until this case, we denied all such requests.

Regrettably, the Court now dismisses the case as moot. If the Court were right on the law, I would of course approve that disposition. Under the Constitution, our authority is limited to deciding actual cases or controversies, and if this were no longer a live controversy — that is, if it were now moot — we would be compelled to dismiss. But if a case is on our docket and we have jurisdiction, we have an obligation to decide it.

Thus, in this case, we must apply the well-established standards for determining whether a case is moot, and under those standards, we still have a live case before us. It is certainly true that the new City ordinance and the new State law give petitioners *most of* what they sought, but that is not the test for mootness. Instead, "a case 'becomes moot only when it is *impossible* for a court to grant *any effectual relief whatever* to the prevailing party.'" "'As long as the parties have a concrete interest, *however small*, in the outcome of the litigation, the case is not moot.'"

Respondents have failed to meet this "heavy burden." This is so for two reasons. First, the changes in City and State law do not provide petitioners with all the injunctive relief they sought. Second, if we reversed on the merits, the District Court on remand could award damages to remedy the constitutional violation that petitioners suffered.

I

[Justice Alito described the New York ordinance and its repeal.]

II

The Court vacates the judgment of the Court of Appeals, *apparently* on the ground that this case is now moot. And if that is the reason for what the Court has done, the Court is wrong. This case is not moot.

We have been particularly wary of attempts by parties to manufacture mootness in order to evade review. And it is black-letter law that we have a "virtually unflagging" obligation to exercise our jurisdiction.

In this case, the amended City ordinance and the new State law gave petitioners most of what they sought in their complaint, but the new laws did not give them complete relief. It is entirely possible for them to obtain more relief, and therefore this case is not moot. This is so for the following reasons.

First, this case is not moot because the amended City ordinance and new State law do not give petitioners all the *prospective relief* they seek. Petitioners asserted in their complaint that the Second Amendment guarantees them, as holders of premises licenses, "unrestricted access" to ranges, competitions, and second homes outside of New York City, and the new laws do not give them that.

The new City ordinance has limitations that petitioners claim are unconstitutional, namely, that a trip outside the City must be "direc[t]" and travel within the City must be "continuous and uninterrupted." Exactly what these restrictions mean is not clear from the face of the rule, and the City has done little to clarify their reach. Based on all this, we are left with no clear idea where the City draws the line, and the situation is further complicated by the overlay of State law. The new State law appears to prevent the City from penalizing any "direc[t]" trip to a range or competition outside the City, but the State law does not define that limitation. The petitioners wanted to enter competitions in upstate New York more than a five hour drive from the City. Could they stop along the way? And if so, for how long? The State has not explained its understanding of this limitation, and in any event, prosecutorial decisions in New York are generally made by the State's 67 elected district attorneys. The bottom line is that petitioners, who sought "unrestricted access" to out-of-city ranges and competitions, are still subject to restrictions of undetermined meaning.

These restrictions may not seem very important, but that is beside the point for purposes of mootness. Nor does it matter whether, in the end, those restrictions would be found to violate the Second Amendment. All that matters for present purposes is that the City still withholds from petitioners something that they have claimed from the beginning is their constitutional right. It follows that the case is not moot. It is as simple as that.

The case is not moot for a separate and independent reason: If this Court were to hold, as petitioners request and as I believe we should, that 38 N.Y.C.R.R. § 5-23 violated petitioners' Second Amendment right, the District Court on remand could (and probably should) award damages. Petitioners brought their claims under 42 U.S.C. § 1983, which permits the recovery of damages. And while the amended complaint does not expressly seek damages, it is enough that it requests "[a]ny other such further relief as the [c]ourt deems just and proper." Under modern pleading standards, that suffices.

At a minimum, if petitioners succeeded on their challenge to the travel restrictions, they would be eligible for nominal damages. When a plaintiff's constitutional rights have been violated, nominal damages may be awarded without proof of any additional injury.

It is even possible that one or more of the petitioners may be eligible for compensatory damages. To get such relief, they would of course be required to show that they suffered an "actual injury." But petitioners may be able to make such a showing. As discussed above, the failure to include in their complaint specific factual allegations of actual injury would not preclude such recovery. Nor were petitioners obligated to provide information supporting actual injury in opposing the City's motion for summary judgment.

If we were to reverse the judgment below and hold the City's old rule unconstitutional, it would be appropriate to remand the case for proceedings on the question of remedies. We have frequently done this when we reverse a judgment that was entered against the plaintiff on liability grounds.

With this is mind, the possibility of actual damages cannot be ruled out. One or more of the petitioners could seek compensation for out-of-pocket expenses, such as membership fees at in-city ranges. For purposes of determining whether this case is moot, the question is not whether petitioners would actually succeed in obtaining such damages or whether their loss was substantial. If there is a possibility of obtaining damages in any amount, the case is not moot.

III

The *per curiam* provides no sound reason for holding that this case is moot. The *per curiam* states that the City's current rule gave petitioners "the precise relief [they] requested" in their prayer for relief, but that is not so. Petitioners' prayer for relief asks the court to enjoin 38 N.Y.C.R.R. § 5-23 insofar as it "prohibit[s]" travel outside the City to ranges, competitions, and second homes. The new rule's conditions unmistakably continue to prohibit some travel outside the City to those destinations. For this reason, petitioners have not obtained the "unrestricted access" that, they have always maintained, the Second Amendment guarantees. The *per curiam* implies that the current rule, as interpreted at oral argument by counsel for the City, gives petitioners everything that they now seek, but that also is not true. Petitioners still claim the right to "unrestricted access" and counsel's off-the-cuff concessions do not give them that.

The *per curiam*'s main argument appears to go as follows: Petitioners' original claim was a challenge to New York's old rule; this claim is now moot due to the repeal of that rule; and what the petitioners are now asserting is a new claim, namely, that New York's current rule is also unconstitutional.

This argument also misrepresents the nature of the claim asserted in petitioners' complaint. What petitioners claimed in their complaint and still claim is that they are entitled to "unrestricted access" to out-of-city ranges and competitions. The City's replacement of one law denying unrestricted access with another that also denies that access did not change the nature of petitioners' claim or render it moot.

IV

Having shown that this case is not moot, I proceed to the merits of plaintiffs' claim that the City ordinance violated the Second Amendment. This is not a close question. The answer follows directly from *Heller*.

For a similar reason, 38 N.Y.C.R.R. § 5-23 also violated the Second Amendment. We deal here with the same core Second Amendment right, the right to keep a handgun in the home for self-defense. As the Second Circuit "assume[d]," a necessary concomitant of this right is the right to take a gun outside the home for certain purposes. One of these is to take a gun for maintenance or repair, which City law allows. See § 5-22(a)(16). Another is to take a gun outside the home in order to transfer ownership lawfully, which the City also allows. § 5-26(j). And still another is to take a gun to a range in order to gain and maintain the skill necessary to use it responsibly. As we said in *Heller*, "'to bear arms implies something more than the mere keeping [of arms]; it implies the learning to handle and use them in a way that makes those who keep them ready for their efficient use.'"

If history is not sufficient to show that the New York City ordinance is unconstitutional, any doubt is dispelled by the weakness of the City's showing that its travel restriction significantly promoted public safety. Although the courts below claimed to apply heightened scrutiny, there was nothing heightened about what they did.

This case is not moot. The City violated petitioners' Second Amendment right, and we should so hold. I would reverse the judgment of the Court of Appeals and remand the case to the District Court to provide appropriate relief. I therefore respectfully dissent.

Chapter 3

The Federal Executive Power

A. *Inherent Presidential Power*

In *United States v. Nixon* (casebook p. 286), the Supreme Court upheld subpoenas of audiotapes made in the White House that the Watergate special prosecutor wanted to use as evidence in criminal trials. On July 9, 2020, the Court decided two cases concerning subpoenas of financial records from institutions concerning President Trump. In *Trump v. Vance*, the Court considered a state grand jury subpoena of financial records from President Trump's accountants in connection with a criminal investigation of campaign finance violations. In *Trump v. Mazars USA*, the Court considered congressional committee subpoenas of information from financial institutions concerning President Trump.

TRUMP v. VANCE
140 S. Ct. 2412 (2020)

Chief Justice ROBERTS delivered the opinion of the Court.

In our judicial system, "the public has a right to every man's evidence." Since the earliest days of the Republic, "every man" has included the President of the United States. Beginning with Jefferson and carrying on through Clinton, Presidents have uniformly testified or produced documents in criminal proceedings when called upon by federal courts. This case involves — so far as we and the parties can tell — the first *state* criminal subpoena directed to a President. The President contends that the subpoena is unenforceable. We granted certiorari to decide whether Article II and the Supremacy Clause categorically preclude, or require a heightened standard for, the issuance of a state criminal subpoena to a sitting President.

I

In the summer of 2018, the New York County District Attorney's Office opened an investigation into what it opaquely describes as "business transactions involving multiple individuals whose conduct may have violated state law." A year later, the office—acting on behalf of a grand jury—served a subpoena *duces tecum* (essentially a request to produce evidence) on Mazars USA, LLP, the personal accounting firm of President Donald J. Trump. The subpoena directed Mazars to produce financial records relating to the President and business organizations affiliated with him, including "[t]ax returns and related schedules," from "2011 to the present."

The President, acting in his personal capacity, sued the district attorney and Mazars in Federal District Court to enjoin enforcement of the subpoena. He argued that, under Article II and the Supremacy Clause, a sitting President enjoys absolute immunity from state criminal process. He asked the court to issue a "declaratory judgment that the subpoena is invalid and unenforceable while the President is in office" and to permanently enjoin the district attorney "from taking any action to enforce the subpoena." Mazars, concluding that the dispute was between the President and the district attorney, took no position on the legal issues raised by the President.

On the merits, the Court of Appeals agreed with the District Court's denial of a preliminary injunction. Drawing on the 200-year history of Presidents being subject to federal judicial process, the Court of Appeals concluded that "presidential immunity does not bar the enforcement of a state grand jury subpoena directing a third party to produce non-privileged material, even when the subject matter under investigation pertains to the President." It also rejected the argument raised by the United States as *amicus curiae* that a state grand jury subpoena must satisfy a heightened showing of need.

II

In the summer of 1807, all eyes were on Richmond, Virginia. Aaron Burr, the former Vice President, was on trial for treason. Fallen from political grace after his fatal duel with Alexander Hamilton, and with a murder charge pending in New Jersey, Burr followed the path of many down-and-out Americans of his day—he headed West in search of new opportunity. But Burr was a man with outsized ambitions. Together with General James Wilkinson, the Governor of the Louisiana Territory, he hatched a plan to establish a new territory in Mexico, then controlled by Spain. Both men anticipated that war between the United States and Spain was imminent, and when it broke out they intended to invade Spanish territory at the head of a private army.

But while Burr was rallying allies to his cause, tensions with Spain eased and rumors began to swirl that Burr was conspiring to detach States by the Allegheny Mountains from the Union. Wary of being exposed as the principal co-conspirator, Wilkinson took steps to ensure that any blame would fall on Burr. He sent a series of letters to President Jefferson accusing Burr of plotting to attack New Orleans and revolutionize the Louisiana Territory.

Jefferson, who despised his former running mate Burr for trying to steal the 1800 presidential election from him, was predisposed to credit Wilkinson's version of events. The President sent a special message to Congress identifying Burr as the "prime mover" in a plot "against the peace and safety of the Union." According to Jefferson, Burr contemplated either the "severance of the Union" or an attack on Spanish territory. Jefferson acknowledged that his sources contained a "mixture of rumors, conjectures, and suspicions" but, citing Wilkinson's letters, he assured Congress that Burr's guilt was "beyond question."

The trial that followed was "the greatest spectacle in the short history of the republic," complete with a Founder-studded cast. People flocked to Richmond to watch, massing in tents and covered wagons along the banks of the James River, nearly doubling the town's population of 5,000. Burr's defense team included Edmund Randolph and Luther Martin, both former delegates at the Constitutional Convention and renowned advocates. Chief Justice John Marshall, who had recently squared off with the Jefferson administration in *Marbury v. Madison* (1803), presided as Circuit Justice for Virginia. Meanwhile Jefferson, intent on conviction, orchestrated the prosecution from afar, dedicating Cabinet meetings to the case, peppering the prosecutors with directions, and spending nearly $100,000 from the Treasury on the five-month proceedings.

In the lead-up to trial, Burr, taking aim at his accusers, moved for a subpoena *duces tecum* directed at Jefferson. The draft subpoena required the President to produce an October 21, 1806 letter from Wilkinson and accompanying documents, which Jefferson had referenced in his message to Congress. The prosecution opposed the request, arguing that a President could not be subjected to such a subpoena and that the letter might contain state secrets. Following four days of argument, Marshall announced his ruling to a packed chamber.

The President, Marshall declared, does not "stand exempt from the general provisions of the constitution" or, in particular, the Sixth

Amendment's guarantee that those accused have compulsory process for obtaining witnesses for their defense. *United States v. Burr* (CC Va. 1807). At common law the "single reservation" to the duty to testify in response to a subpoena was "the case of the king," whose "dignity" was seen as "incompatible" with appearing "under the process of the court." But, as Marshall explained, a king is born to power and can "do no wrong." The President, by contrast, is "of the people" and subject to the law. According to Marshall, the sole argument for exempting the President from testimonial obligations was that his "duties as chief magistrate demand his whole time for national objects." But, in Marshall's assessment, those demands were "not unremitting." And should the President's duties preclude his attendance at a particular time and place, a court could work that out upon return of the subpoena.

Marshall also rejected the prosecution's argument that the President was immune from a subpoena *duces tecum* because executive papers might contain state secrets. "A subpoena duces tecum," he said, "may issue to any person to whom an ordinary subpoena may issue." As he explained, no "fair construction" of the Constitution supported the conclusion that the right "to compel the attendance of witnesses[ ] does not extend" to requiring those witnesses to "bring[ ] with them such papers as may be material in the defence." And, as a matter of basic fairness, permitting such information to be withheld would "tarnish the reputation of the court." As for "the propriety of introducing any papers," that would "depend on the character of the paper, not on the character of the person who holds it." Marshall acknowledged that the papers sought by Burr could contain information "the disclosure of which would endanger the public safety," but stated that, again, such concerns would have "due consideration" upon the return of the subpoena.

While the arguments unfolded, Jefferson, who had received word of the motion, wrote to the prosecutor indicating that he would—subject to the prerogative to decide which executive communications should be withheld—"furnish on all occasions, whatever the purposes of justice may require." His "personal attendance," however, was out of the question, for it "would leave the nation without" the "sole branch which the constitution requires to be always in function."

Before Burr received the subpoenaed documents, Marshall rejected the prosecution's core legal theory for treason and Burr was accordingly acquitted. Jefferson, however, was not done. Committed to salvaging a conviction, he directed the prosecutors to proceed with a misdemeanor (yes, misdemeanor) charge for inciting war against Spain. Burr then renewed his request for Wilkinson's October 21 letter, which he later received a copy of, and subpoenaed a second letter, dated November 12, 1806, which the prosecutor claimed was privileged. Acknowledging that the President may withhold information to protect public safety, Marshall instructed that Jefferson should "state the particular reasons" for withholding the letter. The court, paying "all proper respect" to those reasons, would then decide whether to compel disclosure. But that decision was averted when the misdemeanor trial was cut short after it became clear that the prosecution lacked the evidence to convict.

In the two centuries since the Burr trial, successive Presidents have accepted Marshall's ruling that the Chief Executive is subject to subpoena. In 1818, President Monroe received a subpoena to testify in a court-martial against one of his appointees. His Attorney General, William Wirt — who had served as a prosecutor during Burr's trial — advised Monroe that, per Marshall's ruling, a subpoena to testify may "be properly awarded to the President." Monroe offered to sit for a deposition and ultimately submitted answers to written interrogatories.

Following Monroe's lead, his successors have uniformly agreed to testify when called in criminal proceedings, provided they could do so at a time and place of their choosing. In 1875, President Grant submitted to a three-hour deposition in the criminal prosecution of a political appointee embroiled in a network of tax-evading whiskey distillers. A century later, President Ford's attempted assassin subpoenaed him to testify in her defense. Ford obliged — from a safe distance — in the first videotaped deposition of a President. President Carter testified via the same means in the trial of two local officials who, while Carter was Governor of Georgia, had offered to contribute to his campaign in exchange for advance warning of any state gambling raids. Two years later, Carter gave videotaped testimony to a federal grand jury investigating whether a fugitive financier had entreated the White House to quash his extradition proceedings. President Clinton testified three times, twice via deposition pursuant to subpoenas in federal criminal trials of associates implicated during the Whitewater investigation, and once by video for a grand jury investigating possible perjury.

The bookend to Marshall's ruling came in 1974 when the question he never had to decide — whether to compel the disclosure of official communications over the objection of the President — came to a head. That spring, the Special Prosecutor appointed to investigate the break-in of the Democratic National Committee Headquarters at the Watergate complex filed an indictment charging seven defendants associated with President Nixon and naming Nixon as an unindicted co-conspirator. As the case moved toward trial, the Special Prosecutor secured a subpoena *duces tecum* directing Nixon to produce, among other things, tape recordings of Oval Office meetings. Nixon moved to quash the subpoena, claiming that the Constitution provides an absolute privilege of confidentiality to all presidential communications. This Court rejected that argument in *United States v. Nixon* (1974), a decision we later described as "unequivocally and emphatically endors[ing] Marshall's" holding that Presidents are subject to subpoena. The Court thus concluded that the President's "generalized assertion of privilege must yield to the demonstrated, specific need for evidence in a pending criminal trial." Two weeks later, President Nixon dutifully released the tapes.

III

The history surveyed above all involved *federal* criminal proceedings. Here we are confronted for the first time with a subpoena issued to the President by a local grand jury operating under the supervision of a *state* court.

In the President's view, that distinction makes all the difference. He argues that the Supremacy Clause gives a sitting President absolute immunity from state criminal subpoenas because compliance with those subpoenas would categorically impair a President's performance of his Article II functions. The Solicitor General, arguing on behalf of the United States, agrees with much of the President's reasoning but does not commit to his bottom line. Instead, the Solicitor General urges us to resolve this case by holding that a state grand jury subpoena for a sitting President's personal records must, at the very least, "satisfy a heightened standard of need," which the Solicitor General contends was not met here.

We begin with the question of absolute immunity. No one doubts that Article II guarantees the independence of the Executive Branch. As the head of that branch, the President "occupies a unique position in the constitutional scheme." His duties, which range from faithfully executing the laws to commanding the Armed Forces, are of unrivaled gravity and breadth. Quite appropriately, those duties come with protections that safeguard the President's ability to perform his vital functions. It follows that States also lack the power to impede the President's execution of those laws.

Marshall's ruling in *Burr*, entrenched by 200 years of practice and our decision in *Nixon*, confirms that *federal* criminal subpoenas do not "rise to the level of constitutionally forbidden impairment of the Executive's ability to perform its constitutionally mandated functions." But the President, joined in part by the Solicitor General, argues that *state* criminal subpoenas pose a unique threat of impairment and thus demand greater protection. To be clear, the President does not contend here that *this* subpoena, in particular, is impermissibly burdensome. Instead he makes a *categorical* argument about the burdens generally associated with state criminal subpoenas, focusing on three: diversion, stigma, and harassment. We address each in turn.

The President's primary contention, which the Solicitor General supports, is that complying with state criminal subpoenas would necessarily divert the Chief Executive from his duties. Indeed, we expressly rejected immunity based on distraction alone 15 years later in *Clinton v. Jones*. There, President Clinton argued that the risk of being "distracted by the need to participate in litigation" entitled a sitting President to absolute immunity from civil liability, not just for official acts, but for private conduct as well. But, the Court concluded, "[w]hile such distractions may be vexing to those subjected to them, they do not ordinarily implicate constitutional . . . concerns."

The same is true of criminal subpoenas. Just as a "properly managed" civil suit is generally "unlikely to occupy any substantial amount of" a President's time or attention, two centuries of experience confirm that a properly tailored criminal subpoena will not normally hamper the performance of the President's constitutional duties. If anything, we expect that in the mine run of cases, where a President is subpoenaed during a proceeding targeting someone else, as Jefferson was, the burden on a President will ordinarily be lighter than the burden of defending against a civil suit.

The President, however, believes the district attorney is investigating him and his businesses. In such a situation, he contends, the "toll that criminal process . . . exacts from the President is even heavier" than the distraction at issue in *Fitzgerald* and *Clinton*, because "criminal litigation" poses unique burdens on the President's time and will generate a "considerable if not overwhelming degree of mental preoccupation."

But the President is not seeking immunity from the diversion occasioned by the prospect of future criminal *liability*. Instead he concedes — consistent with the position of the Department of Justice — that state grand juries are free to investigate a sitting President with an eye toward charging him after the completion of his term. The President's objection therefore must be limited to the *additional* distraction caused by the subpoena itself. But that argument runs up against the 200 years of precedent establishing that Presidents, and their official communications, are subject to judicial process, even when the President is under investigation.

The President next claims that the stigma of being subpoenaed will undermine his leadership at home and abroad. Notably, the Solicitor

General does not endorse this argument, perhaps because we have twice denied absolute immunity claims by Presidents in cases involving allegations of serious misconduct. But even if a tarnished reputation were a cognizable impairment, there is nothing inherently stigmatizing about a President performing "the citizen's normal duty of . . . furnishing information relevant" to a criminal investigation. Nor can we accept that the risk of association with persons or activities under criminal investigation can absolve a President of such an important public duty. Prior Presidents have weathered these associations in federal cases, and there is no reason to think any attendant notoriety is necessarily greater in state court proceedings.

To be sure, the consequences for a President's public standing will likely increase if he is the one under investigation. But, again, the President concedes that such investigations are permitted under Article II and the Supremacy Clause, and receipt of a subpoena would not seem to categorically magnify the harm to the President's reputation.

Additionally, while the current suit has cast the Mazars subpoena into the spotlight, longstanding rules of grand jury secrecy aim to prevent the very stigma the President anticipates. Of course, disclosure restrictions are not perfect. But those who make unauthorized disclosures regarding a grand jury subpoena do so at their peril.

Finally, the President and the Solicitor General warn that subjecting Presidents to state criminal subpoenas will make them "easily identifiable target[s]" for harassment. But we rejected a nearly identical argument in *Clinton*, where then-President Clinton argued that permitting civil liability for unofficial acts would "generate a large volume of politically motivated harassing and frivolous litigation." The President and the Solicitor General nevertheless argue that state criminal subpoenas pose a heightened risk and could undermine the President's ability to "deal fearlessly and impartially" with the States. They caution that, while federal prosecutors are accountable to and removable by the President, the 2,300 district attorneys in this country are responsive to local constituencies, local interests, and local prejudices, and might "use criminal process to register their dissatisfaction with" the President. What is more, we are told, the state courts supervising local grand juries may not exhibit the same respect that federal courts show to the President as a coordinate branch of Government.

We recognize, as does the district attorney, that harassing subpoenas could, under certain circumstances, threaten the independence or effectiveness of the Executive. Even so, in *Clinton* we found that the risk of harassment was not "serious" because federal courts have the tools to deter and, where necessary, dismiss vexatious civil suits. And, while we cannot ignore the possibility that state prosecutors may have political motivations, here again the law already seeks to protect against the predicted abuse.

First, grand juries are prohibited from engaging in "arbitrary fishing expeditions" and initiating investigations "out of malice or an intent to harass." These protections, as the district attorney himself puts it, "apply with special force to a President, in light of the office's unique position as the head of the Executive Branch." And, in the event of such harassment, a President would be entitled to the protection of federal courts. The policy against federal interference in state criminal proceedings, while strong, allows "intervention in those cases where the District Court properly finds that the state proceeding is motivated by a desire to harass or is conducted in bad faith."

Second, contrary to Justice Alito's characterization, our holding does not allow States to "run roughshod over the functioning of [the Executive B]ranch." The Supremacy Clause prohibits state judges and prosecutors from interfering with a President's official duties. Any effort to manipulate a President's policy decisions or to "retaliat[e]" against a President for official acts through issuance of a subpoena, Brief for Respondent Vance 15, 43, would thus be an unconstitutional attempt to "influence" a superior sovereign "exempt" from such obstacles, We generally "assume[ ] that state courts and prosecutors will observe constitutional limitations." Failing that, federal law allows a President to challenge any allegedly unconstitutional influence in a federal forum, as the President has done here.

Given these safeguards and the Court's precedents, we cannot conclude that absolute immunity is necessary or appropriate under Article II or the Supremacy Clause.

We next consider whether a state grand jury subpoena seeking a President's private papers must satisfy a heightened need standard. The Solicitor General would require a threshold showing that the evidence sought is "critical" for "specific charging decisions" and that the subpoena is a "last resort," meaning the evidence is "not available from any other source" and is needed "now, rather than at the end of the President's term." Justice Alito, largely embracing those criteria, agrees that a state criminal subpoena to a President "should not be allowed unless a heightened standard is met."

We disagree, for three reasons. First, such a heightened standard would extend protection designed for official documents to the President's private papers.

Second, neither the Solicitor General nor Justice Alito has established that heightened protection against state subpoenas is necessary for the

Executive to fulfill his Article II functions. Beyond the risk of harassment, which we addressed above, the only justification they offer for the heightened standard is protecting Presidents from "unwarranted burdens." In effect, they argue that even if federal subpoenas to a President are warranted whenever evidence is material, state subpoenas are warranted "only when [the] evidence is essential." But that double standard has no basis in law. For if the state subpoena is not issued to manipulate, the documents themselves are not protected, and the Executive is not impaired, then nothing in Article II or the Supremacy Clause supports holding state subpoenas to a higher standard than their federal counterparts.

Finally, in the absence of a need to protect the Executive, the public interest in fair and effective law enforcement cuts in favor of comprehensive access to evidence. Requiring a state grand jury to meet a heightened standard of need would hobble the grand jury's ability to acquire "all information that might possibly bear on its investigation."

Rejecting a heightened need standard does not leave Presidents with "no real protection." To start, a President may avail himself of the same protections available to every other citizen. These include the right to challenge the subpoena on any grounds permitted by state law, which usually include bad faith and undue burden or breadth.

Furthermore, although the Constitution does not entitle the Executive to absolute immunity or a heightened standard, he is not "relegate[d]" only to the challenges available to private citizens. A President can raise subpoena-specific constitutional challenges, in either a state or federal forum. As previously noted, he can challenge the subpoena as an attempt to influence the performance of his official duties, in violation of the Supremacy Clause. This avenue protects against local political machinations "interposed as an obstacle to the effective operation of a federal constitutional power."

In addition, the Executive can — as the district attorney concedes — argue that compliance with a particular subpoena would impede his constitutional duties. As a result, "once the President sets forth and explains a conflict between judicial proceeding and public duties," or shows that an order or subpoena would "significantly interfere with his efforts to carry out" those duties, "the matter changes." At that point, a court should use its inherent authority to quash or modify the subpoena, if necessary to ensure that such "interference with the President's duties would not occur."

Two hundred years ago, a great jurist of our Court established that no citizen, not even the President, is categorically above the common duty to produce evidence when called upon in a criminal proceeding. We reaffirm that principle today and hold that the President is neither absolutely immune from state criminal subpoenas seeking his private papers nor entitled to a heightened standard of need. The "guard[ ] furnished to this high officer" lies where it always has — in "the conduct of a court" applying established legal and constitutional principles to individual subpoenas in a manner that preserves both the independence of the Executive and the integrity of the criminal justice system.

Justice KAVANAUGH, with whom Justice GORSUCH joins, concurring in the judgment.

The Court today unanimously concludes that a President does not possess absolute immunity from a state criminal subpoena, but also unanimously agrees that this case should be remanded to the District Court, where the President may raise constitutional and legal objections to the subpoena as appropriate. I agree with those two conclusions.

The dispute over this grand jury subpoena reflects a conflict between a State's interest in criminal investigation and a President's Article II interest in performing his or her duties without undue interference. Although this case involves personal information of the President and is therefore not an executive privilege case, the majority opinion correctly concludes based on precedent that Article II and the Supremacy Clause of the Constitution supply some protection for the Presidency against state criminal subpoenas of this sort.

In our system of government, as this Court has often stated, no one is above the law. That principle applies, of course, to a President. At the same time, in light of Article II of the Constitution, this Court has repeatedly declared — and the Court indicates again today — that a court may not proceed against a President as it would against an ordinary litigant.

The question here, then, is how to balance the State's interests and the Article II interests. The longstanding precedent that has applied to federal criminal subpoenas for official, privileged Executive Branch information is *United States v. Nixon* (1974). That landmark case requires that a prosecutor establish a "demonstrated, specific need" for the President's information.

The *Nixon* "demonstrated, specific need" standard is a tried-and-true test that accommodates both the interests of the criminal process and the Article II interests of the Presidency. The *Nixon* standard ensures that a prosecutor's interest in subpoenaed information is sufficiently important to justify an intrusion on the Article II interests of the Presidency. The *Nixon* standard also reduces the risk of subjecting a President to unwarranted burdens, because it provides that a prosecutor may obtain a President's information only in certain defined circumstances.

Because this case again entails a clash between the interests of the criminal process and the Article II interests of the Presidency, I would apply the longstanding *Nixon* "demonstrated, specific need" standard to this case. The majority opinion does not apply the *Nixon* standard in this distinct Article II context, as I would have done. That said, the majority opinion appropriately takes account of some important concerns that also animate *Nixon* and the Constitution's balance of powers. The majority opinion explains that a state prosecutor may not issue a subpoena for a President's personal information out of bad faith, malice, or an intent to harass a President; as a result of prosecutorial impropriety; to seek information that is not relevant to an investigation; that is overly broad or unduly burdensome; to manipulate, influence, or retaliate against a President's official acts or policy decisions; or in a way that would impede, conflict with, or interfere with a President's official duties. All nine Members of the Court agree, moreover, that a President may raise objections to a state criminal subpoena not just in state court but also in federal court. And the majority opinion indicates that, in light of the "high respect that is owed to the office of the Chief Executive," courts "should be particularly meticulous" in assessing a subpoena for a President's personal records.

I agree that the case should be remanded to the District Court for further proceedings, where the President may raise constitutional and legal objections to the state grand jury subpoena as appropriate.

Justice THOMAS, dissenting.

The President argues that he is absolutely immune from the issuance of any subpoena, but that if the Court disagrees, we should remand so that the District Court can develop a record about this particular subpoena. I agree with the majority that the President is not entitled to absolute immunity from *issuance* of the subpoena. But he may be entitled to relief against its *enforcement*. I therefore agree with the President that the proper course is to vacate and remand. If the President can show that "his duties as chief magistrate demand his whole time for national objects," *United States v. Burr* (CC Va. 1807) (Marshall, C. J.), he is entitled to relief from enforcement of the subpoena.

I

The President first argues that he has absolute immunity from the issuance of grand jury subpoenas during his term in office. This Court has recognized absolute immunity for the President from "damages liability predicated on his official acts." *Nixon v. Fitzgerald* (1982). But we have rejected absolute immunity from damages actions for a President's nonofficial conduct, *Clinton v. Jones* (1997), and we have never addressed the question of immunity from a grand jury subpoena.

I agree with the majority that the President does not have absolute immunity from the issuance of a grand jury subpoena. Unlike the majority, however, I do not reach this conclusion based on a primarily functionalist analysis. Instead, I reach it based on the text of the Constitution, which, as understood by the ratifying public and incorporated into an early circuit opinion by Chief Justice Marshall, does not support the President's claim of absolute immunity.

The text of the Constitution explicitly addresses the privileges of some federal officials, but it does not afford the President absolute immunity. Members of Congress are "privileged from Arrest during their Attendance at the Session of their respective Houses, and in going to and returning from the same," except for "Treason, Felony and Breach of the Peace." Art. I, § 6, cl. 1. The Constitution further specifies that, "for any Speech or Debate in either House, they shall not be questioned in any other Place." By contrast, the text of the Constitution contains no explicit grant of absolute immunity from legal process for the President. This original understanding is reflected in an early circuit decision by Chief Justice Marshall, on which the majority partially relies. Based on the evidence of original meaning and Chief Justice Marshall's early interpretation in *Burr*, the better reading of the text of the Constitution is that the President has no absolute immunity from the issuance of a grand jury subpoena.

II

In addition to contesting the issuance of the subpoena, the President also seeks injunctive and declaratory relief against its enforcement. The majority recognizes that the President can seek relief from enforcement, but it does not vacate and remand for the lower courts to address this question. I would do so and instruct them to apply the standard articulated by Chief Justice Marshall in *Burr*: If the President is unable to comply because of his official duties, then he is entitled to injunctive and declaratory relief.

The *Burr* standard places the burden on the President but also requires courts to take pains to respect the demands on the President's time. The Constitution vests the President with extensive powers and responsibilities, and courts are poorly situated to conduct a searching review of the President's assertion that he is unable to comply.

In sum, the demands on the President's time and the importance of his tasks are extraordinary, and the office of the President cannot be delegated to subordinates. A subpoena imposes both demands on the President's limited time and a mental burden, even when the President is not directly engaged in complying. This understanding of the Presidency should guide courts in deciding whether to enforce a subpoena for the President's documents.

Courts must also recognize their own limitations. When the President asserts that matters of foreign affairs or national defense preclude his compliance with a subpoena, the Judiciary will rarely have a basis for rejecting that assertion. Judges "simply lack the relevant information and expertise to second-guess determinations made by the President based on information properly withheld." "[E]ven if the courts could compel the Executive to produce the necessary information" to understand the demands on his time, decisions about that information "are simply not amenable to judicial determination because '[t]hey are delicate, complex, and involve large elements of prophecy.'" The President has at his disposal enormous amounts of classified intelligence regarding the Government's concerns around the globe. His decisionmaking is further informed by experience in matters of foreign affairs, national defense, and intelligence that judges almost always will not have. And his decisionmaking takes into account the full spectrum of the Government's operations, not just the matters directly related to a particular case. Even with perfect information, courts lack the institutional competence to engage in a searching review of the President's reasons for not complying with a subpoena.

I would vacate and remand to allow the District Court to determine whether enforcement of this subpoena should be enjoined because the President's "duties as chief magistrate demand his whole time for national objects." Accordingly, I respectfully dissent.

Justice ALITO, dissenting.

This case is almost certain to be portrayed as a case about the current President and the current political situation, but the case has a much deeper significance. While the decision will of course have a direct effect on President Trump, what the Court holds today will also affect all future Presidents — which is to say, it will affect the Presidency, and that is a matter of great and lasting importance to the Nation.

The event that precipitated this case is unprecedented. Respondent Vance, an elected state prosecutor, launched a criminal investigation of a sitting President and obtained a grand jury subpoena for his records. The specific question before us — whether the subpoena may be enforced — cannot be answered adequately without considering the broader question that frames it: whether the Constitution imposes restrictions on a State's deployment of its criminal law enforcement powers against a sitting President. If the Constitution sets no such limits, then a local prosecutor may prosecute a sitting President. And if that is allowed, it follows *a fortiori* that the subpoena at issue can be enforced. On the other hand, if the Constitution does not permit a State to prosecute a sitting President, the next logical question is whether the Constitution restrains any other prosecutorial or investigative weapons.

These are important questions that go to the very structure of the Government created by the Constitution. In evaluating these questions, two important structural features must be taken into account.

The first is the nature and role of the Presidency. The Presidency, like Congress and the Supreme Court, is a permanent institution created by the Constitution. All three of these institutions are distinct from the human beings who serve in them at any point in time. In the case of Congress or the Supreme Court, the distinction is easy to perceive, since they have multiple Members. But because "[t]he President is the only person who alone composes a branch of government . . . , there is not always a clear line between his personal and official affairs." As a result, the law's treatment of the person who serves as President can have an important effect on the institution, and the institution of the Presidency plays an indispensable role in our constitutional system.

The second structural feature is the relationship between the Federal Government and the States.

Building on this principle of federalism, two centuries of case law prohibit the States from taxing, regulating, or otherwise interfering with the lawful work of federal agencies, instrumentalities, and officers. The Court premised these cases on the principle that "the activities of the Federal Government are free from regulation by any State. No other adjustment of competing enactments or legal principles is possible."

The scenario apparently contemplated by the District Court is striking. If a sitting President were charged in New York County, would he be arrested and fingerprinted? He would presumably be required to appear for arraignment in criminal court, where the judge would set the conditions for his release. Could he be sent to Rikers Island or be required to post bail? Could the judge impose restrictions on his travel? If the President were scheduled to travel abroad—perhaps to attend a G–7 meeting—would he have to get judicial approval? If the President were charged with a complicated offense requiring a long trial, would he have to put his Presidential responsibilities aside for weeks on end while sitting in a Manhattan courtroom? While the trial was in progress, would aides be able to approach him and whisper in his ear about pressing matters?

Would he be able to obtain a recess whenever he needed to speak with an aide at greater length or attend to an urgent matter, such as speaking with a foreign leader? Could he effectively carry out all his essential Presidential responsibilities after the trial day ended and at the same time adequately confer with his trial attorneys regarding his defense? Or should he be expected to give up the right to attend his own trial and be tried in absentia? And if he were convicted, could he be imprisoned? Would aides be installed in a nearby cell?

This entire imagined scene is farcical. The "right of all the People to a functioning government" would be sacrificed. "Does anyone really think, in a country where common crimes are usually brought before state grand juries by state prosecutors, that it is feasible to subject the president—and thus the country—to every district attorney with a reckless mania for self-promotion?" C. Black & P. Bobbitt, Impeachment: A Handbook 112 (2018).

While the prosecution of a sitting President provides the most dramatic example of a clash between the indispensable work of the Presidency and a State's exercise of its criminal law enforcement powers, other examples are easy to imagine. Suppose state officers obtained and sought to execute a search warrant for a sitting President's private quarters in the White House. Suppose a state court authorized surveillance of a telephone that a sitting President was known to use. Or suppose that a sitting President was subpoenaed to testify before a state grand jury and, as is generally the rule, no Presidential aides, even those carrying the so-called "nuclear football," were permitted to enter the grand jury room. What these examples illustrate is a principle that this Court has recognized: legal proceedings involving a sitting President must take the responsibilities and demands of the office into account.

It is not enough to recite sayings like "no man is above the law" and "the public has a right to every man's evidence." These sayings are true—and important—but they beg the question. The law applies equally to all persons, including a person who happens for a period of time to occupy the Presidency. But there is no question that the nature of the office demands in some instances that the application of laws be adjusted at least until the person's term in office ends.

In light of the above, a subpoena like the one now before us should not be enforced unless it meets a test that takes into account the need to prevent interference with a President's discharge of the responsibilities of the office. I agree with the Court that not all such subpoenas should be barred. There may be situations in which there is an urgent and critical need for the subpoenaed information. The situation in the Burr trial, where the documents at issue were sought by a criminal defendant to defend against a charge of treason, is a good example. But in a case like the one at hand, a subpoena should not be allowed unless a heightened standard is met.

Prior cases involving Presidential subpoenas have always applied special, heightened standards. In the Burr trial, Chief Justice Marshall was careful to note that "in no case of this kind would a court be required to proceed against the president as against an ordinary individual," and he held that the subpoena to President Jefferson was permissible only because the prosecutor had shown that the materials sought were "essential to the justice of the [pending criminal] case." *United States v. Burr* (CC Va. 1807).

The Presidency deserves greater protection. Thus, in a case like this one, a prosecutor should be required (1) to provide at least a general description of the possible offenses that are under investigation, (2) to outline how the subpoenaed records relate to those offenses, and (3) to explain why it is important that the records be produced and why it is necessary for production to occur while the President is still in office.

Unlike this rule, which would not undermine any legitimate state interests, the opinion of the Court provides no real protection for the Presidency. The Court discounts the risk of harassment and assumes that state prosecutors will observe constitutional limitations, and I also assume that the great majority of state prosecutors will carry out their responsibilities responsibly. But for the reasons noted, there is a very real risk that some will not.

The subpoena at issue here is unprecedented. Never before has a local prosecutor subpoenaed the records of a sitting President. The Court's decision threatens to impair the functioning of the Presidency and provides no real protection against the use of the subpoena power by the Nation's 2,300+ local prosecutors. Respect for the structure of Government created by the Constitution demands greater protection for an institution that is vital to the Nation's safety and well-being.

TRUMP v. MAZARS USA
140 S. Ct. 2019 (2020)

Chief Justice ROBERTS delivered the opinion of the Court.

Over the course of five days in April 2019, three committees of the U.S. House of Representatives issued four subpoenas seeking information about the finances of President Donald J. Trump, his children, and affiliated businesses. We have held that the House has authority under the

Constitution to issue subpoenas to assist it in carrying out its legislative responsibilities. The House asserts that the financial information sought here — encompassing a decade's worth of transactions by the President and his family — will help guide legislative reform in areas ranging from money laundering and terrorism to foreign involvement in U.S. elections. The President contends that the House lacked a valid legislative aim and instead sought these records to harass him, expose personal matters, and conduct law enforcement activities beyond its authority. The question presented is whether the subpoenas exceed the authority of the House under the Constitution.

We have never addressed a congressional subpoena for the President's information. Two hundred years ago, it was established that Presidents may be subpoenaed during a federal criminal proceeding, *United States v. Burr* (No. 14,692d) (CC Va. 1807) (Marshall, Cir. J.), and earlier today we extended that ruling to state criminal proceedings, Nearly fifty years ago, we held that a federal prosecutor could obtain information from a President despite assertions of executive privilege, *United States v. Nixon* (1974), and more recently we ruled that a private litigant could subject a President to a damages suit and appropriate discovery obligations in federal court, *Clinton v. Jones* (1997).

This case is different. Here the President's information is sought not by prosecutors or private parties in connection with a particular judicial proceeding, but by committees of Congress that have set forth broad legislative objectives. Congress and the President — the two political branches established by the Constitution — have an ongoing relationship that the Framers intended to feature both rivalry and reciprocity. That distinctive aspect necessarily informs our analysis of the question before us.

I

Each of the three committees sought overlapping sets of financial documents, but each supplied different justifications for the requests.

The House Committee on Financial Services issued two subpoenas, both on April 11, 2019. The first, issued to Deutsche Bank, seeks the financial information of the President, his children, their immediate family members, and several affiliated business entities. Specifically, the subpoena seeks any document related to account activity, due diligence, foreign transactions, business statements, debt schedules, statements of net worth, tax returns, and suspicious activity identified by Deutsche Bank. The second, issued to Capital One, demands similar financial information with respect to more than a dozen business entities associated with the President. The Deutsche Bank subpoena requests materials from "2010 through the present," and the Capital One subpoena covers "2016 through the present," but both subpoenas impose no time limitations for certain documents, such as those connected to account openings and due diligence.

According to the House, the Financial Services Committee issued these subpoenas pursuant to House Resolution 206, which called for "efforts to close loopholes that allow corruption, terrorism, and money laundering to infiltrate our country's financial system." Such loopholes, the resolution explained, had allowed "illicit money, including from Russian oligarchs," to flow into the United States through "anonymous shell companies" using investments such as "luxury high-end real estate." The House also invokes the oversight plan of the Financial Services Committee, which stated that the Committee intends to review banking regulation and "examine the implementation, effectiveness, and enforcement" of laws designed to prevent money laundering and the financing of terrorism. The plan further provided that the Committee would "consider proposals to prevent the abuse of the financial system" and "address any vulnerabilities identified" in the real estate market.

On the same day as the Financial Services Committee, the Permanent Select Committee on Intelligence issued an identical subpoena to Deutsche Bank—albeit for different reasons. According to the House, the Intelligence Committee subpoenaed Deutsche Bank as part of an investigation into foreign efforts to undermine the U.S. political process. Committee Chairman Adam Schiff had described that investigation in a previous statement, explaining that the Committee was examining alleged attempts by Russia to influence the 2016 election; potential links between Russia and the President's campaign; and whether the President and his associates had been compromised by foreign actors or interests. Chairman Schiff added that the Committee planned "to develop legislation and policy reforms to ensure the U.S. government is better positioned to counter future efforts to undermine our political process and national security."

Four days after the Financial Services and Intelligence Committees, the House Committee on Oversight and Reform issued another subpoena, this time to the President's personal accounting firm, Mazars USA, LLP. The subpoena demanded information related to the President and several affiliated business entities from 2011 through 2018, including statements of financial condition, independent auditors' reports, financial reports, underlying source documents, and communications between Mazars and the President or his businesses. The subpoena also requested all engagement agreements and contracts "[w]ithout regard to time."

Chairman Elijah Cummings explained the basis for the subpoena in a memorandum to the Oversight Committee. According to the chairman, recent testimony by the President's former personal attorney Michael Cohen, along with several documents prepared by Mazars and supplied by Cohen, raised questions about whether the President had accurately represented his financial affairs. Chairman Cummings asserted that the Committee had "full authority to investigate" whether the President: (1) "may have engaged in illegal conduct before and during his tenure in office," (2) "has undisclosed conflicts of interest that may impair his ability to make impartial policy decisions," (3) "is complying with the Emoluments Clauses of the Constitution," and (4) "has accurately reported his finances to the Office of Government Ethics and other federal entities." "The Committee's interest in these matters," Chairman Cummings concluded, "informs its review of multiple laws and legislative proposals under our jurisdiction."

Petitioners—the President in his personal capacity, along with his children and affiliated businesses—filed two suits challenging the subpoenas.

II

A

The question presented is whether the subpoenas exceed the authority of the House under the Constitution. Historically, disputes over congressional demands for presidential documents have not ended up in court. Instead, they have been hashed out in the "hurly-burly, the give-and-take of the political process between the legislative and the executive."

That practice began with George Washington and the early Congress. In 1792, a House committee requested Executive Branch documents pertaining to General St. Clair's campaign against the Indians in the Northwest Territory, which had concluded in an utter rout of federal forces when they were caught by surprise near the present-day border between Ohio and Indiana. Since this was the first such request from Congress, President Washington called a Cabinet meeting, wishing to take care that his response "be rightly conducted" because it could "become a precedent."

The meeting, attended by the likes of Alexander Hamilton, Thomas Jefferson, Edmund Randolph, and Henry Knox, ended with the Cabinet of "one mind": The House had authority to "institute inquiries" and "call for papers" but the President could "exercise a discretion" over disclosures, "communicat[ing] such papers as the public good would permit" and "refus[ing]" the rest. President Washington then dispatched Jefferson to speak to individual congressmen and "bring them by persuasion into the right channel." The discussions were apparently fruitful, as the House later narrowed its request and the documents were supplied without recourse to the courts.

Jefferson, once he became President, followed Washington's precedent. In early 1807, after Jefferson had disclosed that "sundry persons" were conspiring to invade Spanish territory in North America with a private army, the House requested that the President produce any information in his possession touching on the conspiracy (except for information that would harm the public interest). Jefferson chose not to divulge the entire "voluminous" correspondence on the subject, explaining that much of it was "private" or mere "rumors" and "neither safety nor justice" permitted him to "expos[e] names" apart from identifying the conspiracy's "principal actor": Aaron Burr. Instead of the entire correspondence, Jefferson sent Congress particular documents and a special message summarizing the conspiracy. Neither Congress nor the President asked the Judiciary to intervene.

Ever since, congressional demands for the President's information have been resolved by the political branches without involving this Court. The Reagan and Clinton presidencies provide two modern examples.

This dispute therefore represents a significant departure from historical practice. Although the parties agree that this particular controversy is justiciable, we recognize that it is the first of its kind to reach this Court; that disputes of this sort can raise important issues concerning relations between the branches; that related disputes involving congressional efforts to seek official Executive Branch information recur on a regular basis, including in the context of deeply partisan controversy; and that Congress and the Executive have nonetheless managed for over two centuries to resolve such disputes among themselves without the benefit of guidance from us. Such longstanding practice "'is a consideration of great weight'" in cases concerning "the allocation of power between [the] two elected branches of Government," and it imposes on us a duty of care to ensure that we not needlessly disturb "the compromises and working arrangements that [those] branches . . . themselves have reached." With that in mind, we turn to the question presented.

B

Congress has no enumerated constitutional power to conduct investigations or issue subpoenas, but we have held that each House has power "to secure needed information" in order to legislate. This "power of inquiry — with process to enforce it — is an essential and appropriate auxiliary to the legislative function." Without information, Congress would be shooting in the dark, unable to legislate "wisely or effectively." The congressional power to obtain information is "broad" and "indispensable." It encompasses inquiries into the administration of existing laws, studies of proposed laws, and "surveys of defects in our social, economic or political system for the purpose of enabling the Congress to remedy them."

Because this power is "justified solely as an adjunct to the legislative process," it is subject to several limitations. Most importantly, a congressional subpoena is valid only if it is "related to, and in furtherance of, a legitimate task of the Congress." The subpoena must serve a "valid legislative purpose"; it must "concern[ ] a subject on which legislation 'could be had.'" Furthermore, Congress may not issue a subpoena for the purpose of "law enforcement," because "those powers are assigned under our Constitution to the Executive and the Judiciary." Thus Congress may not use subpoenas to "try" someone "before [a] committee for any crime or wrongdoing." Congress has no "'general' power to inquire into private affairs and compel disclosures," and "there is no congressional power to expose for the sake of exposure." "Investigations conducted solely for the personal aggrandizement of the investigators or to 'punish' those investigated are indefensible."

Finally, recipients of legislative subpoenas retain their constitutional rights throughout the course of an investigation. And recipients have long been understood to retain common law and constitutional privileges with respect to certain materials, such as attorney-client communications and governmental communications protected by executive privilege.

C

The President contends, as does the Solicitor General appearing on behalf of the United States, that the usual rules for congressional subpoenas do not govern here because the President's papers are at issue. They argue for a more demanding standard based in large part on cases involving the Nixon tapes — recordings of conversations between President Nixon and close advisers discussing the break-in at the Democratic National Committee's headquarters at the Watergate complex.

Those cases, the President and the Solicitor General now contend, establish the standard that should govern the House subpoenas here. Quoting *Nixon*, the President asserts that the House must establish a "demonstrated, specific need" for the financial information, just as the Watergate special prosecutor was required to do in order to obtain the tapes. . . . And drawing on *Senate Select Committee*—the D.C. Circuit case refusing to enforce the Senate subpoena for the tapes—the President and the Solicitor General argue that the House must show that the financial information is "demonstrably critical" to its legislative purpose.

We disagree that these demanding standards apply here. Unlike the cases before us, *Nixon* and *Senate Select Committee* involved Oval Office communications over which the President asserted executive privilege. That privilege safeguards the public interest in candid, confidential deliberations within the Executive Branch; it is "fundamental to the operation of Government." As a result, information subject to executive privilege deserves "the greatest protection consistent with the fair administration of justice." We decline to transplant that protection root and branch to cases involving nonprivileged, private information, which by definition does not implicate sensitive Executive Branch deliberations.

The standards proposed by the President and the Solicitor General—if applied outside the context of privileged information—would risk seriously impeding Congress in carrying out its responsibilities. The President and the Solicitor General would apply the same exacting standards to *all* subpoenas for the President's information, without recognizing distinctions between privileged and nonprivileged information, between official and personal information, or between various legislative objectives. Such a categorical approach would represent a significant departure from the longstanding way of doing business between the branches, giving short shrift to Congress's important interests in conducting inquiries to obtain the information it needs to legislate effectively. Confounding the legislature in that effort would be contrary to the principle that: "It is the proper duty of a representative body to look diligently into every affair of government and to talk much about what it sees. It is meant to be the eyes and the voice, and to embody the wisdom and will of its constituents. Unless Congress have and use every means of acquainting itself with the acts and the disposition of the administrative agents of the government, the country must be helpless to learn how it is being served." Legislative inquiries might involve the President in appropriate cases; as noted, Congress's responsibilities extend to "every affair of government." Because the President's approach does not take adequate account of these significant congressional interests, we do not adopt it.

D

The House meanwhile would have us ignore that these suits involve the President. Invoking our precedents concerning investigations that did not target the President's papers, the House urges us to uphold its subpoenas because they "relate[ ] to a valid legislative purpose" or "concern[ ] a subject on which legislation could be had." That approach is appropriate, the House argues, because the cases before us are not "momentous separation-of-powers disputes." Largely following the House's lead, the courts below treated these cases much like any other, applying precedents that do not involve the President's papers.

The House's approach fails to take adequate account of the significant separation of powers issues raised by congressional subpoenas for the President's information. Congress and the President have an ongoing institutional relationship as the "opposite and rival" political branches established by the Constitution. As a result, congressional subpoenas directed at the President differ markedly from congressional subpoenas we have previously reviewed and they bear little resemblance to criminal subpoenas issued to the President in the course of a specific investigation. Unlike those subpoenas, congressional subpoenas for the President's information unavoidably pit the political branches against one another.

Far from accounting for separation of powers concerns, the House's approach aggravates them by leaving essentially no limits on the congressional power to subpoena the President's personal records. Any personal paper possessed by a President could potentially "relate to" a conceivable subject of legislation, for Congress has broad legislative powers that touch a vast number of subjects. The President's financial records could relate to economic reform, medical records to health reform, school transcripts to education reform, and so on. Indeed, at argument, the House was unable to identify *any* type of information that lacks some relation to potential legislation.

Without limits on its subpoena powers, Congress could "exert an imperious controul" over the Executive Branch and aggrandize itself at the President's expense, just as the Framers feared. And a limitless subpoena power would transform the "established practice" of the political branches. Instead of negotiating over information requests, Congress could simply walk away from the bargaining table and compel compliance in court.

The interbranch conflict here does not vanish simply because the subpoenas seek personal papers or because the President sued in his personal capacity. The President is the only person who alone composes a branch of government. As a result, there is not always a clear line between his personal and official affairs. "The interest of the man" is often "connected with the constitutional rights of the place." Given the close connection between the Office of the President and its occupant, congressional demands for the President's papers can implicate the relationship between the branches regardless whether those papers are personal or official. Either way, a demand may aim to harass the President or render him "complaisan[t] to the humors of the Legislature." In fact, a subpoena for personal papers may pose a heightened risk of such impermissible purposes, precisely because of the documents' personal nature and their less evident connection to a legislative task. No one can say that the controversy here is less significant to the relationship between the branches simply because it involves personal papers. Quite the opposite. That appears to be what makes the matter of such great consequence to the President and Congress.

In addition, separation of powers concerns are no less palpable here simply because the subpoenas were issued to third parties. Congressional demands for the President's information present an interbranch conflict no matter where the information is held—it is, after all, the President's information. Were it otherwise, Congress could sidestep constitutional requirements any time a President's information is entrusted to a third party—as occurs with rapidly increasing frequency. Indeed, Congress could declare open season on the President's information held by schools, archives, internet service providers, e-mail clients, and financial institutions. The Constitution does not tolerate such ready evasion; it "deals with substance, not shadows."

E

Congressional subpoenas for the President's personal information implicate weighty concerns regarding the separation of powers. A balanced approach is necessary, one that takes a "considerable impression" from "the practice of the government." We therefore conclude that, in assessing whether a subpoena directed at the President's personal information is "related to, and in furtherance of, a legitimate task of the Congress," courts must perform a careful analysis that takes adequate account of the separation of powers principles at stake, including both the significant legislative interests of Congress and the "unique position" of the President. Several special considerations inform this analysis.

First, courts should carefully assess whether the asserted legislative purpose warrants the significant step of involving the President and his papers. "[O]ccasion[s] for constitutional confrontation between the two branches' should be avoided whenever possible." Congress may not rely on the President's information if other sources could reasonably provide Congress the information it needs in light of its particular legislative objective. The President's unique constitutional position means that Congress may not look to him as a "case study" for general legislation.

Unlike in criminal proceedings, where "[t]he very integrity of the judicial system" would be undermined without "full disclosure of all the facts," efforts to craft legislation involve predictive policy judgments that are "not hamper[ed] . . . in quite the same way" when every scrap of potentially relevant evidence is not available. While we certainly recognize Congress's important interests in obtaining information through appropriate inquiries, those interests are not sufficiently powerful to justify access to the President's personal papers when other sources could provide Congress the information it needs.

Second, to narrow the scope of possible conflict between the branches, courts should insist on a subpoena no broader than reasonably necessary to support Congress's legislative objective. The specificity of the subpoena's request "serves as an important safeguard against unnecessary intrusion into the operation of the Office of the President."

Third, courts should be attentive to the nature of the evidence offered by Congress to establish that a subpoena advances a valid legislative purpose. The more detailed and substantial the evidence of Congress's legislative purpose, the better. That is particularly true when Congress contemplates legislation that raises sensitive constitutional issues, such as legislation concerning the Presidency. In such cases, it is "impossible" to conclude that a subpoena is designed to advance a valid legislative purpose unless Congress adequately identifies its aims and explains why the President's information will advance its consideration of the possible legislation.

Fourth, courts should be careful to assess the burdens imposed on the President by a subpoena. We have held that burdens on the President's time and attention stemming from judicial process and litigation, without more, generally do not cross constitutional lines. But burdens imposed by a congressional subpoena should be carefully scrutinized, for they stem from a rival political branch that has an ongoing relationship with the President and incentives to use subpoenas for institutional advantage.

Other considerations may be pertinent as well; one case every two centuries does not afford enough experience for an exhaustive list.

When Congress seeks information "needed for intelligent legislative action," it "unquestionably" remains "the duty of *all* citizens to cooperate." Congressional subpoenas for information from the President, however, implicate special concerns regarding the separation of powers. The courts below did not take adequate account of those concerns. The judgments of the Courts of Appeals for the D.C. Circuit and the Second

Circuit are vacated, and the cases are remanded for further proceedings consistent with this opinion.

Justice THOMAS, dissenting.

Three Committees of the U.S. House of Representatives issued subpoenas to several accounting and financial firms to obtain the personal financial records of the President, his family, and several of his business entities. The Committees do not argue that these subpoenas were issued pursuant to the House's impeachment power. Instead, they argue that the subpoenas are a valid exercise of their legislative powers.

I would hold that Congress has no power to issue a legislative subpoena for private, nonofficial documents—whether they belong to the President or not. Congress may be able to obtain these documents as part of an investigation of the President, but to do so, it must proceed under the impeachment power. Accordingly, I would reverse the judgments of the Courts of Appeals.

At the time of the founding, the power to subpoena private, nonofficial documents was not included by necessary implication in any of Congress' legislative powers. This understanding persisted for decades and is consistent with the Court's first decision addressing legislative subpoenas, and the majority's variation on that standard today, are without support as applied to private, nonofficial documents.

The Committees argue that Congress wields the same investigatory powers that the British Parliament did at the time of the founding. But this claim overlooks one of the fundamental differences between our Government and the British Government: Parliament was supreme. Congress is not. I have previously explained that "the founding generation did not subscribe to Blackstone's view of parliamentary supremacy."

The subpoenas in these cases also cannot be justified based on the practices of 18th-century American legislatures. *Amici* supporting the Committees resist this conclusion, but the examples they cite materially differ from the legislative subpoenas at issue here. First, *amici* cite investigations in which legislatures sought to compel testimony from government officials on government matters. The subjects included military affairs, taxes, government finances, and the judiciary. But the information sought in these examples was official, not private.

Given that Congress has no exact precursor in England or colonial America, founding-era congressional practice is especially informative about the scope of implied legislative powers. Thus, it is highly probative that no founding-era Congress issued a subpoena for private, nonofficial documents.

I

If the Committees wish to investigate alleged wrongdoing by the President and obtain documents from him, the Constitution provides Congress with a special mechanism for doing so: impeachment. The power to impeach includes a power to investigate and demand documents. Impeachments in the States often involved an investigation.

I express no view today on the boundaries of the power to demand documents in connection with impeachment proceedings. But the power of impeachment provides the House with authority to investigate and hold accountable Presidents who commit high crimes or misdemeanors. That is the proper path by which the Committees should pursue their demands.

II

Congress' legislative powers do not authorize it to engage in a nationwide inquisition with whatever resources it chooses to appropriate for itself. The majority's solution—a nonexhaustive four-factor test of uncertain origin—is better than nothing. But the power that Congress seeks to exercise here has even less basis in the Constitution than the majority supposes. I would reverse in full because the power to subpoena private, nonofficial documents is not a necessary implication of Congress' legislative powers. If Congress wishes to obtain these documents, it should proceed through the impeachment power. Accordingly, I respectfully dissent.

Justice ALITO, dissenting.

Justice Thomas makes a valuable argument about the constitutionality of congressional subpoenas for a President's personal documents. In these cases, however, I would assume for the sake of argument that such subpoenas are not categorically barred. Nevertheless, legislative subpoenas for a President's personal documents are inherently suspicious. Such documents are seldom of any special value in considering potential legislation, and subpoenas for such documents can easily be used for improper non-legislative purposes. Accordingly, courts must be very sensitive to separation of powers issues when they are asked to approve the enforcement of such subpoenas.

Whenever such a subpoena comes before a court, Congress should be required to make more than a perfunctory showing that it is seeking the documents for a legitimate legislative purpose and not for the purpose of exposing supposed Presidential wrongdoing. I agree that the lower courts erred and that these cases must be remanded, but I do not think that the considerations outlined by the Court can be properly satisfied unless the House is required to show more than it has put forward to date.

Specifically, the House should provide a description of the type of legislation being considered, and while great specificity is not necessary, the description should be sufficient to permit a court to assess whether the particular records sought are of any special importance. The House should also spell out its constitutional authority to enact the type of legislation that it is contemplating, and it should justify the scope of the subpoenas in relation to the articulated legislative needs. In addition, it should explain why the subpoenaed information, as opposed to information available from other sources, is needed. Unless the House is required to make a showing along these lines, I would hold that enforcement of the subpoenas cannot be ordered. Because I find the terms of the Court's remand inadequate, I must respectfully dissent.

B. The Constitutional Problems of the Administrative State

3. Checking Administrative Power

The Appointment Power (casebook p. 313)

The Constitution says that the President appoints officers of the United States, but that Congress may vest the appointment of inferior officers in the President, the heads of agencies, or the lower federal courts. But there is no clear definition of who is an officer as opposed to an inferior officer. That is the issue in *United States v. Arthrex* (2020).

UNITED STATES v. ARTHREX
141 S. Ct. 1970 (2021)

Chief Justice ROBERTS delivered the opinion of the Court with respect to Parts I and II.

The validity of a patent previously issued by the Patent and Trademark Office can be challenged before the Patent Trial and Appeal Board, an executive tribunal within the PTO. The Board, composed largely of Administrative Patent Judges appointed by the Secretary of Commerce, has the final word within the Executive Branch on the validity of a challenged patent. Billions of dollars can turn on a Board decision.

Under the Constitution, "[t]he executive Power" is vested in the President, who has the responsibility to "take Care that the Laws be faithfully executed." The Appointments Clause provides that he may be assisted in carrying out that responsibility by officers nominated by him and confirmed by the Senate, as well as by other officers not appointed in that manner but whose work, we have held, must be directed and supervised by an officer who has been. § 2, cl. 2. The question presented is whether the authority of the Board to issue decisions on behalf of the Executive Branch is consistent with these constitutional provisions.

I

The creation of a workable patent system was a congressional priority from the start. The First Congress established the Patent Board — consisting impressively of Secretary of State Thomas Jefferson, Secretary of War Henry Knox, and Attorney General Edmund Randolph — to issue patents for inventions they deemed "sufficiently useful and important." The Patent Board was a short-lived experiment because its members had much else to do.

In 1793, Congress shifted to a registration system administered by the Secretary of State. The Secretary no longer reviewed the substance of patent applications but instead issued patents through a routine process "as a ministerial officer." The courts would make the initial determination of patent validity in a subsequent judicial proceeding, such as an infringement suit. This scheme unsurprisingly resulted in the Executive Branch issuing many invalid patents and the Judicial Branch having to decide many infringement cases.

The present system is administered by the Patent and Trademark Office (PTO), an executive agency within the Department of Commerce "responsible for the granting and issuing of patents" in the name of the United States. Congress has vested the "powers and duties" of the PTO in a sole Director appointed by the President with the advice and consent of the Senate. As agency head, the Director "provid[es] policy direction and management supervision" for PTO officers and employees.

This suit centers on the Patent Trial and Appeal Board (PTAB), an executive adjudicatory body within the PTO established by the Leahy-Smith America Invents Act of 2011. The PTAB sits in panels of at least three members drawn from the Director, the Deputy Director, the Commissioner for Patents, the Commissioner for Trademarks, and more than 200 Administrative Patent Judges (APJs). The Secretary of

Commerce appoints the members of the PTAB (except for the Director), including the APJs at issue in this dispute. Like the 1790 Patent Board, the modern Board decides whether an invention satisfies the standards for patentability on review of decisions by primary examiners.

Through a variety of procedures, the PTAB can also take a second look at patents previously issued by the PTO. One such procedure is inter partes review. Established in 2011, inter partes review is an adversarial process by which members of the PTAB reconsider whether existing patents satisfy the novelty and nonobviousness requirements for inventions. Any person — other than the patent owner himself — can file a petition to institute inter partes review of a patent. The Director can institute review only if, among other requirements, he determines that the petitioner is reasonably likely to prevail on at least one challenged patent claim. Congress has committed the decision to institute inter partes review to the Director's unreviewable discretion. By regulation, the Director has delegated this authority to the PTAB itself.

The Director designates at least three members of the PTAB (typically three APJs) to conduct an inter partes proceeding. The PTAB then assumes control of the process, which resembles civil litigation in many respects. The PTAB must issue a final written decision on all of the challenged patent claims within 12 to 18 months of institution. A party who disagrees with a decision may request rehearing by the PTAB.

The PTAB is the last stop for review within the Executive Branch. A party dissatisfied with the final decision may seek judicial review in the Court of Appeals for the Federal Circuit. At this stage, the Director can intervene before the court to defend or disavow the Board's decision. The Federal Circuit reviews the PTAB's application of patentability standards *de novo* and its underlying factual determinations for substantial evidence. Upon expiration of the time to appeal or termination of any appeal, "the Director shall issue and publish a certificate canceling any claim of the patent finally determined to be unpatentable, confirming any claim of the patent determined to be patentable, and incorporating in the patent by operation of the certificate any new or amended claim determined to be patentable."

Arthrex, Inc. develops medical devices and procedures for orthopedic surgery. In 2015, it secured a patent on a surgical device for reattaching soft tissue to bone without tying a knot, Arthrex soon claimed that Smith & Nephew, Inc. and ArthroCare Corp. (collectively, Smith & Nephew) had infringed the '907 patent, and the dispute eventually made its way to inter partes review in the PTO. Three APJs formed the PTAB panel that conducted the proceeding and ultimately concluded that a prior patent application "anticipated" the invention claimed by the '907 patent, so that Arthrex's patent was invalid.

On appeal to the Federal Circuit, Arthrex raised for the first time an argument premised on the Appointments Clause of the Constitution. That Clause specifies how the President may appoint officers who assist him in carrying out his responsibilities. *Principal* officers must be appointed by the President with the advice and consent of the Senate, while *inferior* officers may be appointed by the President alone, the head of an executive department, or a court. Arthrex argued that the APJs were principal officers and therefore that their appointment by the Secretary of Commerce was unconstitutional. The Government intervened to defend the appointment procedure.

II

The President is "'responsible for the actions of the Executive Branch'" and "'cannot delegate [that] ultimate responsibility or the active obligation to supervise that goes with it.'" The Framers recognized, of course, that "no single person could fulfill that responsibility alone, [and] expected that the President would rely on subordinate officers for assistance."

Today, thousands of officers wield executive power on behalf of the President in the name of the United States. That power acquires its legitimacy and accountability to the public through "a clear and effective chain of command" down from the President, on whom all the people vote. James Madison extolled this "great principle of unity and responsibility in the Executive department," which ensures that "the chain of dependence [will] be preserved; the lowest officers, the middle grade, and the highest, will depend, as they ought, on the President, and the President on the community."

The Appointments Clause provides: "[The President] shall nominate, and by and with the Advice and Consent of the Senate, shall appoint Ambassadors, other public Ministers and Consuls, Judges of the supreme Court, and all other Officers of the United States, whose Appointments are not herein otherwise provided for, and which shall be established by Law: but Congress may by Law vest the Appointment of such inferior Officers, as they think proper, in the President alone, in the Courts of Law, or in the Heads of Departments."

Assigning the nomination power to the President guarantees accountability for the appointees' actions because the "blame of a bad nomination would fall upon the president singly and absolutely." The Appointments

Clause adds a degree of accountability in the Senate, which shares in the public blame "for both the making of a bad appointment and the rejection of a good one."

Only the President, with the advice and consent of the Senate, can appoint noninferior officers, called "principal" officers as shorthand in our cases. The "default manner of appointment" for inferior officers is also nomination by the President and confirmation by the Senate. But the Framers foresaw that "when offices became numerous, and sudden removals necessary, this mode might be inconvenient." Reflecting this concern for "administrative convenience," the Appointments Clause permits Congress to dispense with joint appointment, but only for inferior officers. Congress may vest the appointment of such officers "in the President alone, in the Courts of Law, or in the Heads of Departments."

Congress provided that APJs would be appointed as inferior officers, by the Secretary of Commerce as head of a department. The question presented is whether the nature of their responsibilities is consistent with their method of appointment. As an initial matter, no party disputes that APJs are officers—not "lesser functionaries" such as employees or contractors—because they "exercis[e] significant authority pursuant to the laws of the United States." APJs do so when reconsidering an issued patent, a power that (the Court has held) involves the adjudication of public rights that Congress may appropriately assign to executive officers rather than to the Judiciary.

The starting point for each party's analysis is our opinion in *Edmond* [*v. United States* (1997)]. There we explained that "[w]hether one is an 'inferior' officer depends on whether he has a superior" other than the President. An inferior officer must be "directed and supervised at some level by others who were appointed by Presidential nomination with the advice and consent of the Senate."

In *Edmond*, we applied this test to adjudicative officials within the Executive Branch—specifically, Coast Guard Court of Criminal Appeals judges appointed by the Secretary of Transportation. We held that the judges were inferior officers because they were effectively supervised by a combination of Presidentially nominated and Senate confirmed officers in the Executive Branch.

Congress structured the PTAB differently, providing only half of the "divided" supervision to which judges of the Court of Criminal Appeals were subject. Like the Judge Advocate General, the PTO Director possesses powers of "administrative oversight." The Director fixes the rate of pay for APJs, controls the decision whether to institute inter partes review, and selects the APJs to reconsider the validity of the patent. The Director also promulgates regulations governing inter partes review, issues prospective guidance on patentability issues, and designates past PTAB decisions as "precedential" for future panels. He is the boss, except when it comes to the one thing that makes the APJs officers exercising "significant authority" in the first place — their power to issue decisions on patentability. In contrast to the scheme approved by *Edmond*, no principal officer at any level within the Executive Branch "direct[s] and supervise[s]" the work of APJs in that regard.

Edmond goes a long way toward resolving this dispute. What was "significant" to the outcome there — review by a superior executive officer — is absent here: APJs have the "power to render a final decision on behalf of the United States" without any such review by their nominal superior or any other principal officer in the Executive Branch. The only possibility of review is a petition for rehearing, but Congress unambiguously specified that "[o]nly the Patent and Trial Appeal Board may grant rehearings." Such review simply repeats the arrangement challenged as unconstitutional in this suit.

This "diffusion of power carries with it a diffusion of accountability." The restrictions on review relieve the Director of responsibility for the final decisions rendered by APJs purportedly under his charge. The principal dissent's observation that "the Director alone has the power to take final action to cancel a patent claim or confirm it," simply ignores the undisputed fact that the Director's "power" in that regard is limited to carrying out the ministerial duty that he "shall issue and publish a certificate" canceling or confirming patent claims he had previously allowed, as dictated by the APJs' final decision. The chain of command runs not from the Director to his subordinates, but from the APJs to the Director.

History reinforces the conclusion that the unreviewable executive power exercised by APJs is incompatible with their status as inferior officers. Since the founding, principal officers have directed the decisions of inferior officers on matters of law as well as policy. Early congressional statutes expressly empowered department heads to supervise the work of their subordinates, sometimes by providing for an appeal in adjudicatory proceedings to a Presidentially nominated and Senate confirmed officer.

We hold that the unreviewable authority wielded by APJs during inter partes review is incompatible with their appointment by the Secretary to an inferior office. In reaching this conclusion, we do not attempt to "set forth an exclusive criterion for distinguishing between principal and inferior officers for Appointments Clause purposes." Many decisions by inferior officers do not bind the Executive Branch to exercise executive power in a particular manner, and we do not address supervision outside the context of adjudication. Here, however, Congress has assigned APJs "significant authority" in adjudicating the public rights of private parties, while also insulating their decisions from review and their offices from removal.

III

We turn now to the appropriate way to resolve this dispute given this violation of the Appointments Clause. In general, "when confronting a constitutional flaw in a statute, we try to limit the solution to the problem" by disregarding the "problematic portions while leaving the remainder intact."

Arthrex asks us to hold the entire regime of inter partes review unconstitutional. In its view, any more tailored declaration of unconstitutionality would necessitate a policy decision best left to Congress in the first instance. Because the good cannot be separated from the bad, Arthrex continues, the appropriate remedy is to order outright dismissal of the proceeding below.

In our view, however, the structure of the PTO and the governing constitutional principles chart a clear course: Decisions by APJs must be subject to review by the Director. Congress vested the Director with the "powers and duties" of the PTO, tasked him with supervising APJs, and placed the PTAB "in" the PTO.

In sum, we hold that 35 U.S.C. § 6(c) is unenforceable as applied to the Director insofar as it prevents the Director from reviewing the decisions of the PTAB on his own. The Director may engage in such review and reach his own decision. When reviewing such a decision by the Director, a court must decide the case "conformably to the constitution, disregarding the law" placing restrictions on his review authority in violation of Article II.

Today, we reaffirm and apply the rule from *Edmond* that the exercis of executive power by inferior officers must at some level be subject to the direction and supervision of an officer nominated by the President and confirmed by the Senate. The Constitution therefore forbids the enforcement of statutory restrictions on the Director that insulate the decisions of APJs from his direction and supervision. To be clear, the Director need not review every decision of the PTAB. What matters is that the Director have the discretion to review decisions rendered by APJs. In this way, the President remains responsible for the exercise of executive power—and through him, the exercise of executive power remains accountable to the people.

Justice BREYER, with whom Justice SOTOMAYOR and Justice KAGAN join, concurring in the judgment in part and dissenting in part.

I agree with Justice Thomas' discussion on the merits and I join Parts I and II of his dissent. Two related considerations also persuade me that his conclusion is correct.

First, in my view, the Court should interpret the Appointments Clause as granting Congress a degree of leeway to establish and empower federal offices. Neither that Clause nor anything else in the Constitution describes the degree of control that a superior officer must exercise over the decisions of an inferior officer. Even a small degree of "judicial deference" should prove sufficient to validate the statutes here. For one, the provisions at issue fall well within Article I's grant to Congress of the patent power. Nothing in them represents an effort by the "Legislative Branch [to] aggrandize itself at the expense of the other two branches." There is accordingly no general separation-of-powers defect that has arisen in other cases. For another, Congress' scheme is consistent with our Appointments Clause precedents. Finally, Congress' judgment is unusually clear in this suit, as there is strong evidence that Congress designed the current structure specifically to address constitutional concerns.

Second, I believe the Court, when deciding cases such as these, should conduct a functional examination of the offices and duties in question rather than a formalist, judicial-rules-based approach. In advocating for a "functional approach," I mean an approach that would take account of, and place weight on, why Congress enacted a particular statutory limitation. It would also consider the practical consequences that are likely to follow from Congress' chosen scheme.

More broadly, I see the Court's decision as one part of a larger shift in our separation-of-powers jurisprudence. I continue to believe that a more functional approach to constitutional interpretation in this area is superior. As for this particular suit, the consequences of the majority's rule are clear. The nature of the PTAB calls for technically correct adjudicatory decisions.

But there are further reasons for a functional approach that extend beyond the bounds of patent adjudication. First, the Executive Branch has many different constituent bodies, many different bureaus, many different agencies, many different tasks, many different kinds of employees. Administration comes in many different shapes and sizes. Appreciating this variety is especially important in the context of administrative adjudication, which typically demands decisionmaking (at least where policy made by others is simply applied) that is free of political influence. Are the President and Congress, through judicial insistence upon certain mechanisms for removal or review, to be denied the ability to create independent adjudicators?

Second, the Constitution is not a detailed tax code, and for good reason. The Nation's desires and needs change, sometimes over long periods of time. In the 19th century the Judiciary may not have foreseen the changes that produced the New Deal, along with its accompanying changes in the nature of the tasks that Government was expected to perform. We may not now easily foresee just what kinds of tasks present or future technological changes will call for. The Founders wrote a Constitution that they believed was flexible enough to respond to new needs as those needs developed and changed over the course of decades or centuries. At the same time, they designed a Constitution that would protect certain basic principles. A principle that prevents Congress from affording inferior level adjudicators some decisionmaking independence was not among them.

Finally, the Executive Branch and Congress are more likely than are judges to understand how to implement the tasks that Congress has written into legislation. That understanding encompasses the nature of different mechanisms of bureaucratic control that may apply to the many thousands of administrators who will carry out those tasks. And it includes an awareness of the reasonable limits that can be placed on supervisors to ensure that those working under them enjoy a degree of freedom sufficient to carry out their responsibilities. Considered as a group, unelected judges have little, if any, experience related to this kind of a problem.

This is not to say that the Constitution grants Congress free rein. But in this area of the law a functional approach, when compared with the highly detailed judicial-rules-based approach reflected in the Court's decision, is more likely to prevent inappropriate judicial interference. It embodies, at least to a degree, the philosopher's advice: "Whereof one cannot speak, thereof one must be silent."

In my view, today's decision is both unprecedented and unnecessary, and risks pushing the Judiciary further into areas where we lack both the authority to act and the capacity to act wisely.

Justice THOMAS, with whom Justice BREYER, Justice SOTOMAYOR, and Justice KAGAN join as to Parts I and II, dissenting.

For the very first time, this Court holds that Congress violated the Constitution by vesting the appointment of a federal officer in the head of a department. Just who are these "principal" officers that Congress unsuccessfully sought to smuggle into the Executive Branch without Senate confirmation? About 250 administrative patent judges who sit at the bottom of an organizational chart, nestled under at least two levels of authority. Neither our precedent nor the original understanding of the Appointments Clause requires Senate confirmation of officers inferior to not one, but *two* officers below the President.

I

The Executive Branch is large, and the hierarchical path from President to administrative patent judge is long. At the top sits the President, in whom the executive power is vested. U.S. Const., Below him is the Secretary of Commerce, who oversees the Department of Commerce and its work force of about 46,000. Within that Department is the United States Patent and Trademark Office led by a Director. In the Patent and Trademark Office is the Patent Trial and Appeal Board. Serving on this Board are administrative patent judges.

There are few statutory prerequisites to becoming an administrative patent judge. One must be a "perso[n] of competent legal knowledge and scientific ability" and be "appointed by the Secretary." The Board adjudicates both appellate and trial disputes. See § 6(b). It may directly review certain decisions made by patent examiners, and it may hold its own proceedings to determine the patentability of patent claims. As relevant here, it conducts inter partes review, which "offers a second look at an earlier administrative grant of a patent."

That both the Federal Circuit and this Court would take so much care to ensure that administrative patent judges, appointed as inferior officers, would remain inferior officers at the end of the day suggests that perhaps they were inferior officers to begin with. Instead of rewriting the Director's statutory powers, I would simply leave intact the patent scheme Congress has created.

II

The Court has been careful not to create a rigid test to divide principal officers — those who must be Senate confirmed — from inferior ones. And those analyses invariably result in this Court deferring to Congress' choice of which constitutional appointment process works best. No party (nor the majority) has identified any instance in which this Court has found unconstitutional an appointment that aligns with one of the two processes outlined in the Constitution.

There can be no dispute that administrative patent judges are, in fact, inferior: They are lower in rank to at least two different officers. As part of the Board, they serve in the Patent and Trademark Office, run by a Director "responsible for providing policy direction and management supervision for the Office and for the issuance of patents and the registration of trademarks." That Office, in turn, is "[w]ithin the Department of Commerce" and "subject to the policy direction of the Secretary of Commerce." § 1(a). The Secretary, in consultation with the Director, appoints administrative patent judges.

The Court today appears largely to agree with all of this. "In every respect" save one, the plurality says, "[administrative patent judges] appear to be inferior officers." But instead of finding it persuasive that administrative patent judges seem to be inferior officers—"an understanding consistent with their appointment"—the majority suggests most of *Edmond* is superfluous: All that matters is whether the Director has the statutory authority to individually reverse Board decisions. The problem with that theory is that there is no precedential basis (or historical support) for boiling down "inferior-officer" status to the way Congress structured a particular agency's process for reviewing decisions.

Perhaps the better way to understand the Court's opinion today is as creating a new form of intrabranch separation-of-powers law. Traditionally, the Court's task when resolving Appointments Clause challenges has been to discern whether the challenged official qualifies as a specific sort of officer and whether his appointment complies with the Constitution. If the official's appointment is inconsistent with the constitutional appointment process for the position he holds, then the Court provides a remedy. Otherwise, the Court must conclude that the "appointments at issue in th[e] case are . . . valid."

Today's majority leaves that tried-and-true approach behind. It never expressly tells us whether administrative patent judges are inferior officers or principal. And the Court never tells us whether the appointment process complies with the Constitution. The closest the Court comes is to say that "the source of the constitutional violation" is *not* "the appointment of [administrative patent judges] by the Secretary." Under our precedent and the Constitution's text, that should resolve the suit. If the appointment process for administrative patent judges—appointment by the Secretary—does not violate the Constitution, then administrative patent judges must be inferior officers. And if administrative patent judges are inferior officers and have been properly appointed as such, then the Appointments Clause challenge fails. After all, the Constitution provides that "Congress may by Law vest the Appointment of . . . inferior Officers . . . in the Heads of Departments."

In the end, the Court's remedy underscores that it is ambivalent about the idea of administrative patent judges *actually* being principal officers. Instead of holding as much explicitly, the Court rewrites the statutory text to ensure that the Director can directly review Board decisions.

The Court today draws a new line dividing inferior officers from principal ones. The fact that this line places administrative patent judges on the side of Ambassadors, Supreme Court Justices, and department heads suggests that something is not quite right. At some point, we should take stock of our precedent to see if it aligns with the Appointments Clause's original meaning. But, for now, we must apply the test we have. And, under that test, administrative patent judges are both formally and functionally inferior to the Director and to the Secretary. I respectfully dissent.

The Removal Power (casebook p. 328)

In the cases presented in the casebook, the Court upheld the ability of Congress to limit presidential removal of executive officials if it is a position that ideally should be independent of the President and if the law does not prohibit all removal. In *Seila Law LLC v. Consumer Financial Protection Bureau*, the Court said that it was unconstitutional for Congress to limit the removal of the head of that agency because it was a single person, and not a multi-member body. The Court distinguished the earlier cases that are presented in the casebook, such as *Humphrey's Executor v. United States* and *United States v. Morrison*.

SEILA LAW LLC v. CONSUMER FINANCIAL
PROTECTION BUREAU
140 S. Ct. 2183 (2020)

Chief Justice ROBERTS delivered the opinion of the Court with respect to Parts I, II, and III.

In the wake of the 2008 financial crisis, Congress established the Consumer Financial Protection Bureau (CFPB), an independent regulatory agency tasked with ensuring that consumer debt products are safe and transparent. In organizing the CFPB, Congress deviated from the structure of nearly every other independent administrative agency in our history. Instead of placing the agency under the leadership of a board with multiple members, Congress provided that the CFPB would be led by a single Director, who serves for a longer term than the President and cannot be removed by the President except for inefficiency, neglect, or malfeasance. The CFPB Director has no boss, peers, or voters to report to. Yet the Director wields vast rulemaking, enforcement, and adjudicatory authority over a significant portion of the U.S. economy. The question before us is whether this arrangement violates the Constitution's separation of powers.

Under our Constitution, the "executive Power"—all of it—is "vested in a President," who must "take Care that the Laws be faithfully executed." Because no single person could fulfill that responsibility alone, the Framers expected that the President would rely on subordinate officers for assistance. Ten years ago, in *Free Enterprise Fund v. Public Company Accounting Oversight Bd.* (2010), we reiterated that, "as a general matter," the Constitution gives the President "the authority to remove those who assist him in carrying out his duties." "Without such power, the President could not be held fully accountable for discharging his own responsibilities; the buck would stop somewhere else."

The President's power to remove—and thus supervise—those who wield executive power on his behalf follows from the text of Article II, was settled by the First Congress, and was confirmed in the landmark decision *Myers v. United States* (1926). Our precedents have recognized only two exceptions to the President's unrestricted removal power. In *Humphrey's Executor v. United States* (1935), we held that Congress could create expert agencies led by a *group* of principal officers removable by the President only for good cause. And in *United States v. Perkins* (1886), and *Morrison v. Olson* (1988), we held that Congress could provide tenure protections to certain *inferior* officers with narrowly defined duties.

We are now asked to extend these precedents to a new configuration: an independent agency that wields significant executive power and is run by a single individual who cannot be removed by the President unless certain statutory criteria are met. We decline to take that step. While we need not and do not revisit our prior decisions allowing certain limitations on the President's removal power, there are compelling reasons not to extend those precedents to the novel context of an independent agency led by a single Director. Such an agency lacks a foundation in historical practice and clashes with constitutional structure by concentrating power in a unilateral actor insulated from Presidential control.

We therefore hold that the structure of the CFPB violates the separation of powers. We go on to hold that the CFPB Director's removal protection is severable from the other statutory provisions bearing on the CFPB's authority. The agency may therefore continue to operate, but its Director, in light of our decision, must be removable by the President at will.

I

In the summer of 2007, then-Professor Elizabeth Warren called for the creation of a new, independent federal agency focused on regulating consumer financial products. Professor Warren believed the financial products marketed to ordinary American households — credit cards, student loans, mortgages, and the like — had grown increasingly unsafe due to a "regulatory jumble" that paid too much attention to banks and too little to consumers. To remedy the lack of "coherent, consumer-oriented" financial regulation, she proposed "concentrat[ing] the review of financial products in a single location" — an independent agency modeled after the multimember Consumer Product Safety Commission.

That proposal soon met its moment. Within months of Professor Warren's writing, the subprime mortgage market collapsed, precipitating a financial crisis that wiped out over $10 trillion in American household wealth and cost millions of Americans their jobs, their retirements, and their homes. In the aftermath, the Obama administration embraced Professor Warren's recommendation. Through the Treasury Department, the administration encouraged Congress to establish an agency with a mandate to ensure that "consumer protection regulations" in the financial sector "are written fairly and enforced vigorously." Like Professor Warren, the administration envisioned a traditional independent agency, run by a multimember board with a "diverse set of viewpoints and experiences."

In 2010, Congress acted on these proposals and created the Consumer Financial Protection Bureau (CFPB) as an independent financial regulator within the Federal Reserve System. Dodd-Frank Wall Street Reform and Consumer Protection Act (Dodd-Frank), Congress tasked the CFPB with "implement[ing]" and "enforc[ing]" a large body of financial consumer protection laws to "ensur[e] that all consumers have access to markets for consumer financial products and services and that markets for consumer financial products and services are fair, transparent, and competitive." Congress transferred the administration of 18 existing federal statutes to the CFPB, including the Fair Credit Reporting Act, the Fair Debt Collection Practices Act, and the Truth in Lending Act. In addition, Congress enacted a new prohibition on "any unfair, deceptive, or abusive act or practice" by certain participants in the consumer-finance sector. Congress authorized the CFPB to implement that broad standard (and the 18 pre-existing statutes placed under the agency's purview) through binding regulations.

Congress also vested the CFPB with potent enforcement powers. The agency has the authority to conduct investigations, issue subpoenas and civil investigative demands, initiate administrative adjudications, and prosecute civil actions in federal court. To remedy violations of federal consumer financial law, the CFPB may seek restitution, disgorgement, and injunctive relief, as well as civil penalties of up to $1,000,000 (inflation adjusted) for each day that a violation occurs. Since its inception, the CFPB has obtained over $11 billion in relief for over 25 million consumers, including a $1 billion penalty against a single bank in 2018.

The CFPB's rulemaking and enforcement powers are coupled with extensive adjudicatory authority. The agency may conduct administrative proceedings to "ensure or enforce compliance with" the statutes and regulations it administers. When the CFPB acts as an adjudicator, it has "jurisdiction to grant any appropriate legal or equitable relief." At the close of the proceedings, the hearing officer issues a "recommended decision," and the CFPB Director considers that recommendation and "issue[s] a final decision and order."

Congress's design for the CFPB differed from the proposals of Professor Warren and the Obama administration in one critical respect. Rather than create a traditional independent agency headed by a multimember board or commission, Congress elected to place the CFPB under the leadership of a single Director. The CFPB Director is appointed by the President with the advice and consent of the Senate. The Director serves for a term of five years, during which the President may remove the Director from office only for "inefficiency, neglect of duty, or malfeasance in office."

Unlike most other agencies, the CFPB does not rely on the annual appropriations process for funding. Instead, the CFPB receives funding directly from the Federal Reserve, which is itself funded outside the appropriations process through bank assessments. Each year, the CFPB requests an amount that the Director deems "reasonably necessary to carry out" the agency's duties, and the Federal Reserve grants that request so long as it does not exceed 12% of the total operating expenses of the Federal Reserve (inflation adjusted). In recent years, the CFPB's annual budget has exceeded half a billion dollars.

Seila Law LLC is a California-based law firm that provides debt-related legal services to clients. In 2017, the CFPB issued a civil investigative demand to Seila Law to determine whether the firm had "engag[ed] in unlawful acts or practices in the advertising, marketing, or sale of debt relief services." The demand (essentially a subpoena) directed Seila Law to produce information and documents related to its business practices. Seila Law asked the CFPB to set aside the demand, objecting that the agency's leadership by a single Director removable only for cause violated the separation of powers. We granted certiorari to address the constitutionality of We also requested argument on an additional question: whether, if the CFPB's structure violates the separation of powers, the CFPB Director's removal protection can be severed from the rest of the Dodd-Frank Act.

II

[In Part II of the opinion, Chief Justice Roberts explained that the Court had jurisdiction to decide the constitutional issues.]

III

We hold that the CFPB's leadership by a single individual removable only for inefficiency, neglect, or malfeasance violates the separation of powers. Article II provides that "[t]he executive Power shall be vested in a President," who must "take Care that the Laws be faithfully executed." The entire "executive Power" belongs to the President alone. But because it would be "impossib[le]" for "one man" to "perform all the great business of the State," the Constitution assumes that lesser executive officers will "assist the supreme Magistrate in discharging the duties of his trust."

These lesser officers must remain accountable to the President, whose authority they wield. As Madison explained, "[I]f any power whatsoever is in its nature Executive, it is the power of appointing, overseeing, and controlling those who execute the laws." That power, in turn, generally includes the ability to remove executive officials, for it is "only the authority that can remove" such officials that they "must fear and, in the performance of [their] functions, obey."

The President's removal power has long been confirmed by history and precedent. It "was discussed extensively in Congress when the first executive departments were created" in 1789. "The view that 'prevailed, as most consonant to the text of the Constitution' and 'to the requisite responsibility and harmony in the Executive Department,' was that the executive power included a power to oversee executive officers through removal." (quoting Letter from James Madison to Thomas Jefferson (June 30, 1789) The First Congress's recognition of the President's removal power in 1789 "provides contemporaneous and weighty evidence of the Constitution's meaning," and has long been the "settled and well understood construction of the Constitution."

The Court recognized the President's prerogative to remove executive officials in *Myers v. United States*. Chief Justice Taft, writing for the Court, concluded that Article II "grants to the President" the "general administrative control of those executing the laws, including the power of appointment *and removal* of executive officers." We recently reiterated the President's general removal power in *Free Enterprise Fund*. "Since 1789," we recapped, "the Constitution has been understood to empower the President to keep these officers accountable — by removing them from office, if necessary."

Free Enterprise Fund left in place two exceptions to the President's unrestricted removal power. First, in *Humphrey's Executor*, decided less than a decade after *Myers*, the Court upheld a statute that protected the Commissioners of the FTC from removal except for "inefficiency, neglect of duty, or malfeasance in office." In reaching that conclusion, the Court stressed that Congress's ability to impose such removal restrictions "will depend upon the character of the office." The Court identified several organizational features that helped explain its characterization of the FTC as non-executive. Composed of five members — no more than three from the same political party — the Board was designed to be "non-partisan" and to "act with entire impartiality." The FTC's duties were "neither political nor executive," but instead called for "the trained judgment of a body of experts" "informed by experience." And the Commissioners' staggered, seven-year terms enabled the agency to accumulate technical expertise and avoid a "complete change" in leadership "at any one time."

In short, *Humphrey's Executor* permitted Congress to give for-cause removal protections to a multimember body of experts, balanced along partisan lines, that performed legislative and judicial functions and was said not to exercise any executive power. Consistent with that understanding, the Court later applied "[t]he philosophy of *Humphrey's Executor*" to uphold for-cause removal protections for the members of the War Claims Commission — a three-member "adjudicatory body" tasked with resolving claims for compensation arising from World War II. *Wiener v. United States* (1958).

While recognizing an exception for multimember bodies with "quasi-judicial" or "quasi-legislative" functions, *Humphrey's Executor* reaffirmed the core holding of *Myers* that the President has "unrestrictable power . . . to remove purely executive officers." The Court acknowledged that between purely executive officers on the one hand, and officers that closely resembled the FTC Commissioners on the other, there existed "a field of doubt" that the Court left "for future consideration."

We have recognized a second exception for *inferior* officers in two cases, *United States v. Perkins* and *Morrison v. Olson*. In *Perkins*, we upheld tenure protections for a naval cadet-engineer. And, in *Morrison*, we upheld a provision granting good-cause tenure protection to an independent counsel appointed to investigate and prosecute particular alleged crimes by high-ranking Government officials. Backing away from the reliance in *Humphrey's Executor* on the concepts of "quasi-legislative" and "quasi-judicial" power, we viewed the ultimate question as whether a removal restriction is of "such a nature that [it] impede[s] the President's ability to perform his constitutional duty." Although the independent counsel was a single person and performed "law enforcement functions that typically have been undertaken by officials within the Executive Branch," we concluded that the removal protections did not unduly interfere with the functioning of the Executive Branch because "the independent counsel [was] an inferior officer under the Appointments Clause, with limited jurisdiction and tenure and lacking policymaking or significant administrative authority."

These two exceptions—one for multimember expert agencies that do not wield substantial executive power, and one for inferior officers with limited duties and no policymaking or administrative authority—"represent what up to now have been the outermost constitutional limits of permissible congressional restrictions on the President's removal power."

Neither *Humphrey's Executor* nor *Morrison* resolves whether the CFPB Director's insulation from removal is constitutional. Start with *Humphrey's Executor*. Unlike the New Deal-era FTC upheld there, the CFPB is led by a single Director who cannot be described as a "body of experts" and cannot be considered "non-partisan" in the same sense as a group of officials drawn from both sides of the aisle. Moreover, while the staggered terms of the FTC Commissioners prevented complete turnovers in agency leadership and guaranteed that there would always be some Commissioners who had accrued significant expertise, the CFPB's single-Director structure and five-year term guarantee abrupt shifts in agency leadership and with it the loss of accumulated expertise.

In addition, the CFPB Director is hardly a mere legislative or judicial aid. Instead of making reports and recommendations to Congress, as the 1935 FTC did, the Director possesses the authority to promulgate binding rules fleshing out 19 federal statutes, including a broad prohibition on unfair and deceptive practices in a major segment of the U.S. economy. And instead of submitting recommended dispositions to an Article III court, the Director may unilaterally issue final decisions awarding legal and equitable relief in administrative adjudications. Finally, the Director's enforcement authority includes the power to seek daunting monetary penalties against private parties on behalf of the United States in federal court—a quintessentially executive power not considered in *Humphrey's Executor*.

The logic of *Morrison* also does not apply. Everyone agrees the CFPB Director is not an inferior officer, and her duties are far from limited. Unlike the independent counsel, who lacked policymaking or administrative authority, the Director has the sole responsibility to administer 19 separate consumer-protection statutes that cover everything from credit cards and car payments to mortgages and student loans. It is true that the independent counsel in *Morrison* was empowered to initiate criminal investigations and prosecutions, and in that respect wielded core executive power. But that power, while significant, was trained inward to high-ranking Governmental actors identified by others, and was confined to a specified matter in which the Department of Justice had a potential conflict of interest. By contrast, the CFPB Director has the authority to bring the coercive power of the state to bear on millions of private citizens and businesses, imposing even billion-dollar penalties through administrative adjudications and civil actions.

In light of these differences, the constitutionality of the CFPB Director's insulation from removal cannot be settled by *Humphrey's Executor* or *Morrison* alone.

The question instead is whether to extend those precedents to the "new situation" before us, namely an independent agency led by a single Director and vested with significant executive power. We decline to do so. Such an agency has no basis in history and no place in our constitutional structure. "Perhaps the most telling indication of [a] severe constitutional problem" with an executive entity "is [a] lack of historical precedent" to support it. An agency with a structure like that of the CFPB is almost wholly unprecedented.

In addition to being a historical anomaly, the CFPB's single-Director configuration is incompatible with our constitutional structure. Aside from the sole exception of the Presidency, that structure scrupulously avoids concentrating power in the hands of any single individual. "The Framers recognized that, in the long term, structural protections against abuse of power were critical to preserving liberty." Their solution to governmental power and its perils was simple: divide it. To prevent the "gradual concentration" of power in the same hands, they enabled "[a]mbition . . . to counteract ambition" at every turn. The Federalist No. 51, p. 349 (J. Cooke ed. 1961) (J. Madison).

The Executive Branch is a stark departure from all this division. The Framers viewed the legislative power as a special threat to individual liberty, so they divided that power to ensure that "differences of opinion" and the "jarrings of parties" would "promote deliberation and circumspection" and "check excesses in the majority." By contrast, the Framers thought it necessary to secure the authority of the Executive so that he could carry out his unique responsibilities. As Madison put it, while "the weight of the legislative authority requires that it should be . . . divided, the weakness of the executive may require, on the other hand, that it should be fortified."

The resulting constitutional strategy is straightforward: divide power everywhere except for the Presidency, and render the President directly accountable to the people through regular elections. In that scheme, individual executive officials will still wield significant authority, but that authority remains subject to the ongoing supervision and control of the elected President. Through the President's oversight, "the chain of dependence [is] preserved," so that "the lowest officers, the middle grade, and the highest" all "depend, as they ought, on the President, and the President on the community." 1 Annals of Cong. 499 (J. Madison).

The CFPB's single-Director structure contravenes this carefully calibrated system by vesting significant governmental power in the hands of a single individual accountable to no one. The Director is neither elected by the people nor meaningfully controlled (through the threat of removal) by someone who is. The Director does not even depend on Congress for annual appropriations. Yet the Director may *unilaterally*, without meaningful supervision, issue final regulations, oversee adjudications, set enforcement priorities, initiate prosecutions, and determine what penalties to impose on private parties. With no colleagues to persuade, and no boss or electorate looking over her shoulder, the Director may dictate and enforce policy for a vital segment of the economy affecting millions of Americans.

The CFPB Director's insulation from removal by an accountable President is enough to render the agency's structure unconstitutional. But several other features of the CFPB combine to make the Director's removal protection even more problematic. In addition to lacking the most direct method of presidential control—removal at will—the agency's unique structure also forecloses certain indirect methods of Presidential control.

Because the CFPB is headed by a single Director with a five-year term, some Presidents may not have any opportunity to shape its leadership and thereby influence its activities. A President elected in 2020 would likely not appoint a CFPB Director until 2023, and a President elected in 2028 may *never* appoint one. That means an unlucky President might get elected on a consumer-protection platform and enter office only to find herself saddled with a holdover Director from a competing political party who is dead set *against* that agenda. To make matters worse, the agency's single-Director structure means the President will not have the opportunity to appoint any other leaders—such as a chair or fellow members of a Commission or Board—who can serve as a check on the Director's authority and help bring the agency in line with the President's preferred policies.

The CFPB's receipt of funds outside the appropriations process further aggravates the agency's threat to Presidential control. The President normally has the opportunity to recommend or veto spending bills that affect the operation of administrative agencies. But no similar opportunity exists for the President to influence the CFPB Director. Instead, the Director receives over $500 million per year to fund the agency's chosen priorities. And the Director receives that money from the Federal Reserve, which is itself funded outside of the annual appropriations process. This financial freedom makes it even more likely that the agency will "slip from the Executive's control, and thus from that of the people."

IV

Having concluded that the CFPB's leadership by a single independent Director violates the separation of powers, we now turn to the appropriate remedy. We directed the parties to brief and argue whether the Director's removal protection was severable from the other provisions of the Dodd-Frank Act that establish the CFPB. If so, then the CFPB may continue to exist and operate notwithstanding Congress's unconstitutional attempt to insulate the agency's Director from removal by the President. [The Court concluded that there was severability and thus the rest of the Dodd-Frank Act can remain.] Because we find the Director's removal protection severable from the other provisions of Dodd-Frank that establish the CFPB, we remand for the Court of Appeals to consider whether the civil investigative demand was validly ratified.

A decade ago, we declined to extend Congress's authority to limit the President's removal power to a new situation, never before confronted by the Court. We do the same today. In our constitutional system, the executive power belongs to the President, and that power generally includes the ability to supervise and remove the agents who wield executive power in his stead. While we have previously upheld limits on the President's removal authority in certain contexts, we decline to do so when it comes to principal officers who, acting alone, wield significant executive power.

The Constitution requires that such officials remain dependent on the President, who in turn is accountable to the people.

Justice THOMAS with whom Justice GORSUCH joins, concurring in part and dissenting in part.

The Court's decision today takes a restrained approach on the merits by limiting *Humphrey's Executor v. United States*, rather than overruling it. At the same time, the Court takes an aggressive approach on severability by severing a provision when it is not necessary to do so. I would do the opposite.

Because the Court takes a step in the right direction by limiting *Humphrey's Executor* to "multimember expert agencies that *do not wield substantial executive power*," I join Parts I, II, and III of its opinion. I respectfully dissent from the Court's severability analysis, however, because I do not believe that we should address severability in this case.

I

The decision in *Humphrey's Executor* poses a direct threat to our constitutional structure and, as a result, the liberty of the American people. The Court concludes that it is not strictly necessary for us to overrule that decision. But with today's decision, the Court has repudiated almost every aspect of *Humphrey's Executor*. In a future case, I would repudiate what is left of this erroneous precedent.

Despite the defined structural limitations of the Constitution and the clear vesting of executive power in the President, Congress has increasingly shifted executive power to a *de facto* fourth branch of Government—independent agencies. These agencies wield considerable executive power without Presidential oversight. They are led by officers who are insulated from the President by removal restrictions, "reduc[ing] the Chief Magistrate to [the role of] cajoler-in-chief." But "[t]he people do not vote for the Officers of the United States. They instead look to the President to guide the assistants or deputies subject to his superintendence." Because independent agencies wield substantial power with no accountability to either the President or the people, they "pose a significant threat to individual liberty and to the constitutional system of separation of powers and checks and balances."

Unfortunately, this Court "ha[s] not always been vigilant about protecting the structure of our Constitution," at times endorsing a "more pragmatic, flexible approach" to our Government's design. Our tolerance of independent agencies in *Humphrey's Executor* is an unfortunate example of the Court's failure to apply the Constitution as written. That decision has paved the way for an ever-expanding encroachment on the power of the Executive, contrary to our constitutional design.

Humphrey's Executor laid the foundation for a fundamental departure from our constitutional structure with nothing more than handwaving and obfuscating phrases such as "quasi-legislative" and "quasi-judicial." The exceptional weakness of the reasoning could be a product of the circumstances under which the case was decided — in the midst of a bitter stand-off between the Court and President Roosevelt — or it could be just another example of this Court departing from the strictures of the Constitution for a "more pragmatic, flexible approach" to our government's design. But whatever the motivation, *Humphrey's Executor* does not comport with the Constitution.

Humphrey's Executor relies on one key premise: the notion that there is a category of "quasi-legislative" and "quasi-judicial" power that is not exercised by Congress or the Judiciary, but that is also not part of "the executive power vested by the Constitution in the President."

The problem is that the Court's premise was entirely wrong. The Constitution does not permit the creation of officers exercising "quasi-legislative" and "quasi-judicial powers" in "quasi-legislative" and "quasi-judicial agencies." Nor can Congress create agencies that straddle multiple branches of Government. The Constitution sets out three branches of Government and provides each with a different form of power — legislative, executive, and judicial. Free-floating agencies simply do not comport with this constitutional structure.

Continued reliance on *Humphrey's Executor* to justify the existence of independent agencies creates a serious, ongoing threat to our Government's design. Leaving these unconstitutional agencies in place does not enhance this Court's legitimacy; it subverts political accountability and threatens individual liberty. We have a "responsibility to 'examin[e] without fear, and revis[e] without reluctance,' any 'hasty and crude decisions' rather than leaving 'the character of [the] law impaired, and the beauty and harmony of the [American constitutional] system destroyed by the perpetuity of error.'" We simply cannot compromise when it comes to our Government's structure. Today, the Court does enough to resolve this case, but in the future, we should reconsider *Humphrey's Executor in toto*. And I hope that we will have the will to do so.

II

While I think that the Court correctly resolves the merits of the constitutional question, I do not agree with its decision to sever the removal restriction. [Justice Thomas then disagreed with the majority about severability of the removal provision from the rest of the statute.]

Justice KAGAN, with whom Justice GINSBURG, Justice BREYER, and Justice SOTOMAYOR join, concurring in the judgment with respect to severability and dissenting in part.

Throughout the Nation's history, this Court has left most decisions about how to structure the Executive Branch to Congress and the President, acting through legislation they both agree to. In particular, the Court has commonly allowed those two branches to create zones of administrative independence by limiting the President's power to remove agency heads. The Federal Reserve Board. The Federal Trade Commission (FTC). The National Labor Relations Board. Statute after statute establishing such entities instructs the President that he may not discharge their directors except for cause—most often phrased as inefficiency, neglect of duty, or malfeasance in office. Those statutes, whose language the Court has repeatedly approved, provide the model for the removal restriction before us today. If precedent were any guide, that provision would have survived its encounter with this Court—and so would the intended independence of the Consumer Financial Protection Bureau (CFPB).

Our Constitution and history demand that result. The text of the Constitution allows these common for-cause removal limits. Nothing in it speaks of removal. And it grants Congress authority to organize all the institutions of American governance, provided only that those arrangements allow the President to perform his own constitutionally assigned duties. Still more, the Framers' choice to give the political branches wide discretion over administrative offices has played out through American history in ways that have settled the constitutional meaning. From the first, Congress debated and enacted measures to create spheres of administration—especially of financial affairs—detached from direct presidential control. As the years passed, and governance became ever more complicated, Congress continued to adopt and adapt such measures—confident it had latitude to do so under a Constitution meant to "endure for ages to come." Not every innovation in governance—not every experiment in administrative independence—has proved successful. And debates about the prudence of limiting the President's control over regulatory agencies, including through his removal power, have never abated. But the Constitution—both as originally drafted and as practiced—mostly leaves disagreements about administrative structure to Congress and the President, who have the knowledge and experience needed to address them. Within broad bounds, it keeps the courts—who do not—out of the picture.

The Court today fails to respect its proper role. It recognizes that this Court has approved limits on the President's removal power over heads of agencies much like the CFPB. Agencies possessing similar powers, agencies charged with similar missions, agencies created for similar reasons. The majority's explanation is that the heads of those agencies fall within an "exception"—one for multimember bodies and another for inferior officers—to a "general rule" of unrestricted presidential removal power. And the majority says the CFPB Director does not. That account, though, is wrong in every respect. The majority's general rule does not exist. Its exceptions, likewise, are made up for the occasion—gerrymandered so the CFPB falls outside them. And the distinction doing most of the majority's work—between multimember bodies and single directors—does not respond to the constitutional values at stake. If a removal provision violates the separation of powers, it is because the measure so deprives the President of control over an official as to impede his own constitutional functions. But with or without a for-cause removal provision, the President has at least as much control over an individual as over a commission—and possibly more. That means the constitutional concern is, if anything, ameliorated when the agency has a single head. Unwittingly, the majority shows why courts should stay their hand in these matters. "Compared to Congress and the President, the Judiciary possesses an inferior understanding of the realities of administration" and the way "political power[ ] operates."

In second-guessing the political branches, the majority second-guesses as well the wisdom of the Framers and the judgment of history. It writes in rules to the Constitution that the drafters knew well enough not to put there. It repudiates the lessons of American experience, from the 18th century to the present day. And it commits the Nation to a static version of governance, incapable of responding to new conditions and challenges. Congress and the President established the CFPB to address financial practices that had brought on a devastating recession, and could do so again. Today's decision wipes out a feature of that agency its creators thought fundamental to its mission—a measure of independence from political pressure. I respectfully dissent.

I

The text of the Constitution, the history of the country, the precedents of this Court, and the need for sound and adaptable governance—all stand against the majority's opinion. They point not to the majority's "general rule" of "unrestricted removal power" with two grudgingly applied "exceptions." Rather, they bestow discretion on the legislature to structure administrative institutions as the times demand, so long as the President retains the ability to carry out his constitutional duties. And most relevant here, they give Congress wide leeway to limit the President's removal power in the interest of enhancing independence from politics in regulatory bodies like the CFPB.

What does the Constitution say about the separation of powers—and particularly about the President's removal authority? (Spoiler alert: about the latter, nothing at all.)

The majority offers the civics class version of separation of powers—call it the Schoolhouse Rock definition of the phrase.

There is nothing wrong with that as a beginning (except the adjective "simple"). It is of course true that the Framers lodged three different kinds of power in three different entities. The problem lies in treating the beginning as an ending too—in failing to recognize that the separation of powers is, by design, neither rigid nor complete.

Contrary to the majority's view, then, the founding era closed without any agreement that Congress lacked the power to curb the President's removal authority. And as it kept that question open, Congress took the first steps—which would launch a tradition—of distinguishing financial regulators from diplomatic and military officers. The latter mainly helped the President carry out his own constitutional duties in foreign relations and war. The former chiefly carried out statutory duties, fulfilling functions Congress had assigned to their offices. In addressing the new Nation's finances, Congress had begun to use its powers under the Necessary and Proper Clause to design effective administrative institutions. And that included taking steps to insulate certain officers from political influence.

As the decades and centuries passed, those efforts picked up steam. Confronting new economic, technological, and social conditions, Congress—and often the President—saw new needs for pockets of independence within the federal bureaucracy. And that was especially so, again, when it came to financial regulation. I mention just a few highlights here—times when Congress decided that effective governance depended on shielding technical or expertise-based functions relating to the financial system from political pressure (or the moneyed interests that might lie behind it). Enacted under the Necessary and Proper Clause, those measures — creating some of the Nation's most enduring institutions — themselves helped settle the extent of Congress's power. "[A] regular course of practice," to use Madison's phrase, has "liquidate[d]" constitutional meaning about the permissibility of independent agencies.

Take first Congress's decision in 1816 to create the Second Bank of the United States — "the first truly independent agency in the republic's history." Of the twenty-five directors who led the Bank, the President could appoint and remove only five. Yet the Bank had a greater impact on the Nation than any but a few institutions, regulating the Nation's money supply in ways anticipating what the Federal Reserve does today. Of course, the Bank was controversial — in large part because of its freedom from presidential control. Andrew Jackson chafed at the Bank's independence and eventually fired his Treasury Secretary for keeping public moneys there (a dismissal that itself provoked a political storm). No matter. Innovations in governance always have opponents; administrative independence predictably (though by no means invariably) provokes presidential ire. The point is that by the early 19th century, Congress established a body wielding enormous financial power mostly outside the President's dominion.

The Civil War brought yet further encroachments on presidential control over financial regulators. In response to wartime economic pressures, President Lincoln (not known for his modest view of executive power) asked Congress to establish an office called the Comptroller of the Currency. The statute he signed made the Comptroller removable only with the Senate's consent — a version of the old Hamiltonian idea, though this time required not by the Constitution itself but by Congress. A year later, Congress amended the statute to permit removal by the President alone, but only upon "reasons to be communicated by him to the Senate."

And then, nearly a century and a half ago, the floodgates opened. In 1887, the growing power of the railroads over the American economy led Congress to create the Interstate Commerce Commission. Under that legislation, the President could remove the five Commissioners only "for inefficiency, neglect of duty, or malfeasance in office" — the same standard Congress applied to the CFPB Director. More — many more — for-cause removal provisions followed. In 1913, Congress gave the Governors of the Federal Reserve Board for-cause protection to ensure the agency would resist political pressure and promote economic stability. The next year, Congress provided similar protection to the FTC in the interest of ensuring "a continuous policy" "free from the effect" of "changing [White House] incumbency." The Federal Deposit Insurance Corporation (FDIC), the Securities and Exchange Commission (SEC), the Commodity Futures Trading Commission. By one count, across all subject matter areas, 48 agencies have heads (and below them hundreds more inferior officials) removable only for cause. So year by year by year, the broad sweep of history has spoken to the constitutional question before us: Independent agencies are everywhere.

What is more, the Court's precedents before today have accepted the role of independent agencies in our governmental system. To be sure, the line of our decisions has not run altogether straight. But we have repeatedly upheld provisions that prevent the President from firing regulatory officials except for such matters as neglect or malfeasance. In those decisions, we sounded a caution, insisting that Congress could not impede through removal restrictions the President's performance of his own constitutional duties. (So, to take the clearest example, Congress could not curb the President's power to remove his close military or diplomatic advisers.) But within that broad limit, this Court held, Congress could protect from at-will removal the officials it deemed to need some independence from political pressures. Nowhere do those precedents suggest what the majority announces today: that the President has an "unrestricted removal power" subject to two bounded exceptions.

The deferential approach this Court has taken gives Congress the flexibility it needs to craft administrative agencies. Diverse problems of government demand diverse solutions. They call for varied measures and mixtures of democratic accountability and technical expertise, energy and efficiency. Sometimes, the arguments push toward tight presidential control of agencies. The President's engagement, some people say, can disrupt bureaucratic stagnation, counter industry capture, and make agencies more responsive to public interests. At other times, the arguments favor greater independence from presidential involvement. Insulation from political pressure helps ensure impartial adjudications. It places technical issues in the hands of those most capable of addressing them. It promotes continuity, and prevents short-term electoral interests from distorting policy. (Consider, for example, how the Federal Reserve's independence stops a President trying to win a second term from manipulating interest rates.) Of course, the right balance between presidential control and independence is often uncertain, contested, and value-laden. No mathematical formula governs institutional design; trade-offs are endemic to the enterprise. But that is precisely why the issue is one for the political branches to debate — and then debate again as times change. And it's why courts should stay (mostly) out of the way. Rather than impose rigid rules like the majority's, they should let Congress and the President figure out what blend of independence and political control will best enable an agency to perform its intended functions.

Judicial intrusion into this field usually reveals only how little courts know about governance. Even everything I just said is an over-simplification. It suggests that agencies can easily be arranged on a spectrum, from the most to the least presidentially controlled. But that is not so. A given agency's independence (or lack of it) depends on a wealth of features, relating not just to removal standards, but also to appointments practices, procedural rules, internal organization, oversight regimes, historical traditions, cultural norms, and (inevitably) personal relationships. It is hard to pinpoint how those factors work individually, much less in concert, to influence the distance between an agency and a President. In that light, even the judicial opinions' perennial focus on removal standards is a bit of a puzzle. Removal is only the most obvious, not necessarily the most potent, means of control. That is because informal restraints can prevent Presidents from firing at-will officers—and because other devices can keep officers with for-cause protection under control.

II

As the majority explains, the CFPB emerged out of disaster. The collapse of the subprime mortgage market "precipitat[ed] a financial crisis that wiped out over $10 trillion in American household wealth and cost millions of Americans their jobs, their retirements, and their homes." In that moment of economic ruin, the President proposed and Congress enacted legislation to address the causes of the collapse and prevent a recurrence. An important part of that statute created an agency to protect consumers from exploitative financial practices.

No one had a doubt that the new agency should be independent. The law thus included an ordinary for-cause provision—once again, that the President could fire the CFPB's Director only for "inefficiency, neglect of duty, or malfeasance in office." That standard would allow the President to discharge the Director for a failure to "faithfully execute[ ]" the law, as well as for basic incompetence. But it would not permit removal for policy differences.

The question here, which by now you're well equipped to answer, is whether including that for-cause standard in the statute creating the CFPB violates the Constitution. Applying our longstanding precedent, the answer is clear: It does not. This Court, as the majority acknowledges, has sustained the constitutionality of the FTC and similar independent agencies. The for-cause protections for the heads of those agencies, the Court has found, do not impede the President's ability to perform his own constitutional duties, and so do not breach the separation of powers. There is nothing different here. The CFPB wields the same kind of power as the FTC and similar agencies. And all of their heads receive the same kind of removal protection. No less than those other entities—by now part of the fabric of government—the CFPB is thus a permissible exercise of Congress's power under the Necessary and Proper Clause to structure administration.

The majority focuses on one (it says sufficient) reason: The CFPB Director is singular, not plural. "Instead of placing the agency under the leadership of a board with multiple members," the majority protests, "Congress provided that the CFPB would be led by a single Director."

I'm tempted at this point just to say: No. All I've explained about constitutional text, history, and precedent invalidates the majority's thesis. But I'll set out here some more targeted points, taking step by step the majority's reasoning.

First, as I'm afraid you've heard before, the majority's "exceptions" (like its general rule) are made up. To begin with, our precedents reject the very idea of such exceptions. The independent counsel was very much a person, not a committee. So the idea that *Morrison* is in a separate box from this case doesn't hold up. Similarly, *Humphrey's* and later precedents give no support to the majority's view that the number of people at the apex of an agency matters to the constitutional issue.

By contrast, the CFPB's single-director structure has a fair bit of precedent behind it. The Comptroller of the Currency. The Office of the Special Counsel (OSC). The Social Security Administration (SSA). The Federal Housing Finance Agency (FHFA). Maybe four prior agencies is in the eye of the beholder, but it's hardly nothing.

The majority says a single head is the greater threat because he may wield power "*unilaterally*" and "[w]ith no colleagues to persuade." So the CFPB falls victim to what the majority sees as a constitutional anti-power-concentration principle (with an exception for the President). If you've never heard of a statute being struck down on that ground, you're not alone. It is bad enough to "extrapolat[e]" from the "general constitutional language" of Article II's Vesting Clause an unrestricted removal power constraining Congress's ability to legislate under the Necessary and Proper Clause. It is still worse to extrapolate from the Constitution's general structure (division of powers) and implicit values (liberty) a limit on Congress's express power to create administrative bodies. And more: to extrapolate from such sources a distinction as prosaic as that between the SEC and the CFPB — *i.e.,* between a multi-headed and single-headed agency. That is, to adapt a phrase (or two) from our precedent, "more than" the emanations of "the text will bear."

III

Recall again how this dispute got started. In the midst of the Great Recession, Congress and the President came together to create an agency with an important mission. It would protect consumers from the reckless financial practices that had caused the then-ongoing economic collapse. Not only Congress but also the President thought that the new agency, to fulfill its mandate, needed a measure of independence. So the two political branches, acting together, gave the CFPB Director the same job protection that innumerable other agency heads possess. All in all, those branches must have thought, they had done a good day's work. Relying on their experience and knowledge of administration, they had built an agency in the way best suited to carry out its functions. They had protected the public from financial chicanery and crisis. They had governed.

And now consider how the dispute ends — with five unelected judges rejecting the result of that democratic process. The outcome today will not shut down the CFPB: A different majority of this Court, including all those who join this opinion, believes that *if* the agency's removal provision is unconstitutional, it should be severed. But the majority on constitutionality jettisons a measure Congress and the President viewed as integral to the way the agency should operate. The majority does so even though the Constitution grants to Congress, acting with the President's approval, the authority to create and shape administrative bodies. And even though those branches, as compared to courts, have far greater understanding of political control mechanisms and agency design.

Nothing in the Constitution requires that outcome; to the contrary. "While the Constitution diffuses power the better to secure liberty, it also contemplates that practice will integrate the dispersed powers into a workable government." The Framers took pains to craft a document that would allow the structures of governance to change, as times and needs change.

Our history has stayed true to the Framers' vision. Congress has accepted their invitation to experiment with administrative forms — nowhere more so than in the field of financial regulation. And this Court has mostly allowed it to do so. The result is a broad array of independent agencies, no two exactly alike but all with a measure of insulation from the President's removal power. The Federal Reserve Board; the FTC; the SEC; maybe some you've never heard of. As to each, Congress thought that formal job protection for policymaking would produce regulatory outcomes in greater accord with the long-term public interest. Congress may have been right; or it may have been wrong; or maybe it was some of both. No matter—the branches accountable to the people have decided how the people should be governed.

The CFPB should have joined the ranks. Maybe it will still do so, even under today's opinion: The majority tells Congress that it may "pursu[e] alternative responses" to the identified constitutional defect—"for example, converting the CFPB into a multimember agency." But there was no need to send Congress back to the drawing board. The Constitution does not distinguish between single-director and multimember independent agencies. It instructs Congress, not this Court, to decide on agency design. Because this Court ignores that sensible—indeed, that obvious—division of tasks, I respectfully dissent.

***

The year after *Seila Law* was decided, the Supreme Court applied it to declare unconstitutional removal provisions for another federal agency.

COLLINS v. YELLEN

141 S. Ct. 1761 (2021)

Justice ALITO delivered the opinion of the Court.

Fannie Mae and Freddie Mac are two of the Nation's leading sources of mortgage financing. When the housing crisis hit in 2008, the companies suffered significant losses, and many feared that their troubling financial condition would imperil the national economy. To address that concern, Congress enacted the Housing and Economic Recovery Act of 2008 (Recovery Act). Among other things, that law created the Federal Housing Finance Agency (FHFA), "an independent agency" tasked with regulating the companies and, if necessary, stepping in as their conservator or receiver. At its head, Congress installed a single Director, whom the President could remove only "for cause."

Shortly after the FHFA came into existence, it placed Fannie Mae and Freddie Mac into conservatorship and negotiated agreements for the companies with the Department of Treasury. Under those agreements, Treasury committed to providing each company with up to $100 billion in capital, and in exchange received, among other things, senior preferred shares and quarterly fixed-rate dividends. Four years later, the FHFA and Treasury amended the agreements and replaced the fixed-rate dividend formula with a variable one that required the companies to make quarterly payments consisting of their entire net worth minus a small specified capital reserve. This deal, which the parties refer to as the "third amendment" or "net worth sweep," caused the companies to transfer enormous amounts of wealth to Treasury. It also resulted in a slew of lawsuits, including the one before us today.

A group of Fannie Mae's and Freddie Mac's shareholders challenged the third amendment on statutory and constitutional grounds. And with respect to their constitutional claim, the shareholders argued that the FHFA's structure violates the separation of powers because the Agency is led by a single Director who may be removed by the President only "for cause." [W]e conclude that the FHFA's structure violates the separation of powers, and we remand for further proceedings to determine what remedy, if any, the shareholders are entitled to receive on their constitutional claim.

The Recovery Act's for-cause restriction on the President's removal authority violates the separation of powers. Indeed, our decision last Term in *Seila Law* is all but dispositive. There, we held that Congress could not limit the President's power to remove the Director of the Consumer Financial Protection Bureau (CFPB) to instances of "inefficiency, neglect, or malfeasance." We did "not revisit our prior decisions allowing certain limitations on the President's removal power," but we found "compelling reasons not to extend those precedents to the novel context of an independent agency led by a single Director." "Such an agency," we observed, "lacks a foundation in historical practice and clashes with constitutional structure by concentrating power in a unilateral actor insulated from Presidential control."

A straightforward application of our reasoning in *Seila Law* dictates the result here. The FHFA (like the CFPB) is an agency led by a single Director, and the Recovery Act (like the Dodd-Frank Act) restricts the President's removal power.

Amicus first argues that Congress should have greater leeway to restrict the President's power to remove the FHFA Director because the FHFA's authority is more limited than that of the CFPB. But the nature and breadth of an agency's authority is not dispositive in determining whether Congress may limit the President's power to remove its head. The President's removal power serves vital purposes even when the officer subject to removal is not the head of one of the largest and most powerful agencies. The removal power helps the President maintain a degree of control over the subordinates he needs to carry out his duties as the head of the Executive Branch, and it works to ensure that these subordinates serve the people effectively and in accordance with the policies that the people presumably elected the President to promote. In addition, because the President, unlike agency officials, is elected, this control is essential to subject Executive Branch actions to a degree of electoral accountability. At-will removal ensures that "the lowest officers, the middle grade, and the highest, will depend, as they ought, on the President, and the President on the community." These purposes are implicated whenever an agency does important work, and nothing about the size or role of the FHFA convinces us that its Director should be treated differently from the Director of the CFPB. Courts are not well-suited to weigh the relative importance of the regulatory and enforcement authority of disparate agencies, and we do not think that the constitutionality of removal restrictions hinges on such an inquiry.

But as we explained last Term, the Constitution prohibits even "modest restrictions" on the President's power to remove the head of an agency with a single top officer. The President must be able to remove not just officers who disobey his commands but also those he finds "negligent and inefficient," those who exercise their discretion in a way that is not "intelligen[t] or wis[e]," those who have "different views of policy," those who come "from a competing political party who is dead set against [the President's] agend," and those in whom he has simply lost confidence.

Justice SOTOMAYOR, with whom Justice BREYER joins, concurring in part and dissenting in part.

Prior to 2010, this Court had gone the greater part of a century since it last prevented Congress from protecting an Executive Branch officer from unfettered Presidential removal. Yet today, for the third time in just over a decade, the Court strikes down the tenure protections Congress provided an independent agency's leadership.

Last Term, the Court held in *Seila Law LLC v. Consumer Financial Protection Bureau* (2020), that for-cause removal protection for the Director of the Consumer Financial Protection Bureau (CFPB) violated the separation of powers. As an "independent agency led by a single Director and vested with significant executive power," the Court reasoned, the CFPB had "no basis in history and no place in our constitutional structure." *Seila Law* expressly distinguished the Federal Housing

Finance Agency (FHFA), another independent Agency headed by a single Director, on the ground that the FHFA does not possess "regulatory or enforcement authority remotely comparable to that exercised by the CFPB." Moreover, the Court found it significant that, unlike the CFPB, the FHFA "regulates primarily Government-sponsored enterprises, not purely private actors."

Nevertheless, the Court today holds that the FHFA and CFPB are comparable after all, and that any differences between the two are irrelevant to the constitutional separation of powers. That reasoning cannot be squared with this Court's precedents, least of all last Term's *Seila Law*. I respectfully dissent in part from the Court's opinion and from the corresponding portions of the judgment.

Never before, however, has the Court forbidden simple for-cause tenure protection for an Executive Branch officer who neither exercises significant executive power nor regulates the affairs of private parties. Because the FHFA Director fits that description, this Court's precedent, separation-of-powers principles, and proper respect for Congress all support leaving in place Congress' limits on the grounds upon which the President may remove the Director.

Not only does the FHFA lack significant executive power, the authority it does possess is exercised over other governmental actors. In that respect, the FHFA Director mimics the independent counsel whose tenure protections were upheld in *Morrison* [*v. Olson* (1988)]. The independent counsel, as *Seila Law* noted, could bring criminal prosecutions and thus "wielded core executive power." Separation-of-powers concerns were allayed, however, because "that power, while significant, was trained inward to high-ranking Governmental actors identified by others." In explaining why "[t]he logic of *Morrison*" did "not apply" to the CFPB, *Seila Law* emphasized that the CFPB "has the authority to bring the coercive power of the state to bear on millions of private citizens and businesses."

Historical considerations further confirm the constitutionality of the FHFA Director's independence. Single-director independent agencies with limited executive power, like the FHFA, boast a more storied pedigree than do single-director independent agencies with significant executive power, like the CFPB. Consider three such examples, each discussed in *Seila Law*. First, the Comptroller of the Currency, who was briefly independent from Presidential removal during the Civil War and thereafter retained a lesser form of tenure protection. Second, the Office of Special Counsel, which has been "headed by a single officer since 1978." Third, the Social Security Administration, which has been "run by a single

Administrator since 1994." Like the FHFA, these examples lack "regulatory or enforcement authority remotely comparable to that exercised by the CFPB."

The FHFA also draws on a long tradition of independence enjoyed by financial regulators, including the Comptroller of the Treasury, the Second Bank of the United States, the Federal Reserve Board, the Securities and Exchange Commission, the Commodity Futures Trading Commission, and the Federal Deposit Insurance Corporation.

The Court has proved far too eager in recent years to insert itself into questions of agency structure best left to Congress. In striking down the independence of the FHFA Director, the Court reaches further than ever before, refusing tenure protections to an Agency head who neither wields significant executive power nor regulates private individuals. Troublingly, the Court justifies that result by ignoring the standards it set out just last Term in *Seila Law*. Because I would afford Congress the freedom it has long possessed to make officers like the FHFA Director independent from Presidential control, I respectfully dissent.

G.   The Electoral College (new)

Although the Electoral College has existed since 1787, there are few Supreme Court decisions about it. In *Chiafalo v. Washington*, the Court considered whether a state can require that an elector vote in a particular way. The Court said yes.

CHIAFALO v. WASHINGTON
140 S. Ct. 2316 (2020)

Justice KAGAN delivered the opinion of the Court.

Every four years, millions of Americans cast a ballot for a presidential candidate. Their votes, though, actually go toward selecting members of the Electoral College, whom each State appoints based on the popular returns. Those few "electors" then choose the President.

The States have devised mechanisms to ensure that the electors they appoint vote for the presidential candidate their citizens have preferred. With two partial exceptions, every State appoints a slate of electors selected by the political party whose candidate has won the State's popular vote. Most States also compel electors to pledge in advance to support the nominee of that party. This Court upheld such a pledge requirement decades ago, rejecting the argument that the Constitution "demands absolute freedom for the elector to vote his own choice." *Ray v. Blair* (1952).

Today, we consider whether a State may also penalize an elector for breaking his pledge and voting for someone other than the presidential candidate who won his State's popular vote. We hold that a State may do so.

I

Our Constitution's method of picking Presidents emerged from an eleventh-hour compromise. The issue, one delegate to the Convention remarked, was "the most difficult of all [that] we have had to decide." Despite long debate and many votes, the delegates could not reach an agreement. In the dying days of summer, they referred the matter to the so-called Committee of Eleven to devise a solution. The Committee returned with a proposal for the Electoral College. Just two days later, the delegates accepted the recommendation with but a few tweaks. James Madison later wrote to a friend that the "difficulty of finding an unexceptionable [selection] process" was "deeply felt by the Convention." Because "the final arrangement of it took place in the latter stage of the Session," Madison continued, "it was not exempt from a degree of the hurrying influence produced by fatigue and impatience in all such Bodies: tho' the degree was much less than usually prevails in them." Whether less or not, the delegates soon finished their work and departed for home.

The provision they approved about presidential electors is fairly slim. Article II, § 1, cl. 2 says: "Each State shall appoint, in such Manner as the Legislature thereof may direct, a Number of Electors, equal to the whole Number of Senators and Representatives to which the State may be entitled in the Congress: but no Senator or Representative, or Person holding an Office of Trust or Profit under the United States, shall be appointed an Elector."

The next clause (but don't get attached: it will soon be superseded) set out the procedures the electors were to follow in casting their votes. In brief, each member of the College would cast votes for two candidates in the presidential field. The candidate with the greatest number of votes, assuming he had a majority, would become President. The runner-up would become Vice President. If no one had a majority, the House of Representatives would take over and decide the winner.

That plan failed to anticipate the rise of political parties, and soon proved unworkable. The Nation's first contested presidential election occurred in 1796, after George Washington's retirement. John Adams came in first among the candidates, and Thomas Jefferson second. That meant the leaders of the era's two warring political parties — the Federalists and the Republicans — became President and Vice President respectively. (One might think of this as fodder for a new season of Veep.) Four years later, a different problem arose. Jefferson and Aaron Burr ran that year as a Republican Party ticket, with the former meant to be President and the latter meant to be Vice. For that plan to succeed, Jefferson had to come in first and Burr just behind him. Instead, Jefferson came in first and Burr . . . did too. Every elector who voted for Jefferson also voted for Burr, producing a tie. That threw the election into the House of Representatives, which took no fewer than 36 ballots to elect Jefferson. (Alexander Hamilton secured his place on the Broadway stage — but possibly in the cemetery too — by lobbying Federalists in the House to tip the election to Jefferson, whom he loathed but viewed as less of an existential threat to the Republic.) By then, everyone had had enough of the Electoral College's original voting rules.

The result was the Twelfth Amendment, whose main part provided that electors would vote separately for President and Vice President. The Amendment, ratified in 1804, says:

"The Electors shall meet in their respective states and vote by ballot for President and Vice-President . . . ; they shall name in their ballots the person voted for as President, and in distinct ballots the person voted for as Vice-President, and they shall make distinct lists of all persons voted for as President, and of all persons voted for as Vice-President, and of the number of votes for each, which lists they shall sign and certify, and transmit sealed to [Congress, where] the votes shall then be counted."

The Amendment thus brought the Electoral College's voting procedures into line with the Nation's new party system.

Within a few decades, the party system also became the means of translating popular preferences within each State into Electoral College ballots. In the Nation's earliest elections, state legislatures mostly picked the electors, with the majority party sending a delegation of its choice to the Electoral College. By 1832, though, all States but one had introduced popular presidential elections. At first, citizens voted for a slate of electors put forward by a political party, expecting that the winning slate would vote for its party's presidential (and vice presidential) nominee in the Electoral College. By the early 20th century, citizens in most States voted for the presidential candidate himself; ballots increasingly did not even list the electors. After the popular vote was counted, States appointed the electors chosen by the party whose presidential nominee had won statewide, again expecting that they would vote for that candidate in the Electoral College.

In the 20th century, many States enacted statutes meant to guarantee that outcome — that is, to prohibit so-called faithless voting. Rather than just assume that party-picked electors would vote for their party's winning nominee, those States insist that they do so. As of now, 32 States and the District of Columbia have such statutes on their books. They are typically called pledge laws because most demand that electors take a formal oath or pledge to cast their ballot for their party's presidential (and vice presidential) candidate. Others merely impose that duty by law. Either way, the statutes work to ensure that the electors vote for the candidate who got the most statewide votes in the presidential election.

Most relevant here, States began about 60 years ago to back up their pledge laws with some kind of sanction. By now, 15 States have such a system. Almost all of them immediately remove a faithless elector from his position, substituting an alternate whose vote the State reports instead. A few States impose a monetary fine on any elector who flouts his pledge. Washington is one of the 15 States with a sanctions-backed pledge law designed to keep the State's electors in line with its voting citizens. As all States now do, Washington requires political parties fielding presidential candidates to nominate a slate of electors. On Election Day, the State gives voters a ballot listing only the candidates themselves. When the vote comes in, Washington moves toward appointing the electors chosen by the party whose candidate won the statewide count. But before the appointment can go into effect, each elector must "execute [a] pledge" agreeing to "mark [her] ballots" for the presidential (and vice presidential) candidate of the party nominating her. And the elector must comply with that pledge, or else face a sanction. At the time relevant here, the punishment was a civil fine of up to $1,000.

This case involves three Washington electors who violated their pledges in the 2016 presidential election. That year, Washington's voters chose Hillary Clinton over Donald Trump for President. The State thus appointed as its electors the nominees of the Washington State Democratic Party. Among those Democratic electors were petitioners Peter Chiafalo, Levi Guerra, and Esther John (the Electors). All three pledged to support Hillary Clinton in the Electoral College. But as that vote approached, they decided to cast their ballots for someone else. The three hoped they could encourage other electors — particularly those from States Donald Trump had carried — to follow their example. The idea was to deprive him of a majority of electoral votes and throw the election into the House of Representatives. So the three Electors voted for Colin Powell for President. But their effort failed. Only seven electors across the Nation cast faithless votes — the most in a century, but well short of the goal.

Candidate Trump became President Trump. And, more to the point here, the State fined the Electors $1,000 apiece for breaking their pledges to support the same candidate its voters had.

The Electors challenged their fines in state court, arguing that the Constitution gives members of the Electoral College the right to vote however they please.

II

As the state court recognized, this Court has considered elector pledge requirements before. Some seventy years ago Edmund Blair tried to become a presidential elector in Alabama. Like all States, Alabama lodged the authority to pick electors in the political parties fielding presidential candidates. And the Alabama Democratic Party required a pledge phrased much like Washington's today. No one could get on the party's slate of electors without agreeing to vote in the Electoral College for the Democratic presidential candidate. Blair challenged the pledge mandate. He argued that the "intention of the Founders was that [presidential] electors should exercise their judgment in voting." The pledge requirement, he claimed, "interfere[d] with the performance of this constitutional duty to select [a president] according to the best judgment of the elector."

Our decision in *Ray* rejected that challenge. "Neither the language of Art. II, § 1, nor that of the Twelfth Amendment," we explained, prohibits a State from appointing only electors committed to vote for a party's presidential candidate. Nor did the Nation's history suggest such a bar. To the contrary, "[h]istory teaches that the electors were expected to support the party nominees" as far back as the earliest contested presidential elections. "[L]ongstanding practice" thus "weigh[ed] heavily" against Blair's claim. And current voting procedures did too. The Court noted that by then many States did not even put electors' names on a presidential ballot. The whole system presupposed that the electors, because of either an "implied" or an "oral pledge," would vote for the candidate who had won the State's popular election.

Ray, however, reserved a question not implicated in the case: Could a State enforce those pledges through legal sanctions? Or would doing so violate an elector's "constitutional freedom" to "vote as he may choose" in the Electoral College? Today, we take up that question. We uphold Washington's penalty-backed pledge law for reasons much like those given in *Ray*. The Constitution's text and the Nation's history both support allowing a State to enforce an elector's pledge to support his party's nominee — and the state voters' choice — for President.

Article II, § 1's appointments power gives the States far-reaching authority over presidential electors, absent some other constitutional constraint. As noted earlier, each State may appoint electors "in such Manner as the Legislature thereof may direct." This Court has described that clause as "conveying the broadest power of determination" over who becomes an elector. And the power to appoint an elector (in any manner) includes power to condition his appointment—that is, to say what the elector must do for the appointment to take effect. A State can require, for example, that an elector live in the State or qualify as a regular voter during the relevant time period. Or more substantively, a State can insist (as *Ray* allowed) that the elector pledge to cast his Electoral College ballot for his party's presidential nominee, thus tracking the State's popular vote. Or—so long as nothing else in the Constitution poses an obstacle—a State can add, as Washington did, an associated condition of appointment: It can demand that the elector actually live up to his pledge, on pain of penalty. Which is to say that the State's appointment power, barring some outside constraint, enables the enforcement of a pledge like Washington's.

And nothing in the Constitution expressly prohibits States from taking away presidential electors' voting discretion as Washington does. The Constitution is barebones about electors. Article II includes only the instruction to each State to appoint, in whatever way it likes, as many electors as it has Senators and Representatives (except that the State may not appoint members of the Federal Government). The Twelfth Amendment then tells electors to meet in their States, to vote for President and Vice President separately, and to transmit lists of all their votes to the President of the United States Senate for counting. Appointments and procedures and . . . that is all.

The Framers could have done it differently; other constitutional drafters of their time did. In the founding era, two States—Maryland and Kentucky—used electoral bodies selected by voters to choose state senators (and in Kentucky's case, the Governor too). The Constitutions of both States, Maryland's drafted just before and Kentucky's just after the U.S. Constitution, incorporated language that would have made this case look quite different. Both state Constitutions required all electors to take an oath "to elect without favour, affection, partiality, or prejudice, such persons for Senators, as they, in their judgment and conscience, believe best qualified for the office."

The Electors argue that three simple words stand in for more explicit language about discretion. Article II, § 1 first names the members of the Electoral College: "electors." The Twelfth Amendment then says that electors shall "vote" and that they shall do so by "ballot." The "plain meaning" of those terms, the Electors say, requires electors to have "freedom of choice." If the States could control their votes, "the electors would not be 'Electors,' and their 'vote by Ballot' would not be a 'vote.'"

But those words need not always connote independent choice. Suppose a person always votes in the way his spouse, or pastor, or union tells him to. We might question his judgment, but we would have no problem saying that he "votes" or fills in a "ballot." In those cases, the choice is in someone else's hands, but the words still apply because they can signify a mechanical act. Or similarly, suppose in a system allowing proxy voting (a common practice in the founding era), the proxy acts on clear instructions from the principal, with no freedom of choice. Still, we might well say that he cast a "ballot" or "voted," though the preference registered was not his own. For that matter, some elections give the voter no real choice because there is only one name on a ballot (consider an old Soviet election, or even a down-ballot race in this country). Yet if the person in the voting booth goes through the motions, we consider him to have voted. The point of all these examples is to show that although voting and discretion are usually combined, voting is still voting when discretion departs. Maybe most telling, switch from hypotheticals to the members of the Electoral College. For centuries now, as we'll later show, almost all have considered themselves bound to vote for their party's (and the state voters') preference. . . . Yet there is no better description for what they do in the Electoral College than "vote" by "ballot." And all these years later, everyone still calls them "electors"—and not wrongly, because even though they vote without discretion, they do indeed elect a President.

"Long settled and established practice" may have "great weight in a proper interpretation of constitutional provisions." The history going the opposite way is one of anomalies only. The Electors stress that since the founding, electors have cast some 180 faithless votes for either President or Vice President. And more than a third of the faithless votes come from 1872, when the Democratic Party's nominee (Horace Greeley) died just after Election Day. Putting those aside, faithless votes represent just one-half of one percent of the total. Still, the Electors counter, Congress has counted all those votes. But because faithless votes have never come close to affecting an outcome, only one has ever been challenged. True enough, that one was counted. But the Electors cannot rest a claim of historical tradition on one counted vote in over 200 years. And anyway, the State appointing that elector had no law requiring a pledge or otherwise barring his use of discretion. Congress's deference to a state decision to tolerate a faithless vote is no ground for rejecting a state decision to penalize one.

III

The Electors' constitutional claim has neither text nor history on its side. Article II and the Twelfth Amendment give States broad power over electors, and give electors themselves no rights. Early in our history, States decided to tie electors to the presidential choices of others, whether legislatures or citizens. Except that legislatures no longer play a role, that practice has continued for more than 200 years. Among the devices States have long used to achieve their object are pledge laws, designed to impress on electors their role as agents of others. A State follows in the same tradition if, like Washington, it chooses to sanction an elector for breaching his promise. Then too, the State instructs its electors that they have no ground for reversing the vote of millions of its citizens. That direction accords with the Constitution — as well as with the trust of a Nation that here, We the People rule.

Justice THOMAS, with whom Justice GORSUCH joins as to Part II, concurring in the judgment.

The Court correctly determines that States have the power to require Presidential electors to vote for the candidate chosen by the people of the State. I disagree, however, with its attempt to base that power on Article II. In my view, the Constitution is silent on States' authority to bind electors in voting. I would resolve this case by simply recognizing that "[a]ll powers that the Constitution neither delegates to the Federal Government nor prohibits to the States are controlled by the people of each State."

I

The Constitution does not address — expressly or by necessary implication — whether States have the power to require that Presidential electors vote for the candidates chosen by the people. Article II, § 1, and the Twelfth Amendment provide for the election of the President through a body of electors. But neither speaks directly to a State's power over elector voting.

The only provision in the Constitution that arguably addresses a State's power over Presidential electors is Clause 2 of Article II, § 1. That Clause provides, in relevant part, that "[e]ach State shall appoint, in such Manner as the Legislature thereof may direct, a Number of Electors." As I have previously explained, this language "imposes an affirmative obligation on the States" to establish the manner for appointing electors. By using the term "shall," "the Clause expressly requires action by the States." This obligation to provide the manner of appointing electors does not expressly delegate power to States; it simply imposes an affirmative duty.

In short, the Constitution does not speak to States' power to require Presidential electors to vote for the candidates chosen by the people. The Court's attempt to ground such a power in Article II's text falls short. Rather than contort the language of both Article II and the state statute, I would acknowledge that the Constitution simply says nothing about the States' power in this regard.

When the Constitution is silent, authority resides with the States or the people. This allocation of power is both embodied in the structure of our Constitution and expressly required by the Tenth Amendment. The application of this fundamental principle should guide our decision here.

Chapter 5

The Structure of the Constitution's Protection of Civil Rights and Civil Liberties

B. The Application of the Bill of Rights to the States

3. The Incorporation of the Bill of Rights into the Due Process Clause of the Fourteenth Amendment

The Content of Incorporated Rights (casebook p. 531)

The Supreme Court almost always has held that the content of the Bill of Rights' requirements are the same whether applied directly to the federalgovernment or via incorporation to state and local governments. An important exception was for the requirement for unanimous jury verdicts in criminal cases. In *Apodaca v. Oregon* (casebook p. 532), the Court held that states did not have to have unanimous jury verdicts. Oregon and Louisiana were the only states that did not require this.

In *Ramos v. Louisiana*, 140 S. Ct. 1390 (2020), the Court overruled *Apodaca* and held that the requirement for unanimous jury verdicts applies to the states. Justice Gorsuch wrote the following.

RAMOS v. LOUISIANA
140 S. Ct. 1390 (2020)

Justice GORSUCH announced the judgment of the Court and delivered the opinion of the Court.

Why do Louisiana and Oregon allow nonunanimous convictions? Though it's hard to say why these laws persist, their origins are clear. Louisiana first endorsed nonunanimous verdicts for serious crimes at a constitutional convention in 1898. According to one committee chairman, the avowed purpose of that convention was to "establish the supremacy of the white race," and the resulting document included many of the trappings of the Jim Crow era: a poll tax, a combined literacy and property ownership test, and a grandfather clause that in practice exempted white residents from the most onerous of these requirements.

Nor was it only the prospect of African-Americans voting that concerned the delegates. Just a week before the convention, the U.S. Senate passed a resolution calling for an investigation into whether Louisiana was systemically excluding African-Americans from juries. Seeking to avoid unwanted national attention, and aware that this Court would strike down any policy of overt discrimination against African-American jurors as a violation of the Fourteenth Amendment, the delegates sought to undermine African-American participation on juries in another way. With a careful eye on racial demographics, the convention delegates sculpted a "facially race-neutral" rule permitting 10-to-2 verdicts in order "to ensure that African-American juror service would be meaningless."

Adopted in the 1930s, Oregon's rule permitting nonunanimous verdicts can be similarly traced to the rise of the Ku Klux Klan and efforts to dilute "the influence of racial, ethnic, and religious minorities on Oregon juries." In fact, no one before us contests any of this; courts in both Louisiana and Oregon have frankly acknowledged that race was a motivating factor in the adoption of their States' respective nonunanimity rules.

We took this case to decide whether the Sixth Amendment right to a jury trial — as incorporated against the States by way of the Fourteenth Amendment — requires a unanimous verdict to convict a defendant of a serious offense. Louisiana insists that this Court has never definitively passed on the question and urges us to find its practice consistent with the Sixth Amendment. By contrast, the dissent doesn't try to defend Louisiana's law on Sixth or Fourteenth Amendment grounds; tacitly, it seems to admit that the Constitution forbids States from using nonunanimous juries. Yet, unprompted by Louisiana, the dissent suggests our precedent requires us to rule for the State anyway. What explains all this? To answer the puzzle, it's necessary to say a bit more about the merits of the question presented, the relevant precedent, and, at last, the consequences that follow from saying what we know to be true.

The Sixth Amendment promises that "[i]n all criminal prosecutions, the accused shall enjoy the right to a speedy and public trial, by an impartial jury of the State and district wherein the crime shall have been committed, which district shall have been previously ascertained by law." The Amendment goes on to preserve other rights for criminal defendants but says nothing else about what a "trial by an impartial jury" entails.

One of these requirements was unanimity. Wherever we might look to determine what the term "trial by an impartial jury trial" meant at the time of the Sixth Amendment's adoption—whether it's the common law, state practices in the founding era, or opinions and treatises written soon afterward—the answer is unmistakable. A jury must reach a unanimous verdict in order to convict.

There can be no question either that the Sixth Amendment's unanimity requirement applies to state and federal criminal trials equally. This Court has long explained that the Sixth Amendment right to a jury trial is "fundamental to the American scheme of justice" and incorporated against the States under the Fourteenth Amendment. This Court has long explained, too, that incorporated provisions of the Bill of Rights bear the same content when asserted against States as they do when asserted against the federal government. So if the Sixth Amendment's right to a jury trial requires a unanimous verdict to support a conviction in federal court, it requires no less in state court.

Justice SOTOMAYOR, concurring.

I write separately, however, to underscore three points. First, overruling precedent here is not only warranted, but compelled. Second, the interests at stake point far more clearly to that outcome than those in other recent cases. And finally, the racially biased origins of the Louisiana and Oregon laws uniquely matter here.

Justice THOMAS, concurring in the judgment.

I agree with the Court that petitioner Evangelisto Ramos' felony conviction by a nonunanimous jury was unconstitutional. I write separately because I would resolve this case based on the Court's longstanding view that the Sixth Amendment includes a protection against nonunanimous felony guilty verdicts, without undertaking a fresh analysis of the meaning of "trial . . . by an impartial jury." I also would make clear that this right applies against the States through the Privileges or Immunities Clause of the Fourteenth Amendment, not the Due Process Clause.

Justice ALITO, with whom THE CHIEF JUSTICE joins, and with whom Justice KAGAN joins, dissenting.

The doctrine of *stare decisis* gets rough treatment in today's decision. Lowering the bar for overruling our precedents, a badly fractured majority casts aside an important and long-established decision with little regard for the enormous reliance the decision has engendered. If the majority's approach is not just a way to dispose of this one case, the decision marks an important turn.

Nearly a half century ago in *Apodaca v. Oregon* (1972), the Court held that the Sixth Amendment permits non-unanimous verdicts in state criminal trials, and in all the years since then, no Justice has even hinted that *Apodaca* should be reconsidered. Understandably thinking that *Apodaca* was good law, the state courts in Louisiana and Oregon have tried thousands of cases under rules that permit such verdicts. But today, the Court does away with *Apodaca* and, in so doing, imposes a potentially crushing burden on the courts and criminal justice systems of those States. The Court, however, brushes aside these consequences and even suggests that the States should have known better than to count on our decision.

To add insult to injury, the Court tars Louisiana and Oregon with the charge of racism for permitting nonunanimous verdicts—even though this Court found such verdicts to be constitutional and even though there are entirely legitimate arguments for allowing them.

I would not overrule. Whatever one may think about the correctness of the decision, it has elicited enormous and entirely reasonable reliance. And before this Court decided to intervene, the decision appeared to have little practical importance going forward. Louisiana has now abolished non-unanimous verdicts, and Oregon seemed on the verge of doing the same until the Court intervened.

Chapter 6

Economic Liberties

D. The Takings Clause

2. Is There a Taking?

Possessory takings (casebook p. 633)

As explained in the casebook, there are two types of takings: possessory takings and regulatory takings. The distinction is important because the former are deemed "per se" takings while the latter are analyzed under a balancing test. The issue in *Cedar Point Nursery v. Hassid* was whether a California law that allowed union organizers access to private property for a limited time to speak to workers was a possessory taking.

CEDAR POINT NURSERY v. HASSID
141 S. Ct. 2063 (2021)

Chief Justice ROBERTS delivered the opinion of the Court.

A California regulation grants labor organizations a "right to take access" to an agricultural employer's property in order to solicit support for unionization. Agricultural employers must allow union organizers onto their property for up to three hours per day, 120 days per year. The question presented is whether the access regulation constitutes a *per se* physical taking under the Fifth and Fourteenth Amendments.

I

The California Agricultural Labor Relations Act of 1975 gives agricultural employees a right to self-organization and makes it an unfair labor practice for employers to interfere with that right. The state Agricultural Labor Relations Board has promulgated a regulation providing, in its current form, that the self-organization rights of employees include "the right of access by union organizers to the premises of an agricultural employer for the purpose of meeting and talking with employees and soliciting their support." Under the regulation, a labor organization may "take access" to an agricultural employer's property for up to four 30-day periods in one calendar year. In order to take access, a labor organization must file a written notice with the Board and serve a copy on the employer. Two organizers per work crew (plus one additional organizer for every 15 workers over 30 workers in a crew) may enter the employer's property for up to one hour before work, one hour during the lunch break, and one hour after work. Organizers may not engage in disruptive conduct, but are otherwise free to meet and talk with employees as they wish. Interference with organizers' right of access may constitute an unfair labor practice, which can result in sanctions against the employer.

Cedar Point Nursery is a strawberry grower in northern California. It employs over 400 seasonal workers and around 100 full-time workers, none of whom live on the property. According to the complaint, in October 2015, at five o'clock one morning, members of the United Farm Workers entered Cedar Point's property without prior notice. The organizers moved to the nursery's trim shed, where hundreds of workers were preparing strawberry plants. Calling through bullhorns, the organizers disturbed operations, causing some workers to join the organizers in a protest and others to leave the worksite altogether. Cedar Point filed a charge against the union for taking access without giving notice. The union responded with a charge of its own, alleging that Cedar Point had committed an unfair labor practice.

Fowler Packing Company is a Fresno-based grower and shipper of table grapes and citrus. It has 1,800 to 2,500 employees in its field operations and around 500 in its packing facility. As with Cedar Point, none of Fowler's workers live on the premises. In July 2015, organizers from the United Farm Workers attempted to take access to Fowler's property, but the company blocked them from entering. The union filed an unfair labor practice charge against Fowler, which it later withdrew.

Believing that the union would likely attempt to enter their property again in the near future, the growers filed suit in Federal District Court against several Board members in their official capacity. The growers argued that the access regulation effected an unconstitutional *per se* physical taking under the Fifth and Fourteenth Amendments by appropriating without compensation an easement for union organizers to enter their property. They requested declaratory and injunctive relief prohibiting the Board from enforcing the regulation against them.

II

A

The Takings Clause of the Fifth Amendment, applicable to the States through the Fourteenth Amendment, provides: "[N]or shall private property be taken for public use, without just compensation." The Founders recognized that the protection of private property is indispensable to the promotion of individual freedom. As John Adams tersely put it, "[p]roperty must be secured, or liberty cannot exist." This Court agrees, having noted that protection of property rights is "necessary to preserve freedom" and "empowers persons to shape and to plan their own destiny in a world where governments are always eager to do so for them."

When the government physically acquires private property for a public use, the Takings Clause imposes a clear and categorical obligation to provide the owner with just compensation. The Court's physical takings jurisprudence is "as old as the Republic." The government commits a physical taking when it uses its power of eminent domain to formally condemn property. The same is true when the government physically takes possession of property without acquiring title to it. And the government likewise effects a physical taking when it occupies property — say, by recurring flooding as a result of building a dam. These sorts of physical appropriations constitute the "clearest sort of taking," and we assess them using a simple, *per se* rule: The government must pay for what it takes.

When the government, rather than appropriating private property for itself or a third party, instead imposes regulations that restrict an owner's ability to use his own property, a different standard applies. Our jurisprudence governing such use restrictions has developed more recently. Before the 20th century, the Takings Clause was understood to be limited to physical appropriations of property. In *Pennsylvania Coal Co. v. Mahon* (1922), however, the Court established the proposition that "while property may be regulated to a certain extent, if regulation goes too far it will be recognized as a taking."

Our cases have often described use restrictions that go "too far" as "regulatory takings." But that label can mislead. Government action that physically appropriates property is no less a physical taking because it arises from a regulation. That explains why we held that an administrative reserve requirement compelling raisin growers to physically set aside a percentage of their crop for the government constituted a physical rather than a regulatory taking. The essential question is not, as the Ninth Circuit seemed to think, whether the government action at issue comes garbed as a regulation (or statute, or ordinance, or miscellaneous decree). It is whether the government has physically taken property for itself or someone else — by whatever means — or has instead restricted a property owner's ability to use his own property. Whenever a regulation results in a physical appropriation of property, a *per se* taking has occurred, and *Penn Central* has no place.

B

The access regulation appropriates a right to invade the growers' property and therefore constitutes a *per se* physical taking. The regulation grants union organizers a right to physically enter and occupy the growers' land for three hours per day, 120 days per year. Rather than restraining the growers' use of their own property, the regulation appropriates for the enjoyment of third parties the owners' right to exclude.

The right to exclude is "one of the most treasured" rights of property ownership. According to Blackstone, the very idea of property entails "that sole and despotic dominion which one man claims and exercises over the external things of the world, in total exclusion of the right of any other individual in the universe." In less exuberant terms, we have stated that the right to exclude is "universally held to be a fundamental element of the property right," and is "one of the most essential sticks in the bundle of rights that are commonly characterized as property."

Given the central importance to property ownership of the right to exclude, it comes as little surprise that the Court has long treated government-authorized physical invasions as takings requiring just compensation. The Court has often described the property interest taken as a servitude or an easement.

The upshot of this line of precedent is that government-authorized invasions of property — whether by plane, boat, cable, or beachcomber — are physical takings requiring just compensation. As in those cases, the government here has appropriated a right of access to the growers' property, allowing union organizers to traverse it at will for three hours a day, 120 days a year. The regulation appropriates a right to physically invade the growers' property — to literally "take access," as the regulation provides. It is therefore a *per se* physical taking under our precedents. Accordingly, the growers' complaint states a claim for an uncompensated taking in violation of the Fifth and Fourteenth Amendments.

C

The Ninth Circuit saw matters differently, as do the Board and the dissent. In the decision below, the Ninth Circuit took the view that the access regulation did not qualify as a *per se* taking because, although it grants a right to physically invade the growers' property, it does not allow for permanent and continuous access "24 hours a day, 365 days a year." The dissent likewise concludes that the regulation cannot amount to a *per se* taking because it allows "access short of 365 days a year." That position is insupportable as a matter of precedent and common sense. There is no reason the law should analyze an abrogation of the right to exclude in one manner if it extends for 365 days, but in an entirely different manner if it lasts for 364.

To begin with, we have held that a physical appropriation is a taking whether it is permanent or temporary. Our cases establish that "compensation is mandated when a leasehold is taken and the government occupies property for its own purposes, even though that use is temporary." The duration of an appropriation—just like the size of an appropriation,—bears only on the amount of compensation. [W]e have recognized that physical invasions constitute takings even if they are intermittent as opposed to continuous.

The Board also takes issue with the growers' premise that the access regulation appropriates an easement. In the Board's estimation, the regulation does not exact a true easement in gross under California law because the access right may not be transferred, does not burden any particular parcel of property, and may not be recorded. This, the Board says, reinforces its conclusion that the regulation does not take a constitutionally protected property interest from the growers. The dissent agrees, suggesting that the access right cannot effect a *per se* taking because it does not require the growers to grant the union organizers an easement as defined by state property law.

These arguments misconstrue our physical takings doctrine. As a general matter, it is true that the property rights protected by the Takings Clause are creatures of state law. But no one disputes that, without the access regulation, the growers would have had the right under California law to exclude union organizers from their property. And no one disputes that the access regulation took that right from them. The Board cannot absolve itself of takings liability by appropriating the growers' right to exclude in a form that is a slight mismatch from state easement law. Under the Constitution, property rights "cannot be so easily manipulated."

Our decisions consistently reflect this intuitive approach. We have recognized that the government can commit a physical taking either by appropriating property through a condemnation proceeding or by simply "enter[ing] into physical possession of property without authority of a court order." In the latter situation, the government's intrusion does not vest it with a property interest recognized by state law, such as a fee simple or a leasehold. Yet we recognize a physical taking all the same. Any other result would allow the government to appropriate private property without just compensation so long as it avoids formal condemnation. We have never tolerated that outcome. Instead, we followed our traditional rule: Because the government appropriated a right to invade, compensation was due. That same test governs here.

The Board and the dissent further contend that our decision in *Prune Yard Shopping Center v. Robins* (1980), establishes that the access regulation cannot qualify as a *per se* taking. There the California Supreme Court held that the State Constitution protected the right to engage in leafleting at the Prune Yard, a privately owned shopping center. The shopping center argued that the decision had taken without just compensation its right to exclude. Applying the *Penn Central* factors, we held that no compensable taking had occurred.

The Board and the dissent argue that *Prune Yard* shows that limited rights of access to private property should be evaluated as regulatory rather than *per se* takings. We disagree. Unlike the growers' properties, the Prune Yard was open to the public, welcoming some 25,000 patrons a day. Limitations on how a business generally open to the public may treat individuals on the premises are readily distinguishable from regulations granting a right to invade property closed to the public.

D

In its thoughtful opinion, the dissent advances a distinctive view of property rights. The dissent encourages readers to consider the issue "through the lens of ordinary English," and contends that, so viewed, the "regulation does not *appropriate* anything." Rather, the access regulation merely "*regulates* . . . the owners' right to exclude," so it must be assessed "under *Penn Central*'s fact-intensive test." According to the dissent, this kind of latitude toward temporary invasions is a practical necessity for governing in our complex modern world.

With respect, our own understanding of the role of property rights in our constitutional order is markedly different. In "ordinary English" "appropriation" means "*taking* as one's own," 1 Oxford English Dictionary 587 (2d ed. 1989) (emphasis added), and the regulation expressly grants to labor organizers the "right to *take* access." We cannot agree that the right to exclude is an empty formality, subject to modification at the government's pleasure. On the contrary, it is a "fundamental element of the property right," that cannot be balanced away. Our cases establish that appropriations of a right to invade are *per se* physical takings, not use restrictions subject to *Penn Central*: "[W]hen [government] planes use private airspace to approach a government airport, [the government] is required to pay for that share no matter how small." With regard to the complexities of modern society, we think they only reinforce the importance of safeguarding the basic property rights that help preserve individual liberty, as the Founders explained.

III

The Board, seconded by the dissent, warns that treating the access regulation as a *per se* physical taking will endanger a host of state and federal government activities involving entry onto private property. That fear is unfounded.

First, our holding does nothing to efface the distinction between trespass and takings. Isolated physical invasions, not undertaken pursuant to a granted right of access, are properly assessed as individual torts rather than appropriations of a property right. This basic distinction is firmly grounded in our precedent. *Second*, many government-authorized physical invasions will not amount to takings because they are consistent with longstanding background restrictions on property rights. These background limitations also encompass traditional common law privileges to access private property. One such privilege allowed individuals to enter property in the event of public or private necessity.

Third, the government may require property owners to cede a right of access as a condition of receiving certain benefits, without causing a taking. Under this framework, government health and safety inspection regimes will generally not constitute takings. When the government conditions the grant of a benefit such as a permit, license, or registration on allowing access for reasonable health and safety inspections, both the nexus and rough proportionality requirements of the constitutional conditions framework should not be difficult to satisfy.

None of these considerations undermine our determination that the access regulation here gives rise to a *per se* physical taking. Unlike a mere trespass, the regulation grants a formal entitlement to physically invade the growers' land. Unlike a law enforcement search, no traditional background principle of property law requires the growers to admit union organizers onto their premises. And unlike standard health and safety inspections, the access regulation is not germane to any benefit provided to agricultural employers or any risk posed to the public. The access regulation amounts to simple appropriation of private property.

The access regulation grants labor organizations a right to invade the growers' property. It therefore constitutes a *per se* physical taking.

Justice BREYER, with whom Justice SOTOMAYOR and Justice KAGAN join, dissenting.

A California regulation provides that representatives of a labor organization may enter an agricultural employer's property for purposes of union organizing. They may do so during four months of the year, one hour before the start of work, one hour during an employee lunch break, and one hour after work. The question before us is how to characterize this regulation for purposes of the Constitution's Takings Clause.

Does the regulation *physically appropriate* the employers' property? If so, there is no need to look further; the Government must pay the employers "just compensation." Or does the regulation simply *regulate* the employers' property rights? If so, then there is every need to look further; the government need pay the employers "just compensation" only if the regulation "goes too far."

The Court holds that the provision's "access to organizers" requirement amounts to a physical appropriation of property. In its view, virtually every government-authorized invasion is an "appropriation." But this regulation does not "appropriate" anything; it regulates the employers' right to exclude others. At the same time, our prior cases make clear that the regulation before us allows only a *temporary* invasion of a landowner's property and that this kind of temporary invasion amounts to a taking only if it goes "too far." In my view, the majority's conclusion threatens to make many ordinary forms of regulation unusually complex or impractical. And though the majority attempts to create exceptions to narrow its rule, the law's need for feasibility suggests that the majority's framework is wrong. With respect, I dissent from the majority's conclusion that the regulation is a *per se* taking.

I

[T]he question before us is whether the access regulation falls within one of two narrow categories of government conduct that are *per se* takings. The first is when "'the government directly appropriates private property for its own use.'" The second is when the government causes a permanent physical occupation of private property. It does not.

Initially it may help to look at the legal problem—a problem of characterization—through the lens of ordinary English. The word "regulation" rather than "appropriation" fits this provision in both label and substance.

It is contained in Title 8 of the California Code of Regulations. It was adopted by a state regulatory board, namely, the California Agricultural Labor Relations Board, in 1975. It is embedded in a set of related detailed regulations that describe and limit the access at issue.

At the same time, the provision only awkwardly fits the terms "physical taking" and "physical appropriation." The "access" that it grants union organizers does not amount to any traditional property interest in land. It does not, for example, take from the employers, or provide to the organizers, any freehold estate (*e.g.*, a fee simple, fee tail, or life estate); any concurrent estate (*e.g.*, a joint tenancy, tenancy in common, or tenancy by the entirety); or any leasehold estate (*e.g.*, a term of years, periodic tenancy, or tenancy at will). Nor (as all now agree) does it provide the organizers with a formal easement or access resembling an easement, as the employers once argued, since it does not burden any particular parcel of property.

The majority concludes that the regulation nonetheless amounts to a physical taking of property because, the majority says, it "appropriates" a "right to invade" or a "right to exclude" others. It thereby likens this case to cases in which we have held that appropriation of property rights amounts to a physical *per se* taking.

It is important to understand, however, that, technically speaking, the majority is wrong. The regulation does not *appropriate* anything. It does not take from the owners a right to invade (whatever that might mean). It does not give the union organizations the right to exclude anyone. It does not give the government the right to exclude anyone. What does it do? It gives union organizers the right temporarily to invade a portion of the property owners' land. It thereby limits the landowners' right to exclude certain others. The regulation *regulates* (but does not *appropriate*) the owners' right to exclude.

Why is it important to understand this technical point? Because only then can we understand the issue before us. That issue is whether a regulation that *temporarily* limits an owner's right to exclude others from property *automatically* amounts to a Fifth Amendment taking. Under our cases, it does not.

Our cases draw a distinction between regulations that provide permanent rights of access and regulations that provide nonpermanent rights of access. They either state or hold that the first type of regulation is a taking *per se,* but the second kind is a taking only if it goes "too far." And they make this distinction for good reason.

Now consider *PruneYard Shopping Center v. Robins* (1980). We there considered the status of a state constitutional requirement that a privately owned shopping center permit other individuals to enter upon, and to use, the property to exercise their rights to free speech and petition. We held that this requirement was not a *per se* taking in part because (even though the individuals may have "'physically invaded'" the owner's property) "[t]here [wa]s nothing to suggest that preventing [the owner] from prohibiting this sort of activity w[ould] unreasonably impair the value or use of th[e] property as a shopping center," and the owner could "adop[t] time, place, and manner regulations that w[ould] minimize any interference with its commercial functions."

As these cases have used the terms, the regulation here at issue provides access that is "temporary," not "permanent." At the same time, *PruneYard*'s holding that the taking was "temporary" (and hence not a *per se* taking) fits this case almost perfectly. There the regulation gave nonowners the right to enter privately owned property for the purpose of speaking generally to others, about matters of their choice, subject to reasonable time, place, and manner restrictions. The regulation before us grants a far smaller group of people the right to enter landowners' property for far more limited times in order to speak about a specific subject. Employers have more power to control entry by setting work hours, lunch hours, and places of gathering. On the other hand, as the majority notes, the shopping center in *PruneYard* was open to the public generally. All these factors, however, are the stuff of which regulatory-balancing, not absolute *per se*, rules are made.

The persistence of the permanent/temporary distinction that I have described is not surprising. That distinction serves an important purpose. We live together in communities. Modern life in these communities requires different kinds of regulation. Some, perhaps many, forms of regulation require access to private property (for government officials or others) for different reasons and for varying periods of time. Most such temporary-entry regulations do not go "too far." And it is impractical to compensate every property owner for any brief use of their land. As we have frequently said, "[g]overnment hardly could go on if to some extent values incident to property could not be diminished without paying for every such change in the general law." Thus, the law has not, and should not, convert all temporary-access-permitting regulations into *per se* takings automatically requiring compensation.

Consider the large numbers of ordinary regulations in a host of different fields that, for a variety of purposes, permit temporary entry onto (or an "invasion of ") a property owner's land. They include activities ranging from examination of food products to inspections for compliance with preschool licensing requirements.

The majority tries to deal with the adverse impact of treating these, and other, temporary invasions as if they were *per se* physical takings by creating a series of exceptions from its *per se* rule. It says: (1) "Isolated physical invasions, not undertaken pursuant to a granted right of access, are properly assessed as individual torts rather than appropriations of a property right." It also would except from its *per se* rule (2) government access that is "consistent with longstanding background restrictions on property rights," including "traditional common law privileges to access private property." And it adds that (3) "the government may require property owners to cede a right of access as a condition of receiving certain benefits, without causing a taking."

How well will this new system work? I suspect that the majority has substituted a new, complex legal scheme for a comparatively simpler old one. As to the first exception, what will count as "isolated"? How is an "isolated physical invasion" different from a "temporary" invasion, sufficient under present law to invoke *Penn Central*? And where should one draw the line between trespass and takings? Imagine a school bus that stops to allow public school children to picnic on private land. Do three stops a year place the stops outside the exception? One stop every week? Buses from one school? From every school? Under current law a court would know what question to ask. The stops are temporary; no one assumes a permanent right to stop; thus the court will ask whether the school district has gone "too far." Under the majority's approach, the court must answer a new question (apparently about what counts as "isolated").

As to the second exception, a court must focus on "traditional common law privileges to access private property." Just what are they? We have said before that the government can, without paying compensation, impose a limitation on land that "inhere[s] in the title itself, in the restrictions that background principles of the State's law of property and nuisance already place upon land ownership." But we defined a very narrow set of such background principles. To these the majority adds "public or private necessity," the enforcement of criminal law "under certain circumstances," and reasonable searches. Do only those exceptions that existed in, say, 1789 count? Should courts apply those privileges as they existed at that time, when there were no union organizers? Or do we bring some exceptions (but not others) up to date, *e.g.*, a necessity exception for preserving animal habitats?

As to the third, what is the scope of the phrase "certain benefits"? Does it include the benefit of being able to sell meat labeled "inspected" in interstate commerce? What about the benefit of having electricity? Of sewage collection? Of internet accessibility? Myriad regulatory schemes based on just these sorts of benefits depend upon intermittent, temporary government entry onto private property.

Labor peace (brought about through union organizing) is one such benefit, at least in the view of elected representatives. They wrote laws that led to rules governing the organizing of agricultural workers. Many of them may well have believed that union organizing brings with it "benefits," including community health and educational benefits, higher standards of living, and (as I just said) labor peace. A landowner, of course, may deny the existence of these benefits, but a landowner might do the same were a regulatory statute to permit brief access to verify proper preservation of wetlands or the habitat enjoyed by an endangered species or, for that matter, the safety of inspected meat. So, if a regulation authorizing temporary access for purposes of organizing agricultural workers falls outside of the Court's exceptions and is a *per se* taking, then to what other forms of regulation does the Court's *per se* conclusion also apply?

II

Finally, I touch briefly on remedies, which the majority does not address. The Takings Clause prohibits the Government from taking private property for public use without "just compensation." But the employers do not seek compensation. They seek only injunctive and declaratory relief. Indeed, they did not allege any damages. On remand, California should have the choice of foreclosing injunctive relief by providing compensation.

Chapter 8

Fundamental Rights Under Due Process and Equal Protection

D. Constitutional Protection for Reproductive Autonomy

3. The Right to Abortion

b. *Government Regulation of Abortions* (casebook p. 981)

In *Whole Woman's Health v. Hellerstedt* (2016) (casebook p. 982), the Court declared unconstitutional a Texas law that required that a doctor have admitting privileges at a hospital within 30 miles in order to perform an abortion. In *June Medical Services L.L.C. v. Russo*, the Court, 5-4, declared unconstitutional an identical Louisiana requirement.

JUNE MEDICAL SERVICES L.L.C. v. RUSSO

140 S. Ct. 2103 (2020)

Justice BREYER announced the judgment of the Court and delivered an opinion, in which Justice GINSBURG, Justice SOTOMAYOR, and Justice KAGAN join.

In *Whole Woman's Health v. Hellerstedt* (2016), we held that "'[u]nnecessary health regulations that have the purpose or effect of pre-senting a substantial obstacle to a woman seeking an abortion impose an undue burden on the right'" and are therefore "constitutionally invalid." We explained that this standard requires courts independently to review the legislative findings upon which an abortion-related statute rests and to weigh the law's "asserted benefits against the burdens" it imposes on abortion access.

The Texas statute at issue in *Whole Woman's Health* required abortion providers to hold "'active admitting privileges at a hospital'" within 30 miles of the place where they perform abortions. Reviewing the record for ourselves, we found ample evidence to support the District Court's finding that the statute did not further the State's asserted interest in protecting women's health. The evidence showed, moreover, that conditions on admitting privileges that served no "relevant credentialing function," "help[ed] to explain" the closure of half of Texas' abortion clinics. Those closures placed a substantial obstacle in the path of Texas women seeking an abortion. And that obstacle, "when viewed in light of the virtual absence of any health benefit," imposed an "undue burden" on abortion access in violation of the Federal Constitution.

In this case, we consider the constitutionality of a Louisiana statute, Act 620, that is almost word-for-word identical to Texas' admitting-privileges law. As in *Whole Woman's Health,* the District Court found that the statute offers no significant health benefit. It found that conditions on admitting privileges common to hospitals throughout the State have made and will continue to make it impossible for abortion providers to obtain conforming privileges for reasons that have nothing to do with the State's asserted interests in promoting women's health and safety. And it found that this inability places a substantial obstacle in the path of women seeking an abortion. As in *Whole Woman's Health*, the substantial obstacle the Act imposes, and the absence of any health-related benefit, led the District Court to conclude that the law imposes an undue burden and is therefore unconstitutional.

The Court of Appeals agreed with the District Court's interpretation of the standards we have said apply to regulations on abortion. It thought, however, that the District Court was mistaken on the facts. We disagree. We have examined the extensive record carefully and conclude that it supports the District Court's findings of fact. Those findings mirror those made in *Whole Woman's Health* in every relevant respect and require the same result. We consequently hold that the Louisiana statute is unconstitutional.

I

In March 2014, five months after Texas' admitting-privileges requirement forced the closure of half of that State's abortion clinics, Louisiana's Legislature began to hold hearings to consider a substantially identical proposal. As was true in Texas, Louisiana law already required abortion providers *either* to possess local hospital admitting privileges *or* to have a patient "transfer" arrangement with a physician who had such privileges. The new law eliminated that flexibility. Act 620 requires any doctor who performs abortions to hold "active admitting privileges at a hospital that is located not further than thirty miles from the location at which the abortion is performed or induced and that provides obstetrical or gynecological health care services."

The statute defines "active admitting privileges" to mean that the doctor must be "a member in good standing" of the hospital's "medical staff . . . with the ability to admit a patient and to provide diagnostic and surgical services to such patient." Failure to comply may lead to fines of up to $4,000 per violation, license revocation, and civil liability.

A few weeks before Act 620 was to take effect in September 2014, three abortion clinics and two abortion providers filed a lawsuit in Federal District Court. They alleged that Act 620 was unconstitutional because (among other things) it imposed an undue burden on the right of their patients to obtain an abortion.

Because the issues before us in this case primarily focus upon the factual findings (and fact-related determinations) of the District Court, we set forth only the essential findings here, giving greater detail in the analysis that follows.

With respect to the Act's asserted benefits, the District Court found that:

- "[A]bortion in Louisiana has been extremely safe, with particularly low rates of serious complications." The "testimony of clinic staff and physicians demonstrated" that it "rarely . . . is necessary to transfer patients to a hospital: far less than once a year, or less than one per several thousand patients." And "[w]hether or not a patient's treating physician has admitting privileges is not relevant to the patient's care."
- There was accordingly "'no significant health-related problem that the new law helped to cure.' The record does not contain any evidence that complications from abortion were being treated improperly, nor any evidence that any negative outcomes could have been avoided if the abortion provider had admitting privileges at a local hospital."
- There was also "no credible evidence in the record that Act 620 would further the State's interest in women's health beyond that which is already insured under existing Louisiana law."

Turning to Act 620's impact on women's access to abortion, the District Court found that:

- Approximately 10,000 women obtain abortions in Louisiana each year. At the outset of this litigation, those women were served by six doctors at five abortion clinics. he time the court rendered its decision, two of those clinics had closed, and one of the doctors (Doe 4) had retired, leaving only Does 1, 2, 3, 5, and 6.

- "[N]otwithstanding the good faith efforts of Does 1, 2, 4, 5 and 6 to comply with the Act by getting active admitting privileges at a hospital within 30 miles of where they perform abortions, they have had very limited success for reasons related to Act 620 and not related to their competence."
- These doctors' inability to secure privileges was "caused by Act 620 working in concert with existing laws and practices," including hospital bylaws and criteria that "preclude or, at least greatly discourage, the granting of privileges to abortion providers."
- These requirements establish that admitting privileges serve no "'relevant credentialing function'" because physicians may be denied privileges "for reasons unrelated to competency."
- They also make it "unlikely that the [a]ffected clinics will be able to comply with the Act by recruiting new physicians who have or can obtain admitting privileges."
- Doe 3 testified credibly "that, as a result of his fears, and the demands of his private OB/GYN practice, if he is the last physician performing abortion in either the entire state or in the northern part of the state, he will not continue to perform abortions
- Enforcing the admitting-privileges requirement would therefore "result in a drastic reduction in the number and geographic distribution of abortion providers, reducing the number of clinics to one, or at most two, and leaving only one, or at most two, physicians providing abortions in the entire state," Does 3 and 5, who would only be allowed to practice in Shreveport and New Orleans. Depending on whether Doe 3 stopped practicing, or whether his retirement was treated as legally relevant, the impact would be a 55%–70% reduction in capacity.
- "The result of these burdens on women and providers, taken together and in context, is that many women seeking a safe, legal abortion in Louisiana will be unable to obtain one. Those who can will face substantial obstacles in exercising their constitutional right to choose abortion due to the dramatic reduction in abortion services."
- In sum, "Act 620 does not advance Louisiana's legitimate interest in protecting the health of women seeking abortions. Instead, Act 620 would increase the risk of harm to women's health by dramatically reducing the availability of safe abortion in Louisiana."

II

[Justice Breyer concluded that the doctors had standing to raise the rights of their patients. This part of the opinion is found in Chapter 2 of this Supplement.]

III

Turning to the merits, we apply the constitutional standards set forth in our earlier abortion-related cases, and in particular in *Casey* and *Whole Woman's Health*. At the risk of repetition, we remind the reader of the standards we described above. In *Whole Woman's Health*, we quoted *Casey* in explaining that "'a statute which, while furthering [a] valid state interest has the effect of placing a substantial obstacle in the path of a woman's choice cannot be considered a permissible means of serving its legitimate ends.'" We added that "'*[u]nnecessary* health regulations'" impose an unconstitutional "'undue burden'" if they have "'the purpose or effect of presenting a substantial obstacle to a woman seeking an abortion.'"

We went on to explain that, in applying these standards, courts must "consider the burdens a law imposes on abortion access together with the benefits those laws confer." We cautioned that courts "must review legislative 'factfinding under a deferential standard.'" But they "must not 'place dispositive weight' on those 'findings,'" for the courts "'retai[n] an independent constitutional duty to review factual findings where constitutional rights are at stake.'"

We held in *Whole Woman's Health* that the trial court faithfully applied these standards. It "considered the evidence in the record—including expert evidence, presented in stipulations, depositions, and testimony." It "then weighed the asserted benefits" of the law "against the burdens" it imposed on abortion access. And it concluded that the balance tipped against the statute's constitutionality. The District Court in this suit did the same.

We start from the premise that a district court's findings of fact, "whether based on oral or other evidence, must not be set aside unless clearly erroneous, and the reviewing court must give due regard to the trial court's opportunity to judge the witnesses' credibility." In "'applying [this] standard to the findings of a district court sitting without a jury, appellate courts must constantly have in mind that their function is not to decide factual issues *de novo*.'" Where "the district court's account of the evidence is plausible in light of the record viewed in its entirety, the court of appeals may not reverse it even though convinced that had it been sitting as the trier of fact, it would have weighed the evidence differently."

Under that familiar standard, we find that the testimony and other evidence contained in the extensive record developed over the 6-day trial support the District Court's ultimate conclusion that, "[e]ven if Act 620 could be said to further women's health to some marginal degree, the burdens it imposes far outweigh any such benefit, and thus the Act imposes an unconstitutional undue burden."

IV.   THE DISTRICT COURT'S SUBSTANTIAL-OBSTACLE DETERMINATION

The District Court found that enforcing the admitting-privileges require- ment would "result in a drastic reduction in the number and geographic distribution of abortion providers." In light of demographic, economic, and other evidence, the court concluded that this reduction would make it impossible for "many women seeking a safe, legal abortion in Louisiana . . . to obtain one" and that it would impose "substantial obsta- cles" on those who could.

A.   ACT 620'S EFFECT ON ABORTION PROVIDERS

We begin with the District Court's findings in respect to Act 620's impact on abortion providers. As we have said, the court found that the Act would prevent Does 1, 2, and 6 from providing abortions. And it found that the Act would bar Doe 5 from working in his Baton Rouge-based clinic, rele- gating him to New Orleans.

In *Whole Woman's Health*, we said that, by presenting "direct testi- mony" from doctors who had been unable to secure privileges, and "plau- sible inferences to be drawn from the timing of the clinic closures" around the law's effective date, the plaintiffs had "satisfied their burden" to estab- lish that the Texas admitting-privileges requirement caused the closure of those clinics.

The evidence on which the District Court relied in this case is even stron- ger and more detailed. The District Court supervised Does 1, 2, 5, and 6 for over a year and a half as they tried, and largely failed, to obtain conforming privileges from 13 relevant hospitals. The court heard direct evidence that some of the doctors' applications were denied for reasons that had nothing to do with their ability to perform abortions safely. It also compiled cir- cumstantial evidence that explains why other applications were denied and explains why, given the costs of applying and the reputational risks that accompany rejection, some providers could have chosen in good faith *not* to apply to every qualifying hospital. That circumstantial evidence includes documents and testimony that described the processes Louisiana hospitals follow when considering applications for admitting privileges, including requirements like the ones we cited in *Whole Woman's Health* that are unre- lated to a doctor's competency to perform abortions.

The evidence shows, among other things, that the fact that hospital admissions for abortion are vanishingly rare means that, unless they also maintain active OB/GYN practices, abortion providers in Louisiana are unlikely to have any recent in-hospital experience. Yet such experience can well be a precondition to obtaining privileges. Doe 2, a board-certified OB/GYN with nearly 40 years' experience, testified that he had not "done any in-hospital work in ten years" and that just two of his patients in the preceding 5 years had required hospitalization. As a result, he was unable to comply with one hospital's demand that he produce data on "patient admissions and management, consultations and procedures performed" in-hospital before his application could be "processed." Doe 1, a board-certified family doctor with over 10 years' experience, was similarly unable to "submit documentation of hospital admissions and management of patients."

The evidence also shows that many providers, even if they could initially obtain admitting privileges, would be unable to keep them. That is because, unless they have a practice that requires regular in-hospital care, they will lose the privileges for failing to use them. Doe 6, a board-certified OB/GYN practitioner with roughly 50 years' experience, provides only medication abortions. Of the thousands of women he served over the decade before the District Court's decision, during which he also performed surgical abortions, just two required a direct transfer to a hospital and one of them was treated without being admitted. That safety record would make it impossible for Doe 6 to maintain privileges at any of the many Louisiana hospitals that require newly appointed physicians to undergo a process of "focused professional practice evaluation," in which they are observed by hospital staff as they perform in-hospital procedures.); cf. Record 10755 (requiring an "on-going review" of practice "in the Operating Room"). And it would likewise disqualify him at hospitals that require physicians to admit a minimum number of patients, either initially or on an ongoing basis.

The evidence also shows that opposition to abortion played a significant role in some hospitals' decisions to deny admitting privileges. Some hospitals expressly bar anyone with privileges from performing abortions. Still other hospitals have requirements that abortion providers cannot satisfy because of the hostility they face in Louisiana.

Just as in *Whole Woman's Health*, the experiences of the individual doctors in this case support the District Court's factual finding that Louisiana's admitting-privileges requirement, like that in Texas' law, serves no "'relevant credentialing function.'"

B.   ACT 620'S IMPACT ON ABORTION ACCESS

The District Court drew from the record evidence, including the factual findings we have just discussed, several conclusions in respect to the
burden that Act 620 is likely to impose upon women's ability to access
abortions in Louisiana. To better understand the significance of these conclusions, the reader should keep in mind the geographic distribution of the
doctors and their clinics.

As we have seen, enforcing the admitting-privileges requirement would
eliminate Does 1, 2, and 6. The District Court credited Doe 3's uncontra-
dicted, in-court testimony that he would stop performing abortions if he
was the last provider in northern So the departure of Does 1 and 2 would
also eliminate Doe 3. That would leave only Doe 5. And Doe 5's inability
to obtain privileges in the Baton Rouge area would leave Louisiana with
just one clinic with one provider to serve the 10,000 women annually who
seek abortions in the State.

Working full time in New Orleans, Doe 5 would be able to absorb no
more than about 30% of the annual demand for abortions in Louisiana.
And because Doe 5 does not perform abortions beyond 18 weeks, women
between 18 weeks and the state legal limit of 20 weeks would have little
or no way to exercise their constitutional right to an abortion.

Those women not altogether prevented from obtaining an abortion
would face other burdens. As in *Whole Woman's Health*, the reduction
in abortion providers caused by Act 620 would inevitably mean "longer
waiting times, and increased crowding." The District Court heard testimony that delays in obtaining an abortion increase the risk that a woman
will experience complications from the procedure and may make it impossible for her to choose a noninvasive medication abortion.

Taken together, we think that these findings and the evidence that under-
lies them are sufficient to support the District Court's conclusion that Act
620 would place substantial obstacles in the path of women seeking an
abortion in Louisiana.

V.   BENEFITS

We turn finally to the law's asserted benefits. The District Court found that
there was "'no significant health-related problem that the new law helped
to cure.'" It found that the admitting-privileges requirement "[d]oes [n]ot
[p]rotect [w]omen's [h]ealth," provides "no significant health benefits,"
and makes no improvement to women's health "compared to prior law."

Our examination of the record convinces us that these findings are not "clearly erroneous."

As in *Whole Woman's Health*, the State introduced no evidence "showing that patients have better outcomes when their physicians have admitting privileges" or "of any instance in which an admitting privileges requirement would have helped even one woman obtain better treatment."

VI. CONCLUSION

We conclude, in light of the record, that the District Court's significant factual findings — both as to burdens and as to benefits — have ample evidentiary support. None is "clearly erroneous." Given the facts found, we must also uphold the District Court's related factual and legal determinations. These include its determination that Louisiana's law poses a "substantial obstacle" to women seeking an abortion; its determination that the law offers no significant health-related benefits; and its determination that the law consequently imposes an "undue burden" on a woman's constitutional right to choose to have an abortion. We also agree with its ultimate legal conclusion that, in light of these findings and our precedents, Act 620 violates the Constitution.

VII

As a postscript, we explain why we have found unconvincing several further arguments that the State has made. First, the State suggests that the record supports the Court of Appeals' conclusion that Act 620 poses no substantial obstacle to the abortion decision. This argument misconceives the question before us. "The question we must answer" is "not whether the [Fifth] Circuit's interpretation of the facts was clearly erroneous, but whether the *District Court's* finding[s were] clearly erroneous." As we have explained, we think the District Court's factual findings here are plausible in light of the record as a whole. Nothing in the State's briefing furnishes a basis to disturb that conclusion.

Second, the State says that the record does not show that Act 620 will burden *every* woman in Louisiana who seeks an abortion. True, but beside the point. As we stated in *Casey*, a State's abortion-related law is unconstitutional on its face if "it will operate as a substantial obstacle to a woman's choice to undergo an abortion" in "a large fraction of the cases in which [it] is relevant." In *Whole Woman's Health*, we reaffirmed that standard. We made clear that the phrase refers to a large fraction of "those women for whom the provision is an actual rather than an irrelevant restriction." That standard, not an "every woman" standard, is the standard that must govern in this case.

This case is similar to, nearly identical with, *Whole Woman's Health.* And the law must consequently reach a similar conclusion. Act 620 is unconstitutional.

Chief Justice ROBERTS, concurring in the judgment.

In July 2013, Texas enacted a law requiring a physician performing an abortion to have "active admitting privileges at a hospital . . . located not further than 30 miles from the location at which the abortion is performed." The law caused the number of facilities providing abortions to drop in half. In *Whole Woman's Health v. Hellerstedt* (2016), the Court concluded that Texas's admitting privileges requirement "places a substantial obstacle in the path of women seeking a previability abortion" and therefore violated the Due Process Clause of the Fourteenth Amendment

I joined the dissent in *Whole Woman's Health* and continue to believe that the case was wrongly decided. The question today however is not whether *Whole Woman's Health* was right or wrong, but whether to adhere to it in deciding the present case.

Today's case is a challenge from several abortion clinics and providers to a Louisiana law nearly identical to the Texas law struck down four years ago in *Whole Woman's Health.* The law would reduce the number of clinics from three to "one, or at most two," and the number of physicians providing abortions from five to "one, or at most two," and "therefore cripple women's ability to have an abortion in Louisiana."

The legal doctrine of *stare decisis* requires us, absent special circumstances, to treat like cases alike. The Louisiana law imposes a burden on access to abortion just as severe as that imposed by the Texas law, for the same reasons. Therefore Louisiana's law cannot stand under our precedents.

I

Stare decisis ("to stand by things decided") is the legal term for fidelity to precedent. Black's Law Dictionary 1696 (11th ed. 2019). It has long been "an established rule to abide by former precedents, where the same points come again in litigation; as well to keep the scale of justice even and steady, and not liable to waver with every new judge's opinion." This principle is grounded in a basic humility that recognizes today's legal issues are often not so different from the questions of yesterday and that we are not the first ones to try to answer them.

Adherence to precedent is necessary to "avoid an arbitrary discretion in the courts." The Federalist No. 78, p. 529 (J. Cooke ed. 1961) (A. Hamilton). The constraint of precedent distinguishes the judicial "method and philosophy from those of the political and legislative process." The doctrine also brings pragmatic benefits. Respect for precedent "promotes the evenhanded, predictable, and consistent development of legal principles, fosters reliance on judicial decisions, and contributes to the actual and perceived integrity of the judicial process." It is the "means by which we ensure that the law will not merely change erratically, but will develop in a principled and intelligible fashion." In that way, "*stare decisis* is an old friend of the common lawyer."

Stare decisis is not an "inexorable command." But for precedent to mean anything, the doctrine must give way only to a rationale that goes beyond whether the case was decided correctly. The Court accordingly considers additional factors before overruling a precedent, such as its admin[i]strability, its fit with subsequent factual and legal developments, and the reliance interests that the precedent has engendered. *Stare decisis* principles also determine how we handle a decision that itself departed from the cases that came before it. In those instances, "[r]emaining true to an 'intrinsically sounder' doctrine established in prior cases better serves the values of *stare decisis* than would following" the recent departure. *Stare decisis* is pragmatic and contextual, not "a mechanical formula of adherence to the latest decision."

II

Both Louisiana and the providers agree that the undue burden standard announced in *Casey* provides the appropriate framework to analyze Louisiana's law. Neither party has asked us to reassess the constitutional validity of that standard. *Casey* reaffirmed "the most central principle of *Roe v. Wade*," "a woman's right to terminate her pregnancy before viability." At the same time, it recognized that the State has "important and legitimate interests in . . . protecting the health of the pregnant woman and in protecting the potentiality of human life."

Under *Casey*, the State may not impose an undue burden on the woman's ability to obtain an abortion. "A finding of an undue burden is a shorthand for the conclusion that a state regulation has the purpose or effect of placing a substantial obstacle in the path of a woman seeking an abortion of a nonviable fetus." Laws that do not pose a substantial obstacle to abortion access are permissible, so long as they are "reasonably related" to a legitimate state interest.

After faithfully reciting this standard, the Court in *Whole Woman's Health* added the following observation: "The rule announced in *Casey* . . . requires that courts consider the burdens a law imposes on abortion access together with the benefits those laws confer." The plurality repeats today that the undue burden standard requires courts "to weigh the law's asserted benefits against the burdens it imposes on abortion access."

In this context, courts applying a balancing test would be asked in essence to weigh the State's interests in "protecting the potentiality of human life" and the health of the woman, on the one hand, against the woman's liberty interest in defining her "own concept of existence, of meaning, of the universe, and of the mystery of human life" on the other. There is no plausible sense in which anyone, let alone this Court, could objectively assign weight to such imponderable values and no meaningful way to compare them if there were. Attempting to do so would be like "judging whether a particular line is longer than a particular rock is heavy," Pretending that we could pull that off would require us to act as legislators, not judges, and would result in nothing other than an "unanalyzed exercise of judicial will" in the guise of a "neutral utilitarian calculus."

Nothing about *Casey* suggested that a weighing of costs and benefits of an abortion regulation was a job for the courts. On the contrary, we have explained that the "traditional rule" that "state and federal legislatures [have] wide discretion to pass legislation in areas where there is medical and scientific uncertainty" is "consistent with *Casey*." *Casey* instead focuses on the existence of a substantial obstacle, the sort of inquiry familiar to judges across a variety of contexts.

Whole Woman's Health held that Texas's admitting privileges requirement placed "a substantial obstacle in the path of women seeking a previability abortion," independent of its discussion of benefits. Because Louisiana's admitting privileges requirement would restrict women's access to abortion to the same degree as Texas's law, it also cannot stand under our precedent.

So too here. "While a physician's competency is a factor in assessing an applicant for admitting privileges" in Louisiana, "it is only one factor that hospitals consider in whether to grant privileges." Louisiana hospitals "may deny privileges or decline to consider an application for privileges for myriad reasons unrelated to competency," including "the physician's expected usage of the hospital and intent to admit and treat patients there, the number of patients the physician has treated in the hospital in the recent past, the needs of the hospital, the mission of the hospital, or the business model of the hospital."

Stare decisis instructs us to treat like cases alike. The result in this case is controlled by our decision four years ago invalidating a nearly identical Texas law. The Louisiana law burdens women seeking previability abortions to the same extent as the Texas law, according to factual findings that are not clearly erroneous. For that reason, I concur in the judgment of the Court that the Louisiana law is unconstitutional.

Justice THOMAS, dissenting.

Today a majority of the Court perpetuates its ill-founded abortion jurisprudence by enjoining a perfectly legitimate state law and doing so without jurisdiction. As is often the case with legal challenges to abortion regulations, this suit was brought by abortionists and abortion clinics.

But those decisions created the right to abortion out of whole cloth, without a shred of support from the Constitution's text. Our abortion precedents are grievously wrong and should be overruled. Because we have neither jurisdiction nor constitutional authority to declare Louisiana's duly enacted law unconstitutional, I respectfully dissent.

Even if the plaintiffs had standing, the Court would still lack the authority to enjoin Louisiana's law, which represents a constitutionally valid exercise of the State's traditional police powers.

But today's decision is wrong for a far simpler reason: The Constitution does not constrain the States' ability to regulate or even prohibit abortion. This Court created the right to abortion based on an amorphous, unwritten right to privacy, which it grounded in the "legal fiction" of substantive due process. As the origins of this jurisprudence readily demonstrate, the putative right to abortion is a creation that should be undone.

Roe is grievously wrong for many reasons, but the most fundamental is that its core holding—that the Constitution protects a woman's right to abort her unborn child—finds no support in the text of the Fourteenth Amendment. *Roe* suggests that the Due Process Clause's reference to "liberty" could provide a textual basis for its novel privacy right. But that Clause does not guarantee liberty *qua* liberty. Rather, it expressly contemplates the *deprivation* of liberty and requires only that such deprivations occur through "due process of law." But, whatever the precise requirements of the Due Process Clause, "the notion that a constitutional provision that guarantees only 'process' before a person is deprived of life, liberty, or property could define the substance of those rights strains credulity for even the most casual user of words."

More specifically, the idea that the Framers of the Fourteenth Amendment understood the Due Process Clause to protect a right to abortion is farcical. 1868, when the Fourteenth Amendment was ratified, a majority of the States and numerous Territories had laws on the books that limited (and in many cases nearly prohibited) abortion. It would no doubt shock the public at that time to learn that one of the new constitutional Amendments contained hidden within the interstices of its text a right to abortion. The fact that it took this Court over a century to find that right all but proves that it was more than hidden—it simply was not (and is not) there.

Justice ALITO, with whom Justice GORSUCH joins, with whom Justice THOMAS joins, and with whom Justice KAVANAUGH joins as to Parts I, II, and III, dissenting.

The majority bills today's decision as a facsimile of *Whole Woman's Health v. Hellerstedt*, (2016), and it's true they have something in common. In both, the abortion right recognized in this Court's decisions is used like a bulldozer to flatten legal rules that stand in the way.

Today's decision claims new victims. The divided majority cannot agree on what the abortion right requires, but it nevertheless strikes down a Louisiana law, Act 620, that the legislature enacted for the asserted purpose of protecting women's health. To achieve this end, the majority misuses the doctrine of *stare decisis*, invokes an inapplicable standard of appellate review, and distorts the record.

The plurality eschews the constitutional test set out in *Casey* and instead employs the balancing test adopted in *Whole Woman's Health*. The plurality concludes that the Louisiana law does nothing to protect the health of women, but that is disproved by substantial evidence in the record. And the plurality upholds the District Court's finding that the Louisiana law would cause a drastic reduction in the number of abortion providers in the State even though this finding was based on an erroneous legal standard and a thoroughly inadequate factual inquiry.

The Chief Justice stresses the importance of *stare decisis* and thinks that precedent, namely *Whole Woman's Health,* dooms the Louisiana law. But at the same time, he votes to overrule *Whole Woman's Health* insofar as it changed the *Casey* test.

For these reasons, I cannot join the decision of the Court. I would remand the case to the District Court and instruct that court, before proceeding any further, to require the joinder of a plaintiff with standing. If a proper plaintiff is added, the District Court should conduct a new trial and determine, based on proper evidence, whether enforcement of Act 620 would diminish the number of abortion providers in the State to such a degree that women's access to abortions would be substantially impaired. In making that determination, the court should jettison the nebulous "good faith" test that it used in judging whether the physicians who currently lack admitting privileges would be able to obtain privileges and thus continue to perform abortions if Act 620 were permitted to take effect. Because the doctors in question (many of whom are or were plaintiffs in this case) stand to lose, not gain, by obtaining privileges, the court should require the plaintiffs to show that these doctors sought admitting privileges with the degree of effort that they would expend if their personal interests were at stake.

Justice GORSUCH, dissenting.

The judicial power is constrained by an array of rules. Rules about the deference due the legislative process, the standing of the parties before us, the use of facial challenges to invalidate democratically enacted statutes, and the award of prospective relief. Still more rules seek to ensure that any legal tests judges may devise are capable of neutral and principled administration. Individually, these rules may seem prosaic. But, collectively, they help keep us in our constitutionally assigned lane, sure that we are in the business of saying what the law is, not what we wish it to be.

Today's decision doesn't just overlook one of these rules. It overlooks one after another. And it does so in a case touching on one of the most controversial topics in contemporary politics and law, exactly the context where this Court should be leaning most heavily on the rules of the judicial process. In truth, *Roe v. Wade* (1973), is not even at issue here. The real question we face concerns our willingness to follow the traditional constraints of the judicial process when a case touching on abortion enters the courtroom.

When confronting a constitutional challenge to a law, this Court ordinarily reviews the legislature's factual findings under a "deferential" if not "[u]ncritical" standard. When facing such a challenge, too, this Court usually accepts that "the public interest has been declared in terms well-nigh conclusive" by the legislature's adoption of the law — so we may review the law only for its constitutionality, not its wisdom. Today, however, the plurality declares that the law before us holds no benefits for the public and bears too many social costs. All while sharing virtually nothing about the facts that led the legislature to conclude otherwise. The law might as well have fallen from the sky.

Of course, that's hardly the case. In Act 620, Louisiana's legislature found that requiring abortion providers to hold admitting privileges at a hospital within 30 miles of the clinic where they perform abortions would serve the public interest by protecting women's health and safety. Those in today's majority never bother to say so, but it turns out that Act 620's admitting privileges requirement for abortion providers tracks longstanding state laws governing physicians who perform relatively low-risk procedures like colonoscopies, Lasik eye surgeries, and steroid injections at ambulatory surgical centers. In fact, the Louisiana legislature passed Act 620 only after extensive hearings at which experts detailed how the Act would promote safer abortion treatment—by providing "a more thorough evaluation mechanism of physician competency," promoting "continuity of care" following abortion, enhancing inter-physician communication, and preventing patient abandonment.

Testifying physicians explained, for example, that abortions carry inherent risks including uterine perforation, hemorrhage, cervical laceration, infection, retained fetal body parts, and missed ectopic pregnancy. Unsurprisingly, those risks are minimized when the physician providing the abortion is competent. Yet, unlike hospitals which undertake rigorous credentialing processes, Louisiana's abortion clinics historically have done little to ensure provider competence. Clinics have failed to perform background checks or to inquire into the training of doctors they brought on board. Clinics have even hired physicians whose specialties were unrelated to abortion—including a radiologist and an ophthalmologist. Requiring hospital admitting privileges, witnesses testified, would help ensure that clinics hire competent professionals and provide a mechanism for ongoing peer review of physician proficiency. Loss of admitting privileges, as well, might signal a problem meriting further investigation by state officials. At least one Louisiana abortion provider's loss of admitting privileges following a patient's death alerted the state licensing board to questions about his competence, and ultimately resulted in restrictions on his practice.

The legislature also heard testimony that Louisiana's clinics and the physicians who work in them have racked up dozens of citations for safety and ethical violations in recent years. Violations have included failing to use sterile equipment, maintaining unsanitary conditions, failing to monitor patients' vital signs, permitting improper administration of medications by unauthorized persons, and neglecting to obtain informed consent from patients. Some clinics have failed to maintain supplies of emergency medications and medical equipment for treating surgical complications. One clinic used single-use hoses and tubes on multiple patients, and the solution needed to sterilize instruments was changed so infrequently that it often had pieces of tissue floating in it. Hospital credentialing processes, witnesses suggested, could help prevent such violations. In the course of the credentialing process, physicians' prior safety lapses, including criminal violations and medical malpractice suits, would be revealed and investigated, and incompetent doctors might be weeded out.

The legislature heard, too, from affected women and emergency room physicians about clinic doctors' record of abandoning their patients. One woman testified that, while she was hemorrhaging, her abortion provider told her, "'You're on your own. Get out.'" Eventually, the woman went to a hospital where an emergency room physician removed fetal body parts that the abortion provider had left in her body. Another patient who complained of severe pain following her abortion was told simply to go home and lie down. When she decided for herself to go to the emergency room, physicians discovered a tear in her uterus and a large hematoma containing a fetal head. The woman required an emergency hysterectomy. In another case, a clinic physician allowed a patient to bleed for three hours, yet a clinic employee testified that the physician would not let her call 911 because of possible media involvement. In the end, the employee called anyway and emergency room personnel discovered that the woman had a perforated uterus and a needed a hysterectomy. A different physician explained that she routinely treats abortion complications in the emergency room when the physician who performed the abortion lacks admitting privileges. In her experience, that situation "puts a woman's health at an unnecessary, unacceptable risk that results from a delay of care . . . and a lack of continuity of care." Admitting privileges would mitigate these risks, she testified, because "the physician who performed the procedure would be the one best equipped to evaluate and treat the patient."

Nor did the legislature neglect to consider the law's potential burdens. As witnesses explained, the admitting privileges requirement in Act 620 for abortion clinic providers would parallel existing requirements for many physicians who work at ambulatory surgical centers. And there is no indication this parallel admitting privileges requirement has led to the closing of any surgical centers or otherwise presented obstacles to quality care in Louisiana. Further, legislators learned that at least one Louisiana abortion provider already had qualifying admitting privileges, suggesting other competent abortion providers would be able to comply with the new regulation as well.

Next consider our rules about facial challenges. Generally, courts decide the constitutionality of statutes as applied to specific people in specific situations and disfavor facial challenges seeking to forestall a law's application in every circumstance. The reasons for this rule are many. Not least, when a court focuses on the parties before it, it is able to assess the law's application within a real factual context, rather than left to imagine "every conceivable situation which might possibly arise in the application of complex and comprehensive legislation." Importantly, too, as-applied challenges reduce the risk that a court will "short circuit the democratic process" by interfering with legislation any more than necessary to remedy a complaining party's injury.

As a result, the path for a litigant pursuing a facial challenge is deliberately difficult. Typically, a plaintiff seeking to render a law unenforceable in all of its applications must show that the law cannot be constitutionally applied against *anyone* in *any* situation.

Today, it seems any of these standards would demand too much. Instead of asking whether the law has a "substantial number of unconstitutional applications" compared to its "legitimate sweep," the plurality asks whether the law will impose a " 'substantial obstacle' " for a " 'large fraction'" of "'those women for whom the provision is an actual rather than an irrelevant restriction.'" Concededly, the two tests sound similar—after all, who could say whether a "substantial number" is more or less than a "large fraction"? But notice the switch at the end, where the plurality limits our focus to women for whom the law is an "actual" restriction. Because of that limitation, it doesn't matter how many women continue to have convenient access to abortions: Any woman not burdened by the challenged law is deemed "irrelevant" to the analysis. So instead of asking how the law's unconstitutional applications compare to its legitimate sweep, the plurality winds up asking only whether the law burdens a very large fraction of the people that it burdens. The words might sound familiar, but this circular test is unlike anything we apply to facial challenges anywhere else.

Abandoning our usual caution with facial challenges leads, predictably, to overbroad conclusions. Suppose that for a substantial number of women Louisiana's law imposes no burden at all. These women might live in an area well-served by well-qualified abortion providers who can easily obtain admitting privileges. No one could dispute the law is constitutional as applied to these women and providers. But suppose the law makes it difficult to obtain an abortion on the other side of the State, where qualified providers are fewer and farther between. Under the standard applied today, it seems the entire law would fall statewide, notwithstanding its undeniable constitutionality in many applications.

Even when it comes to assessing the law's effects on the subset of women deemed "relevant," this case proves unusual. Normally, to obtain a prospective injunction like the one approved today, a plaintiff must show that irreparable injury is not just possible, but likely. Yet, nothing like that standard can be found at work today.

The plaintiffs allege that statewide enforcement of Act 620 would irreparably injure Louisiana women by making it difficult for them to obtain abortions. To justify injunctive relief on that theory, however, it can't be enough to show that the law would induce any particular doctor or clinic to stop providing abortions. Instead, the plaintiffs would have to show that a sufficient number of clinics would close (without enough new clinics opening) so that supply would no longer meet demand for abortion in the State. And when assessing claims like *that*, we usually proceed with caution, aware of the "the difficulties and uncertainties involved in determining how [a] relevant market" would behave in response to changed circumstances. At a minimum, we expect one change in a marketplace—such as the introduction of a new regulation—will induce other responsive changes. When "the claim is one that simply makes no economic sense," too, the plaintiffs "must come forward with more persuasive evidence to support their claim than would otherwise be necessary."

Rather than follow these rules, today's decision proceeds to accept one speculative proposition after another to arrive at what can only be called a worst case scenario.

Today's decision also appears to assume that, if Louisiana's law took effect, not a single hospital would amend its rules to permit abortion providers easier access to admitting privileges; no clinic would choose to relocate closer to a hospital that offers admitting privileges rather than permanently close its doors; the prospect of significant unmet demand would not prompt a single Louisiana doctor with established admitting privileges to begin performing abortions; and unmet demand would not induce even one out-of-state abortion provider to relocate to Louisiana.

All these assumptions are open to question. Hospitals can (and do) change their policies in response to regulations. Clinic operators have opened, closed, and relocated clinics numerous times. There are hundreds of OB/GYNs with active admitting privileges in Louisiana who could lawfully perform abortions tomorrow. Millions of Americans move between States every year to pursue their profession. Yet with conditions ripe for market entry and expansion, today's decision foresees nothing but clinic closures and unmet demand.

To arrive at today's result, rules must be brushed aside and shortcuts taken. While the concurrence parts ways with the plurality at the last turn, the road both travel leads us to a strangely open space, unconstrained by many of the neutral principles that normally govern the judicial process. The temptation to proceed this direction, closer with each step toward an unobstructed exercise of will, may be always with us, a danger inherent in judicial review. But it is an impulse this Court normally strives mightily to resist. Today, in a highly politicized and contentious arena, we prove unwilling, or perhaps unable, to resist that temptation. Either way, respectfully, it is a sign we have lost our way.

Justice KAVANAUGH, dissenting.

A threshold question in this case concerns the proper standard for evaluating state abortion laws. Today, five Members of the Court reject the *Whole Woman's Health* cost-benefit standard. A different five Members of the Court conclude that Louisiana's admitting-privileges law is unconstitutional because it "would restrict women's access to abortion to the same degree as" the Texas law in *Whole Woman's Health*.

I agree with the first of those two conclusions. But I respectfully dissent from the second because, in my view, additional factfinding is necessary to properly evaluate Louisiana's law. As Justice Alito thoroughly and carefully explains, the factual record at this stage of plaintiffs' facial, pre-enforcement challenge does not adequately demonstrate that the three relevant doctors (Does 2, 5, and 6) cannot obtain admitting privileges or, therefore, that any of the three Louisiana abortion clinics would close as a result of the admitting-privileges law. In short, I agree with Justice Alito that the Court should remand the case for a new trial and additional factfinding under the appropriate legal standards.

Chapter 9

First Amendment: Freedom of Expression

B. Free Speech Methodology

1. The Distinction Between Content-Based and Content-Neutral Laws

a. The Importance of the Distinction (casebook p. 1186)

In *Barr v. American Association of Political Consultants*, the Court reaffirmed that content-based restrictions on speech must meet strict scrutiny. The Court struck down a provision of the federal law that exempted government debt collection from the prohibition of robocalls to cellphones. The decision was splintered because the Court divided over the question of whether the entire law should be struck down or whether this provision was severable. The Court concluded the latter and declared unconstitutional only the provision which was the content-based restriction.

BARR v. AMERICAN ASSOCIATION OF POLITICAL
CONSULTANTS
140 S. Ct. 2335 (2020)

Justice KAVANAUGH announced the judgment of the Court and delivered an opinion, in which THE CHIEF JUSTICE and Justice ALITO join, and in which Justice THOMAS joins as to Parts I and II.

Americans passionately disagree about many things. But they are largely united in their disdain for robocalls. The Federal Government receives a staggering number of complaints about robocalls—3.7 million complaints in 2019 alone. The States likewise field a constant barrage of complaints.

For nearly 30 years, the people's representatives in Congress have been fighting back. As relevant here, the Telephone Consumer Protection Act of 1991, known as the TCPA, generally prohibits robocalls to cell phones and home phones. But a 2015 amendment to the TCPA allows robo-calls that are made to collect debts owed to or guaranteed by the Federal Government, including robocalls made to collect many student loan and mortgage debts.

This case concerns robocalls to cell phones. Plaintiffs in this case are political and nonprofit organizations that want to make political robocalls to cell phones. Invoking the First Amendment, they argue that the 2015 government-debt exception unconstitutionally favors debt-collection speech over political and other speech. As relief from that unconstitutional law, they urge us to invalidate the entire 1991 robocall restriction, rather than simply invalidating the 2015 government-debt exception.

Six Members of the Court today conclude that Congress has impermissibly favored debt-collection speech over political and other speech, in violation of the First Amendment. Applying traditional severability principles, seven Members of the Court conclude that the entire 1991 robocall restriction should not be invalidated, but rather that the 2015 government-debt exception must be invalidated and severed from the remainder of the statute. As a result, plaintiffs still may not make political robocalls to cell phones, but their speech is now treated equally with debt-collection speech.

I

In 1991, Congress passed and President George H. W. Bush signed the Telephone Consumer Protection Act. The Act responded to a torrent of vociferous consumer complaints about intrusive robocalls. A growing number of telemarketers were using equipment that could automatically dial a telephone number and deliver an artificial or prerecorded voice message. At the time, more than 300,000 solicitors called more than 18 million Americans every day. Consumers were "outraged" and considered robocalls an invasion of privacy "regardless of the content or the initiator of the message."

In enacting the TCPA, Congress found that banning robocalls was "the only effective means of protecting telephone consumers from this nuisance and privacy invasion." To that end, the TCPA imposed various restrictions on the use of automated telephone equipment. In plain English, the TCPA prohibited almost all robocalls to cell phones.

Twenty-four years later, in 2015, Congress passed and President Obama signed the Bipartisan Budget Act. In addition to making other unrelated changes to the U.S. Code, that Act amended the TCPA's restriction on robocalls to cell phones. It stated:

(a) In General.—Section 227(b) of the Communications Act of 1934 is amended—

    (1) in paragraph (1)—

        (A) in subparagraph (A)(iii), by inserting ', unless such call is made solely to collect a debt owed to or guaranteed by the United States' after 'charged for the call.' 129 Stat. 588.

In other words, Congress carved out a new government-debt exception to the general robocall restriction.

Plaintiffs in this case are the American Association of Political Consultants and three other organizations that participate in the political system. Plaintiffs and their members make calls to citizens to discuss candidates and issues, solicit donations, conduct polls, and get out the vote. Plaintiffs believe that their political outreach would be more effective and efficient if they could make robocalls to cell phones. But because plaintiffs are not in the business of collecting government debt, prohibits them from making those robocalls.

II

Above "all else, the First Amendment means that government" generally "has no power to restrict expression because of its message, its ideas, its subject matter, or its content."

The Court's precedents allow the government to "constitutionally impose reasonable time, place, and manner regulations" on speech, but the precedents restrict the government from discriminating "in the regulation of expression on the basis of the content of that expression." Content-based laws are subject to strict scrutiny. By contrast, content-neutral laws are subject to a lower level of scrutiny.

Section 227(b)(1)(A)(iii) generally bars robocalls to cell phones. Since the 2015 amendment, the law has exempted robocalls to collect government debt. The initial First Amendment question is whether the robocall restriction, with the government-debt exception, is content-based. The answer is yes.

As relevant here, a law is content-based if "a regulation of speech 'on its face' draws distinctions based on the message a speaker conveys." That description applies to a law that "singles out specific subject matter for differential treatment." For example, "a law banning the use of sound trucks for political speech—and only political speech—would be a content-based regulation, even if it imposed no limits on the political viewpoints that could be expressed."

Under § 227(b)(1)(A)(iii), the legality of a robocall turns on whether it is "made solely to collect a debt owed to or guaranteed by the United States." A robocall that says, "Please pay your government debt" is legal. A robocall that says, "Please donate to our political campaign" is illegal. That is about as content-based as it gets. Because the law favors speech made for collecting government debt over political and other speech, the law is a content-based restriction on speech.

The Government advances three main arguments for deeming the statute content-neutral, but none is persuasive. *First*, the Government suggests that draws distinctions based on speakers (authorized debt collectors), not based on content. But that is not the law in front of us. This statute singles out calls "made solely to collect a debt owed to or guaranteed by the United States," not all calls from authorized debt collectors. In any event, "the fact that a distinction is speaker based" does not "automatically render the distinction content neutral." Indeed, the Court has held that "'laws favoring some speakers over others demand strict scrutiny when the legislature's speaker preference reflects a content preference.'"

Second, the Government argues that the legality of a robocall under the statute depends simply on whether the caller is engaged in a particular economic activity, not on the content of speech. We disagree. The law here focuses on whether the caller is *speaking* about a particular topic.

Third, according to the Government, if this statute is content-based because it singles out debt-collection speech, then so are statutes that *regulate* debt collection, like the Fair Debt Collection Practices Act. That slippery-slope argument is unpersuasive in this case. "[T]he First Amendment does not prevent restrictions directed at commerce or conduct from imposing incidental burdens on speech." The law here "does not simply have an effect on speech, but is directed at certain content and is aimed at particular speakers."

In short, the robocall restriction with the government-debt exception is content-based. Under the Court's precedents, a "law that is content based" is "subject to strict scrutiny." The Government concedes that it cannot satisfy strict scrutiny to justify the government-debt exception. We agree. The Government's stated justification for the government-debt exception is collecting government debt. Although collecting government debt is no doubt a worthy goal, the Government concedes that it has not sufficiently justified the differentiation between government-debt collection speech and other important categories of robocall speech, such as political speech, charitable fundraising, issue advocacy, commercial advertising, and the like.

III

Having concluded that the 2015 government-debt exception created an unconstitutional exception to the 1991 robocall restriction, we must decide whether to invalidate the entire 1991 robocall restriction, or instead to invalidate and sever the 2015 government-debt exception. [Justice Kavanaugh then concluded that the content-based provision was severable.]

In 1991, Congress enacted a general restriction on robocalls to cell phones. In 2015, Congress carved out an exception that allowed robocalls made to collect government debt. In doing so, Congress favored debt-collection speech over plaintiffs' political speech. We hold that the 2015 government-debt exception added an unconstitutional exception to the law. We cure that constitutional violation by invalidating the 2015 government-debt exception and severing it from the remainder of the statute.

Justice SOTOMAYOR, concurring in the judgment.

I agree with much of the partial dissent's explanation that strict scrutiny should not apply to all content-based distinctions. In my view, however, the government-debt exception in 47 U.S.C. § 227(b) still fails intermediate scrutiny because it is not "narrowly tailored to serve a significant governmental interest." Even under intermediate scrutiny, the Government has not explained how a debt-collection robocall about a government-backed debt is any less intrusive or could be any less harassing than a debt-collection robocall about a privately backed debt. As the Fourth Circuit noted, the government-debt exception is seriously underinclusive because it permits "many of the intrusive calls that the automated call ban was enacted to prohibit." The Government could have employed far less restrictive means to further its interest in collecting debt, such as "secur[ing] consent from the debtors to make debt-collection calls" or "plac[ing] the calls itself." Nor has the Government "sufficiently justified the differentiation between government-debt collection speech and other important categories of robocall speech, such as political speech, charitable fundraising, issue advocacy, commercial advertising, and the like."

Nevertheless, I agree that the offending provision is severable.

Justice BREYER, with whom Justice GINSBURG and Justice KAGAN join, concurring in the judgment with respect to severability and dissenting in part.

A federal statute forbids, with some exceptions, making automatically dialed or prerecorded telephone calls (called robocalls) to cell phones.

This case concerns one of these exceptions, which applies to calls "made solely to collect a debt owed to or guaranteed by the United States." A majority of the Court holds that the exception violates the Constitution's First Amendment. In my view, it does not.

The plurality finds the government-debt exception unconstitutional primarily by applying a logical syllogism: (1) "Content-based laws are subject to strict scrutiny." (2) The exception is based on "content." (3) Hence, the exception is subject to "strict scrutiny." And the Government concedes that the exception cannot survive "strict scrutiny" examination.

The problem with that approach, which reflexively applies strict scrutiny to all content-based speech distinctions, is that it is divorced from First Amendment values. This case primarily involves commercial regulation — namely, debt collection. And, in my view, there is no basis here to apply "strict scrutiny" based on "content-discrimination."

To appreciate why, it is important to understand at least one set of values that underlie the First Amendment and the related reasons why courts scrutinize some speech restrictions strictly. The concept is abstract but simple: "We the People of the United States" have created a government of laws enacted by elected representatives. For our government to remain a *democratic* republic, the people must be free to generate, debate, and discuss both general and specific ideas, hopes, and experiences. The people must then be able to transmit their resulting views and conclusions to their elected representatives, which they may do directly, or indirectly through the shaping of public opinion. The object of that transmission is to influence the public policy enacted by elected representatives. As this Court has explained, "[t]he First Amendment was fashioned to assure unfettered interchange of ideas for the bringing about of political and social changes desired by the people."

In other words, the free marketplace of ideas is not simply a debating society for expressing thought in a vacuum. It is in significant part an instrument for "bringing about . . . political and social chang[e]." The representative democracy that "We the People" have created insists that this be so.

It is thus no surprise that our First Amendment jurisprudence has long reflected these core values. This Court's cases have provided heightened judicial protection for political speech, public forums, and the expression of all viewpoints on any given issue.

From a democratic perspective, however, it is equally important that courts not use the First Amendment in a way that would threaten the workings of ordinary regulatory programs posing little threat to the free marketplace of ideas enacted as result of that public discourse. As a general matter, the strictest scrutiny should not apply indiscriminately to the very "political and social changes desired by the people"—that is, to those government programs which the "unfettered interchange of ideas" has sought to achieve. Otherwise, our democratic system would fail, not through the inability of the people to speak or to transmit their views to government, but because of an elected government's inability to translate those views into action.

Thus, once again, it is not surprising that this Court has applied less strict standards when reviewing speech restrictions embodied in government regulatory programs. This Court, for example, has applied a "rational basis" standard for reviewing those restrictions when they have only indirect impacts on speech. And it has applied a mid-level standard of review—often termed "intermediate scrutiny"—when the government directly restricts protected commercial speech.

This account of well-established principles at the core of the First Amendment demonstrates the problem with the plurality's approach. To reflexively treat all content-based distinctions as subject to strict scrutiny regardless of context or practical effect is to engage in an analysis untethered from the First Amendment's objectives. And in this case, strict scrutiny is inappropriate. Recall that the exception at issue here concerns debt collection—specifically a method for collecting government-owned or -backed debt. Regulation of debt collection does not fall on the first side of the democratic equation. It has next to nothing to do with the free marketplace of ideas or the transmission of the people's thoughts and will to the government. It has everything to do with the second side of the equation, that is, with government response to the public will through ordinary commercial regulation. To apply the strictest level of scrutiny to the economically based exemption here is thus remarkable.

I recognize that the underlying cell phone robocall restriction primarily concerns a means of communication. And that fact, as I discuss below, triggers some heightened scrutiny, reflected in an intermediate scrutiny standard. Strict scrutiny and its strong presumption of unconstitutionality, however, have no place here.

Consider prescription drug labels, securities forms, and tax statements. A government agency might reasonably specify just what information the form or label must contain and further provide that the form or label may not contain other information (thereby excluding political statements). No one would think that the exclusion of political speech, say, from a drug label, means that courts must examine all other regulatory exceptions with strict scrutiny. Put differently, it is hard to imagine that such exceptions threaten political speech in the marketplace of ideas, or have any significant impact on the free exchange of ideas. To treat those exceptions as presumptively unconstitutional would work a significant transfer of authority from legislatures and agencies to courts, potentially inhibiting the creation of the very government programs for which the people (after debate) have voiced their support, despite those programs' minimal speech-related harms. Given the values at the heart of the First Amendment, that interpretation threatens to stand that Amendment on its head. It could also lead the Court to water down the strict scrutiny standard, which would limit speech protections in situations where strict scrutiny's strong protections should properly apply.

If, as I have argued, the First Amendment does not support the mechanical conclusion that content discrimination automatically triggers strict scrutiny, what role might content discrimination play? The plurality is correct when it quotes this Court as having said that the government may not discriminate "'in the regulation of expression on the basis of the content of that expression.'" If, however, this Court is to apply the First Amendment consistently with the democratic values embodied within that Amendment, that kind of statement must reflect a rule of thumb applicable only in certain circumstances.

Indeed, that must be so given that this Court's First Amendment jurisprudence itself ties the constitutional protection speech receives to the content or purpose of that speech. The Court has held that entire categories of speech—for example, obscenity, fraud, and speech integral to criminal conduct—are generally unprotected by the First Amendment entirely because of their content. As Justice Stevens pointed out, "our entire First Amendment jurisprudence creates a regime based on the content of speech." Given that this Court looks to the nature and content of speech to determine whether, or to what extent, the First Amendment protects it, it makes little sense to treat *every* content-based distinction Congress has made as presumptively unconstitutional.

That said, I am not arguing for the abolition of the concept of "content discrimination." There are times when using content discrimination to trigger scrutiny is eminently reasonable. Specifically, when content-based distinctions are used as a method for suppressing particular viewpoints or threatening the neutrality of a traditional public forum, content discrimination triggering strict scrutiny is generally appropriate.

Neither of those situations is present here. Outside of these circumstances, content discrimination can at times help determine the strength of a government justification or identify a potential interference with the free marketplace of ideas. But, as I have explained, this case is not about protecting the marketplace of ideas. It is not about the formation of public opinion or the transmission of the people's will to elected representatives. It is fundamentally about a method of regulating debt collection.

I would examine the validity of the regulation at issue here using a First Amendment standard that (unlike strict scrutiny) does not strongly presume that a regulation that affects speech is unconstitutional. However, given that the government-debt exception does directly impact a means of communication, the appropriate standard requires a closer look at the restriction than does a traditional "rational basis" test. A proper inquiry should examine the seriousness of the speech-related harm, the importance of countervailing objectives, the likelihood that the restriction will achieve those objectives, and whether there are other, less restrictive ways of doing so. Narrow tailoring in this context, however, does not necessarily require the use of the least-restrictive means of furthering those objectives. That inquiry ultimately evaluates a restriction's speech-related harms in light of its justifications. We have typically called this approach "intermediate scrutiny," though we have sometimes referred to it as an assessment of "fit," sometimes called it "proportionality," and sometimes just applied it without using a label.

Applying this Court's intermediate scrutiny analysis, I would begin by asking just what the First Amendment harm is here. Indeed, looking at the government-debt exception in context, we can see that the practical effect of the exception, taken together with the rest of the statute, is to put *non*-government debt collectors at a disadvantage. Their speech operates in the same sphere as government-debt collection speech, communicates comparable messages, and yet does not have the benefit of a particular instrument of communication (robocalls). While this is a speech-related harm, debt-collection speech is both commercial and highly regulated. The speech-related harm at issue here — and any related effect on the marketplace of ideas — is modest.

What, then, is the justification for this harm? The purpose of the exception is to further the protection of the public fisc. That protection is an important governmental interest. Private debt typically involves private funds; public debt typically involves funds that, in principle, belong to all of us, and help to implement numerous governmental policies that the people support.

Finally, is the exception narrowly tailored? Its limited scope shows that it is. Congress has minimized any speech-related harm by tying the exception directly to the Government's interest in preserving the public fisc. The statutory text makes clear that calls will only fall within the bounds of that exception if they are "made *solely* to collect" Government debt.

Thus, the exception cannot be used to permit communications unrelated or less directly related to that public fiscal interest.

The upshot is that the government-debt exception, taken in context, inflicts some speech-related harm. But the harm, as I have explained, is related not to public efforts to develop ideas or transmit them to the Government, but to the Government's response to those efforts, which here takes the form of highly regulated commercial communications. Moreover, there is an important justification for that harm, and the exception is narrowly tailored to further that goal. Given those facts, the government-debt exception should survive intermediate First Amendment scrutiny.

For the reasons described above, I would find that the government-debt exception does not violate the First Amendment.

Justice GORSUCH, with whom Justice THOMAS joins as to Part II, concurring in the judgment in part and dissenting in part.

I agree with Justice Kavanaugh that the provision of the Telephone Consumer Protection Act before us violates the First Amendment. Respectfully, however, I disagree about why that is so and what remedial consequences should follow. [Justice Gorsuch would have invalidated the entire statute.]

4.   What Is an Infringement of Freedom of Speech?

Unconstitutional Conditions (casebook p. 1294)

In *Agency for International Development v. Alliance for Open Society International* (2013) (casebook p. 1306), the Court held that it violated the First Amendment for the government to require as a condition of federal funding that organizations adopt a policy expressing opposition to prostitution and human trafficking. In *Agency for International Development v. Alliance for Open Society International*, 140 S. Ct. 2082 (2020), the Court held that this did not violate the First Amendment when applied to the foreign affiliates of American entities. Justice Kavanaugh, writing for the Court in a 5-3 decision (Justice Kagan was recused), declared: "[I]t is long settled as a matter of American constitutional law that foreign citizens outside U.S. territory do not possess rights under the U.S. Constitution." Because the foreign affiliates were separately incorporated entities and because they were foreign, the Court concluded that the First Amendment did not apply.

D.   What Places Are Available for Speech?

3.   Speech in Authoritarian Environments

c.   *Schools* (casebook, p. 1582)

In *Mahanoy Area School District v. B.L.*, the Supreme Court returned to the issue of student speech for the first time in over a decade. Unlike the earlier cases, this involved student speech off-campus, over the weekend, and over social media. It is the first time the Court has ruled in favor of students in a speech case since *Tinker v. Des Moines Board of Education* (1969) (casebook, p. 1583).

MAHANOY AREA SCHOOL DISTRICT v. B.L.
141 S. Ct. 2038 (2021)

Justice BREYER delivered the opinion of the Court.

A public high school student used, and transmitted to her Snapchat friends, vulgar language and gestures criticizing both the school and the school's cheerleading team. The student's speech took place outside of school hours and away from the school's campus. In response, the school suspended the student for a year from the cheerleading team.

I

B. L. was a student at Mahanoy Area High School, a public school in Mahanoy City, Pennsylvania. At the end of her freshman year, B. L. tried out for a position on the school's varsity cheerleading squad and for right fielder on a private softball team. She did not make the varsity cheerleading team or get her preferred softball position, but she was offered a spot on the cheerleading squad's junior varsity team. B. L. did not accept the coach's decision with good grace, particularly because the squad coaches had placed an entering freshman on the varsity team.

That weekend, B. L. and a friend visited the Cocoa Hut, a local convenience store. There, B. L. used her smartphone to post two photos on Snapchat, a social media application that allows users to post photos and videos that disappear after a set period of time. B. L. posted the images to her Snapchat "story," a feature of the application that allows any person in the user's "friend" group (B. L. had about 250 "friends") to view the images for a 24 hour period.

The first image B. L. posted showed B. L. and a friend with middle fingers raised; it bore the caption: "Fuck school fuck softball fuck cheer fuck everything." The second image was blank but for a caption, which read: "Love how me and [another student] get told we need a year of jv before we make varsity but tha[t] doesn't matter to anyone else?" The caption also contained an upside-down smiley-face emoji.

B. L.'s Snapchat "friends" included other Mahanoy Area High School students, some of whom also belonged to the cheerleading squad. At least one of them, using a separate cellphone, took pictures of B. L.'s posts and shared them with other members of the cheerleading squad. One of the students who received these photos showed them to her mother (who was a cheerleading squad coach), and the images spread. That week, several cheerleaders and other students approached the cheerleading coaches "visibly upset" about B. L.'s posts. Questions about the posts persisted during an Algebra class taught by one of the two coaches.

After discussing the matter with the school principal, the coaches decided that because the posts used profanity in connection with a school extracurricular activity, they violated team and school rules. As a result, the coaches suspended B. L. from the junior varsity cheerleading squad for the upcoming year. B. L.'s subsequent apologies did not move school officials. The school's athletic director, principal, superintendent, and school board, all affirmed B. L.'s suspension from the team. In response, B. L., together with her parents, filed this lawsuit in Federal District Court.

The District Court found in B. L.'s favor. It first granted a temporary restraining order and a preliminary injunction ordering the school to reinstate B. L. to the cheerleading team. In granting B. L.'s subsequent motion for summary judgment, the District Court found that B. L.'s Snapchats had not caused substantial disruption at the school. Cf. *Tinker v. Des Moines Independent Community School Dist.* (1969).

On appeal, a panel of the Third Circuit affirmed the District Court's conclusion. [T]he Court said that [b]ecause B. L.'s speech took place off campus, the panel concluded that the *Tinker* standard did not apply and the school consequently could not discipline B. L. for engaging in a form of pure speech.

II

We have made clear that students do not "shed their constitutional rights to freedom of speech or expression," even "at the school house gate." But we have also made clear that courts must apply the First Amendment "in light of the special characteristics of the school environment." One such characteristic, which we have stressed, is the fact that schools at times stand *in loco parentis*, *i.e.*, in the place of parents.

This Court has previously outlined three specific categories of student speech that schools may regulate in certain circumstances: (1) "indecent," "lewd," or "vulgar" speech uttered during a school assembly on school grounds, (2) speech, uttered during a class trip, that promotes "illegal drug use", and (3) speech that others may reasonably perceive as "bear[ing] the imprimatur of the school," such as that appearing in a school-sponsored newspaper. Finally, in *Tinker*, we said schools have a special interest in regulating speech that "materially disrupts classwork or involves substantial disorder or invasion of the rights of others." These special characteristics call for special leeway when schools regulate speech that occurs under its supervision.

Unlike the Third Circuit, we do not believe the special characteristics that give schools additional license to regulate student speech always disappear when a school regulates speech that takes place off campus. The school's regulatory interests remain significant in some off-campus circumstances. The parties' briefs, and those of *amici*, list several types of off-campus behavior that may call for school regulation. These include serious or severe bullying or harassment targeting particular individuals; threats aimed at teachers or other students; the failure to follow rules concerning lessons, the writing of papers, the use of computers, or participation in other online school activities; and breaches of school security devices, including material maintained within school computers.

[T]he Third Circuit's rule basically, if not entirely, would deny the off-campus applicability of *Tinker's* highly general statement about the nature of a school's special interests. Particularly given the advent of computer-based learning, we hesitate to determine precisely which of many school-related off-campus activities belong on such a list. Neither do we now know how such a list might vary, depending upon a student's age, the nature of the school's off-campus activity, or the impact upon the school itself. Thus, we do not now set forth a broad, highly general First Amendment rule stating just what counts as "off campus" speech and whether or how ordinary First Amendment standards must give way off campus to a school's special need to prevent, *e.g.*, substantial disruption of learning-related activities or the protection of those who make up a school community.

We can, however, mention three features of off-campus speech that often, even if not always, distinguish schools' efforts to regulate that speech from their efforts to regulate on-campus speech. Those features diminish the strength of the unique educational characteristics that might call for special First Amendment leeway.

First, a school, in relation to off-campus speech, will rarely stand *in loco parentis*. The doctrine of *in loco parentis* treats school administrators as standing in the place of students' parents under circumstances where the children's actual parents cannot protect, guide, and discipline them. Geographically speaking, off-campus speech will normally fall within the zone of parental, rather than school-related, responsibility.

Second, from the student speaker's perspective, regulations of off-campus speech, when coupled with regulations of on-campus speech, include all the speech a student utters during the full 24-hour day. That means courts must be more skeptical of a school's efforts to regulate off-campus speech, for doing so may mean the student cannot engage in that kind of speech at all. When it comes to political or religious speech that occurs outside school or a school program or activity, the school will have a heavy burden to justify intervention.

Third, the school itself has an interest in protecting a student's unpopular expression, especially when the expression takes place off campus. America's public schools are the nurseries of democracy. Our representative democracy only works if we protect the "marketplace of ideas." This free exchange facilitates an informed public opinion, which, when transmitted to lawmakers, helps produce laws that reflect the People's will. That protection must include the protection of unpopular ideas, for popular ideas have less need for protection. Thus, schools have a strong interest in ensuring that future generations understand the workings in practice of the well-known aphorism, "I disapprove of what you say, but I will defend to the death your right to say it."

Given the many different kinds of off-campus speech, the different potential school-related and circumstance-specific justifications, and the differing extent to which those justifications may call for First Amendment leeway, we can, as a general matter, say little more than this: Taken together, these three features of much off-campus speech mean that the leeway the First Amendment grants to schools in light of their special characteristics is diminished. We leave for future cases to decide where, when, and how these features mean the speaker's off-campus location will make the critical difference. This case can, however, provide one example.

III

Consider B. L.'s speech. Putting aside the vulgar language, the listener would hear criticism, of the team, the team's coaches, and the school — in a word or two, criticism of the rules of a community of which B. L. forms a part. This criticism did not involve features that would place it outside the First Amendment's ordinary protection. B. L.'s posts, while crude, did not amount to fighting words. And while B. L. used vulgarity, her speech was not obscene as this Court has understood that term. To the contrary, B. L. uttered the kind of pure speech to which, were she an adult, the First Amendment would provide strong protection.

Consider too when, where, and how B. L. spoke. Her posts appeared outside of school hours from a location outside the school. She did not identify the school in her posts or target any member of the school community with vulgar or abusive language. B. L. also transmitted her speech through a personal cellphone, to an audience consisting of her private circle of Snapchat friends. These features of her speech, while risking transmission to the school itself, nonetheless diminish the school's interest in punishing B. L.'s utterance.

But what about the school's interest, here primarily an interest in prohibiting students from using vulgar language to criticize a school team or its coaches — at least when that criticism might well be transmitted to other students, team members, coaches, and faculty? We can break that general interest into three parts.

First, we consider the school's interest in teaching good manners and consequently in punishing the use of vulgar language aimed at part of the school community. The strength of this anti-vulgarity interest is weakened considerably by the fact that B. L. spoke outside the school on her own time.

Second, the school argues that it was trying to prevent disruption, if not within the classroom, then within the bounds of a school-sponsored extra-curricular activity. But we can find no evidence in the record of the sort of "substantial disruption" of a school activity or a threatened harm to the rights of others that might justify the school's action. Rather, the record shows that discussion of the matter took, at most, 5 to 10 minutes of an Algebra class "for just a couple of days" and that some members of the cheerleading team were "upset" about the content of B. L.'s Snapchats. But when one of B. L.'s coaches was asked directly if she had "any reason to think that this particular incident would disrupt class or school activities other than the fact that kids kept asking . . . about it," she responded simply, "No." As we said in *Tinker*, "for the State in the person of school officials to justify prohibition of a particular expression of opinion, it must be able to show that its action was caused by something more than a mere desire to avoid the discomfort and unpleasantness that always accompany an unpopular viewpoint." The alleged disturbance here does not meet *Tinker*'s demanding standard.

Third, the school presented some evidence that expresses (at least indirectly) a concern for team morale. One of the coaches testified that the school decided to suspend B. L., not because of any specific negative impact upon a particular member of the school community, but "based on the fact that there was negativity put out there that could impact students in the school." There is little else, however, that suggests any serious decline in team morale — to the point where it could create a substantial interference in, or disruption of, the school's efforts to maintain team cohesion. As we have previously said, simple "undifferentiated fear or apprehension . . . is not enough to overcome the right to freedom of expression."

It might be tempting to dismiss B. L.'s words as unworthy of the robust First Amendment protections discussed herein. But sometimes it is necessary to protect the superfluous in order to preserve the necessary. "We cannot lose sight of the fact that, in what otherwise might seem a trifling and annoying instance of individual distasteful abuse of a privilege, these fundamental societal values are truly implicated."

Justice THOMAS, dissenting.

B. L., a high school student, sent a profanity-laced message to hundreds of people, including classmates and teammates. The message included a picture of B. L. raising her middle finger and captioned "F*** school" and "f*** cheer." This message was juxtaposed with another, which explained that B. L. was frustrated that she failed to make the varsity cheerleading squad. The cheerleading coach responded by disciplining B. L.

The Court overrides that decision — without even mentioning the 150 years of history supporting the coach. Using broad brushstrokes, the majority outlines the scope of school authority. When students are on campus, the majority says, schools have authority *in loco parentis* — that is, as substitutes of parents — to discipline speech and conduct. Off campus, the authority of schools is somewhat less. At that level of generality, I agree. But the majority omits important detail. What authority does a school have when it operates *in loco parentis*? How much less authority do schools have over off-campus speech and conduct? And how does a court decide if speech is on or off campus?

Disregarding these important issues, the majority simply posits three vague considerations and reaches an outcome. A more searching review reveals that schools historically could discipline students in circumstances like those presented here. Because the majority does not attempt to explain why we should not apply this historical rule and does not attempt to tether its approach to anything stable, I respectfully dissent.

While the majority entirely ignores the relevant history, I would begin the assessment of the scope of free-speech rights incorporated against the States by looking to "what 'ordinary citizens' at the time of [the Fourteenth Amendment's] ratification would have understood" the right to encompass. Cases and treatises from that era reveal that public schools retained substantial authority to discipline students. As I have previously explained, that authority was near plenary while students were at school. Authority also extended to when students were traveling to or from school. And, although schools had less authority after a student returned home, it was well settled that they still could discipline students for off-campus speech or conduct that had a proximate tendency to harm the school environment.

Perhaps the most familiar example applying this rule is a case where a student, after returning home from school, used "disrespectful language" against a teacher—he called the teacher "old"—"in presence of the [teacher] and of some of his fellow pupils." The Vermont Supreme Court held that the teacher could discipline a student for this speech because the speech had "a direct and immediate tendency to injure the school, to subvert the master's authority, and to beget disorder and insubordination."

This rule was widespread. It was consistent with "the universal custom" in New England. Various cases, treatises, and school manuals endorsed it.

If there is a good constitutional reason to depart from this historical rule, the majority and the parties fail to identify it. I would thus apply the rule. Assuming that B. L.'s speech occurred off campus, the purpose and effect of B. L.'s speech was "to degrade the [program and cheerleading staff]" in front of "other pupils," thus having "a direct and immediate tendency to . . . subvert the [cheerleading coach's] authority." As a result, the coach had authority to discipline B. L.

Our modern doctrine is not to the contrary. "[T]he penalties imposed in this case were unrelated to any political viewpoint" or religious viewpoint. And although the majority sugar coats this speech as "criticism," it is well settled that schools can punish "vulgar" speech—at least when it occurs on campus.

The majority declines to consider any of this history, instead favoring a few pragmatic guideposts. This is not the first time the Court has chosen intuition over history when it comes to student speech. The larger problem facing us today is that our student-speech cases are untethered from any textual or historical foundation. That failure leads the majority to miss much of the analysis relevant to these kinds of cases.

The Court's failure to explain itself in *Tinker* needlessly makes this case more difficult. Unlike *Tinker*, which involved a school's authority under a straightforward fact pattern, this case involves speech made in one location but capable of being received in countless others—an issue that has been aggravated exponentially by recent technological advances. The Court's decision not to create a solid foundation in *Tinker*, and now here not to consult the relevant history, predictably causes the majority to ignore relevant analysis.

First, the majority gives little apparent significance to B. L.'s decision to participate in an extracurricular activity. But the historical test suggests that authority of schools over off-campus speech may be greater when students participate in extracurricular programs. So students like B. L. who are active in extracurricular programs have a greater potential, by virtue of their participation, to harm those programs. For example, a profanity-laced screed delivered on social media or at the mall has a much different effect on a football program when done by a regular student than when done by the captain of the football team. So, too, here.

Second, the majority fails to consider whether schools often will have *more* authority, not less, to discipline students who transmit speech through social media. Because off-campus speech made through social media can be received on campus (and can spread rapidly to countless people), it often will have a greater proximate tendency to harm the school environment than will an off-campus in-person conversation.

Third, and relatedly, the majority uncritically adopts the assumption that B. L.'s speech, in fact, was off campus. But, the location of her speech is a much trickier question than the majority acknowledges. Because speech travels, schools sometimes may be able to treat speech as on campus even though it originates off campus. Nobody doubts, for example, that a school has *in loco parentis* authority over a student (and can discipline him) when he passes out vulgar flyers on campus—even if he creates those flyers off campus. The same may be true in many contexts when social media speech is generated off campus but received on campus. But where it is foreseeable and likely that speech will travel onto campus, a school has a stronger claim to treating the speech as on-campus speech.

The Court transparently takes a common-law approach to today's decision. In effect, it states just one rule: Schools can regulate speech less often when that speech occurs off campus. It then identifies this case as an "example" and "leav[es] for future cases" the job of developing this new common-law doctrine. But the Court's foundation is untethered from anything stable, and courts (and schools) will almost certainly be at a loss as to what exactly the Court's opinion today means.

Perhaps there are good constitutional reasons to depart from the historical rule, and perhaps this Court and lower courts will identify and explain these reasons in the future. But because the Court does not do so today, and because it reaches the wrong result under the appropriate historical test, I respectfully dissent.

***

E. Freedom of Association

2. Laws Requiring Disclosure of Membership (casebook p. 1608)

In *Americans for Prosperity Foundation v. Bonta*, the Court declared unconstitutional a California regulation that required non-profits to give to the state the same information it provides the federal government as to its donors. In reading the case, it is important to focus on the level of scrutiny chosen by Chief Justice Roberts: exacting scrutiny, which seems to be in between intermediate and strict scrutiny. Also, it is likely that this will lead to challenges to many other disclosure laws, including the federal law that requires this same information be turned over to the federal government.

AMERICANS FOR PROSPERITY FOUNDATION v. BONTA
141 S. Ct. ___ (2021)

Chief Justice ROBERTS delivered the opinion of the Court, except as to Part II–B–1.

To solicit contributions in California, charitable organizations must disclose to the state Attorney General's Office the identities of their major donors. The State contends that having this information on hand makes it easier to police misconduct by charities. We must decide whether California's disclosure requirement violates the First Amendment right to free association.

I

The California Attorney General's Office is responsible for statewide law enforcement, including the supervision and regulation of charitable fundraising. Under state law, the Attorney General is authorized to "establish and maintain a register" of charitable organizations and to obtain "whatever information, copies of instruments, reports, and records are needed for the establishment and maintenance of the register." In order to operate and raise funds in California, charities generally must register with the Attorney General and renew their registrations annually. Over 100,000 charities are currently registered in the State, and roughly 60,000 renew their registrations each year.

California law empowers the Attorney General to make rules and regulations regarding the registration and renewal process. Pursuant to this regulatory authority, the Attorney General requires charities renewing their registrations to file copies of their Internal Revenue Service Form 990, along with any attachments and schedules. Form 990 contains information regarding tax-exempt organizations' mission, leadership, and finances. Schedule B to Form 990 — the document that gives rise to the present dispute — requires organizations to disclose the names and addresses of donors who have contributed more than $5,000 in a particular tax year (or, in some cases, who have given more than 2 percent of an organization's total contributions).

The petitioners are tax-exempt charities that solicit contributions in California and are subject to the Attorney General's registration and renewal requirements. Americans for Prosperity Foundation is a public charity that is "devoted to education and training about the principles of a free and open society, including free markets, civil liberties, immigration reform, and constitutionally limited government." Thomas More Law Center is a public interest law firm whose "mission is to protect religious freedom, free speech, family values, and the sanctity of human life." Since 2001, each petitioner has renewed its registration and has filed a copy of its Form 990 with the Attorney General, as required by Cal. Code Regs., tit. 11, § 301. Out of concern for their donors' anonymity, however, the petitioners have declined to file their Schedule Bs (or have filed only redacted versions) with the State.

For many years, the petitioners' reluctance to turn over donor information presented no problem because the Attorney General was not particularly zealous about collecting Schedule Bs. That changed in 2010, when the California Department of Justice "ramped up its efforts to enforce charities' Schedule B obligations, sending thousands of deficiency letters to charities that had not complied with the Schedule B requirement." The Law Center and the Foundation received deficiency letters in 2012 and 2013, respectively. When they continued to resist disclosing their contributors' identities, the Attorney General threatened to suspend their registrations and fine their directors and officers. The petitioners each responded by filing suit.

II

A

This Court has "long understood as implicit in the right to engage in activities protected by the First Amendment a corresponding right to associate with others." Protected association furthers "a wide variety of political, social, economic, educational, religious, and cultural ends," and "is especially important in preserving political and cultural diversity and in shielding dissident expression from suppression by the majority." Government infringement of this freedom "can take a number of forms." We have held, for example, that the freedom of association may be violated where a group is required to take in members it does not want, see *id.*, at 623, where individuals are punished for their political affiliation, or where members of an organization are denied benefits based on the organization's message.

We have also noted that "[i]t is hardly a novel perception that compelled disclosure of affiliation with groups engaged in advocacy may constitute as effective a restraint on freedom of association as [other] forms of governmental action." *NAACP v. Alabama ex rel. Patterson* (1958). *NAACP v. Alabama* involved this chilling effect in its starkest form. The NAACP opened an Alabama office that supported racial integration in higher education and public transportation. In response, NAACP members were threatened with economic reprisals and violence. As part of an effort to oust the organization from the State, the Alabama Attorney General sought the group's membership lists. We held that the First Amendment prohibited such compelled disclosure. We explained that "[e]ffective advocacy of both public and private points of view, particularly controversial ones, is undeniably enhanced by group association," and we noted "the vital relationship between freedom to associate and privacy in one's associations." Because NAACP members faced a risk of reprisals if their affiliation with the organization became known—and because Alabama had demonstrated no offsetting interest "sufficient to justify the deterrent effect" of disclosure—we concluded that the State's demand violated the First Amendment.

B

1

NAACP v. Alabama did not phrase in precise terms the standard of review that applies to First Amendment challenges to compelled disclosure. We have since settled on a standard referred to as "exacting scrutiny."

Under that standard, there must be "a substantial relation between the disclosure requirement and a sufficiently important governmental interest." "To withstand this scrutiny, the strength of the governmental interest must reflect the seriousness of the actual burden on First Amendment rights." Such scrutiny, we have held, is appropriate given the "deterrent effect on the exercise of First Amendment rights" that arises as an "inevitable result of the government's conduct in requiring disclosure."

The Law Center (but not the Foundation) argues that we should apply strict scrutiny, not exacting scrutiny. Under strict scrutiny, the government must adopt "the least restrictive means of achieving a compelling state interest," rather than a means substantially related to a sufficiently important interest. The Law Center contends that only strict scrutiny adequately protects the associational rights of charities.

It is true that we first enunciated the exacting scrutiny standard in a campaign finance case. And we have since invoked it in other election-related settings. But exacting scrutiny is not unique to electoral disclosure regimes. Regardless of the type of association, compelled disclosure requirements are reviewed under exacting scrutiny.

2

The Law Center (now joined by the Foundation) argues in the alternative that even if exacting scrutiny applies, such review incorporates a least restrictive means test similar to the one imposed by strict scrutiny. The United States and the Attorney General respond that exacting scrutiny demands no additional tailoring beyond the "substantial relation" requirement noted above. We think that the answer lies between those two positions. While exacting scrutiny does not require that disclosure regimes be the least restrictive means of achieving their ends, it does require that they be narrowly tailored to the government's asserted interest.

The need for narrow tailoring was set forth early in our compelled disclosure cases. In *Shelton v. Tucker*, we considered an Arkansas statute that required teachers to disclose every organization to which they belonged or contributed. We acknowledged the importance of "the right of a State to investigate the competence and fitness of those whom it hires to teach in its schools." But we nevertheless held that the Arkansas statute was invalid because even a "legitimate and substantial" governmental interest "cannot be pursued by means that broadly stifle fundamental personal liberties when the end can be more narrowly achieved."

Shelton stands for the proposition that a substantial relation to an important interest is not enough to save a disclosure regime that is insufficiently tailored. This requirement makes sense. Narrow tailoring is crucial where First Amendment activity is chilled—even if indirectly—"[b]ecause First Amendment freedoms need breathing space to survive." Our more recent decisions confirm the need for tailoring.

Where exacting scrutiny applies, the challenged requirement must be narrowly tailored to the interest it promotes, even if it is not the least restrictive means of achieving that end.

The dissent reads our cases differently. It focuses on the words "broadly stifle" in the quotation from *Shelton* above, and it interprets those words to mean that narrow tailoring is required only for disclosure regimes that "impose a severe burden on associational rights." Because, in the dissent's view, the petitioners have not shown such a burden here, narrow tailoring is not required.

We respectfully disagree. The "government may regulate in the [First Amendment] area only with narrow specificity," and compelled disclosure regimes are no exception. When it comes to "a person's beliefs and associations," "[b]road and sweeping state inquiries into these protected areas . . . discourage citizens from exercising rights protected by the Constitution." Contrary to the dissent, we understand this Court's discussion of rules that are "broad" and "broadly stifle" First Amendment freedoms to refer to the scope of challenged restrictions—their breadth—rather than the severity of any demonstrated burden.

The point is that a reasonable assessment of the burdens imposed by disclosure should begin with an understanding of the extent to which the burdens are unnecessary, and that requires narrow tailoring.

III

The Foundation and the Law Center both argued below that the obligation to disclose Schedule Bs to the Attorney General was unconstitutional on its face and as applied to them. The petitioners renew their facial challenge in this Court, and they argue in the alternative that they are entitled to as-applied relief. For the reasons below, we conclude that California's blanket demand for Schedule Bs is facially unconstitutional.

As explained, exacting scrutiny requires that there be "a substantial relation between the disclosure requirement and a sufficiently important governmental interest," and that the disclosure requirement be narrowly tailored to the interest it promotes.

[T]he narrow tailoring requirement is not satisfied by the disclosure regime.

We do not doubt that California has an important interest in preventing wrongdoing by charitable organizations. It goes without saying that there is a "substantial governmental interest[ ] in protecting the public from fraud." The Attorney General receives complaints each month that identify a range of misconduct, from "misuse, misappropriation, and diversion of charitable assets," to "false and misleading charitable solicitations," to other "improper activities by charities soliciting charitable donations." Such offenses cause serious social harms.

There is a dramatic mismatch, however, between the interest that the Attorney General seeks to promote and the disclosure regime that he has implemented in service of that end. Recall that 60,000 charities renew their registrations each year, and nearly all are required to file a Schedule B. Each Schedule B, in turn, contains information about a charity's top donors — a small handful of individuals in some cases, but hundreds in others. This information includes donors' names and the total contributions they have made to the charity, as well as their addresses.

Given the amount and sensitivity of this information harvested by the State, one would expect Schedule B collection to form an integral part of California's fraud detection efforts. It does not. To the contrary, the record amply supports the District Court's finding that there was not "a single, concrete instance in which pre-investigation collection of a Schedule B did anything to advance the Attorney General's investigative, regulatory or enforcement efforts."

The Attorney General and the dissent contend that alternative means of obtaining Schedule B information — such as a subpoena or audit letter — are inefficient and ineffective compared to up-front collection. It became clear at trial, however, that the Office had not even considered alternatives to the current disclosure requirement. See App. in No. 19–251, at 421 ("I see no reason to change what we've been doing.").

The upshot is that California casts a dragnet for sensitive donor information from tens of thousands of charities each year, even though that information will become relevant in only a small number of cases involving filed complaints. California does not rely on Schedule Bs to initiate investigations, and in all events, there are multiple alternative mechanisms through which the Attorney General can obtain Schedule B information after initiating an investigation. The need for up-front collection is particularly dubious given that California — one of only three States to impose such a requirement, — did not rigorously enforce the disclosure obligation until 2010. Certainly, this is not a regime "whose scope is in proportion to the interest served."

In reality, then, California's interest is less in investigating fraud and more in ease of administration. This interest, however, cannot justify the disclosure requirement. The Attorney General may well prefer to have every charity's information close at hand, just in case. But "the prime objective of the First Amendment is not efficiency." Mere administrative convenience does not remotely "reflect the seriousness of the actual burden" that the demand for Schedule Bs imposes on donors' association rights.

B

The foregoing discussion also makes clear why a facial challenge is appropriate in these cases. We have no trouble concluding here that the Attorney General's disclosure requirement is overbroad. The lack of tailoring to the State's investigative goals is categorical — present in every case — as is the weakness of the State's interest in administrative convenience. Every demand that might chill association therefore fails exacting scrutiny.

The Attorney General tries to downplay the burden on donors, arguing that "there is no basis on which to conclude that California's requirement results in any broad-based chill." He emphasizes that "California's Schedule B requirement is confidential," and he suggests that certain donors — like those who give to noncontroversial charities — are unlikely to be deterred from contributing. He also contends that disclosure to his office imposes no added burdens on donors because tax-exempt charities already provide their Schedule Bs to the IRS.

We are unpersuaded. Our cases have said that disclosure requirements can chill association "[e]ven if there [is] no disclosure to the general public." Exacting scrutiny is triggered by "state action which *may* have the effect of curtailing the freedom to associate," and by the "*possible* deterrent effect" of disclosure. While assurances of confidentiality may reduce the burden of disclosure to the State, they do not eliminate it.

It is irrelevant, moreover, that some donors might not mind — or might even prefer — the disclosure of their identities to the State. The disclosure requirement "creates an unnecessary risk of chilling" in violation of the First Amendment, indiscriminately sweeping up the information of *every* major donor with reason to remain anonymous. The petitioners here, for example, introduced evidence that they and their supporters have been subjected to bomb threats, protests, stalking, and physical violence. Such risks are heightened in the 21st century and seem to grow with each passing year, as "anyone with access to a computer [can] compile a wealth of information about" anyone else, including such sensitive details as a person's home address or the school attended by his children.

The gravity of the privacy concerns in this context is further underscored by the filings of hundreds of organizations as *amici curiae* in support of the petitioners. Far from representing uniquely sensitive causes, these organizations span the ideological spectrum, and indeed the full range of human endeavors. The deterrent effect feared by these organizations is real and pervasive, even if their concerns are not shared by every single charity operating or raising funds in California.

Finally, California's demand for Schedule Bs cannot be saved by the fact that donor information is already disclosed to the IRS as a condition of federal tax-exempt status. For one thing, each governmental demand for disclosure brings with it an additional risk of chill. For another, revenue collection efforts and conferral of tax-exempt status may raise issues not presented by California's disclosure requirement, which can prevent charities from operating in the State altogether.

We are left to conclude that the Attorney General's disclosure requirement imposes a widespread burden on donors' associational rights. And this burden cannot be justified on the ground that the regime is narrowly tailored to investigating charitable wrongdoing, or that the State's interest in administrative convenience is sufficiently important. We therefore hold that the up-front collection of Schedule Bs is facially unconstitutional, because it fails exacting scrutiny in "a substantial number of its applications . . . judged in relation to [its] plainly legitimate sweep."

California has not considered alternatives to indiscriminate up-front disclosure. That is true in every case. And the State's interest in amassing sensitive information for its own convenience is weak. That is true in every case. When it comes to the freedom of association, the protections of the First Amendment are triggered not only by actual restrictions on an individual's ability to join with others to further shared goals. The risk of a chilling effect on association is enough, "[b]ecause First Amendment freedoms need breathing space to survive."

Justice THOMAS, concurring in Parts I, II–A, II–B–2, and III–A, and concurring in the judgment.

The Court correctly holds that California's disclosure requirement violates the First Amendment. It also correctly concludes that the District Court properly enjoined California's attorney general from collecting the forms at issue, which contain sensitive donor information. But, while I agree with much of the Court's opinion, I would approach three issues differently.

First, the bulk of "our precedents . . . require application of strict scrutiny to laws that compel disclosure of protected First Amendment association." California's law fits that description.

Second, the Court holds the law "overbroad" and, thus, invalid in all circumstances. But I continue to have "doubts about [the] origins and application" of our "overbreadth doctrine."

Third, and relatedly, this Court also lacks the power "to 'pronounce that the statute is unconstitutional in *all* applications,'" even if the Court suspects that the law will likely be unconstitutional in every future application as opposed to just a substantial number of its applications. A declaration that the law is "facially" unconstitutional "seems to me no more than an advisory opinion—which a federal court should never issue at all." Courts cannot "strike down statutory text" or resolve the legal rights of litigants not before them.

Despite the Court's use of the term "facially unconstitutional," I join Part III–A, which finds that California's law fails exacting scrutiny, because the Court does not say that it is "provid[ing] relief beyond the parties to the case."

Justice ALITO, with whom Justice GORSUCH joins, concurring in Parts I, II–A, II–B–2, and III, and concurring in the judgment.

I am pleased to join most of The Chief Justice's opinion. In particular, I agree that the exacting scrutiny standard drawn from our election-law jurisprudence has real teeth. It requires both narrow tailoring and consideration of alternative means of obtaining the sought-after information. For the reasons The Chief Justice explains, California's blunderbuss approach to charitable disclosures fails exacting scrutiny and is facially unconstitutional. See *ante,* at 12–19 The question is not even close. And for the same reasons, California's approach necessarily fails strict scrutiny.

The Chief Justice would hold that the particular exacting scrutiny standard in our election-law jurisprudence applies categorically "to First Amendment challenges to compelled disclosure." Justice Thomas, by contrast, would hold that strict scrutiny applies in all such cases. I am not prepared at this time to hold that a single standard applies to all disclosure requirements. And I do not read our cases to have broadly resolved the question in favor of exacting scrutiny.

Because the choice between exacting and strict scrutiny has no effect on the decision in these cases, I see no need to decide which standard should be applied here or whether the same level of scrutiny should apply in all cases in which the compelled disclosure of associations is challenged under the First Amendment.

Justice SOTOMAYOR, with whom Justice BREYER and Justice KAGAN join, dissenting.

Although this Court is protective of First Amendment rights, it typically requires that plaintiffs demonstrate an actual First Amendment burden before demanding that a law be narrowly tailored to the government's interests, never mind striking the law down in its entirety. Not so today. Today, the Court holds that reporting and disclosure requirements must be narrowly tailored even if a plaintiff demonstrates no burden at all. The same scrutiny the Court applied when NAACP members in the Jim Crow South did not want to disclose their membership for fear of reprisals and violence now applies equally in the case of donors only too happy to publicize their names across the websites and walls of the organizations they support.

California oversees nearly a quarter of this Nation's charitable assets. As part of that oversight, it investigates and prosecutes charitable fraud, relying in part on a registry where it collects and keeps charitable organizations' tax forms. The majority holds that a California regulation requiring charitable organizations to disclose tax forms containing the names and contributions of their top donors unconstitutionally burdens the right to associate even if the forms are not publicly disclosed.

In so holding, the Court discards its decades-long requirement that, to establish a cognizable burden on their associational rights, plaintiffs must plead and prove that disclosure will likely expose them to objective harms, such as threats, harassment, or reprisals. It also departs from the traditional, nuanced approach to First Amendment challenges, whereby the degree of means-end tailoring required is commensurate to the actual burdens on associational rights. Finally, it recklessly holds a state regulation facially invalid despite petitioners' failure to show that a substantial proportion of those affected would prefer anonymity, much less that they are objectively burdened by the loss of it.

Today's analysis marks reporting and disclosure requirements with a bull's-eye. Regulated entities who wish to avoid their obligations can do so by vaguely waving toward First Amendment "privacy concerns." It does not matter if not a single individual risks experiencing a single reprisal from disclosure, or if the vast majority of those affected would happily comply. That is all irrelevant to the Court's determination that California's Schedule B requirement is facially unconstitutional. Neither precedent nor common sense supports such a result. I respectfully dissent.

Given the indeterminacy of how disclosure requirements will impact associational rights, this Court requires plaintiffs to demonstrate that a requirement is likely to expose their supporters to concrete repercussions in order to establish an actual burden. It then applies a level of means-end tailoring proportional to that burden. The Court abandons that approach here, instead holding that narrow tailoring applies to disclosure requirements across the board, even if there is no evidence that they burden anyone at all.

Before today, to demonstrate that a reporting or disclosure requirement would chill association, litigants had to show "a reasonable probability that the compelled disclosure of . . . contributors' names will subject them to threats, harassment, or reprisals from either Government officials or private parties." Proof could include "specific evidence of past or present harassment of members due to their associational ties, or of harassment directed against the organization itself," as well as evidence that "fear of community hostility and economic reprisals that would follow public disclosure . . . had discouraged new members from joining" an organization or caused "former members to withdraw." Although the Court has never imposed an "unduly strict requiremen[t] of proof," it has consistently required at least some record evidence demonstrating a risk of such objective harms.

Indeed, the Court has expressly held that parties do not have standing to bring claims where they assert nothing more than that government action will cause a "subjective 'chill.'"

Today, the Court abandons the requirement that plaintiffs demonstrate that they are chilled, much less that they are reasonably chilled. Instead, it presumes (contrary to the evidence, precedent, and common sense) that all disclosure requirements impose associational burdens. For example, the Court explains that there is a risk of chill in this suit because the government requires disclosure of the identity of any donor "with reason to remain anonymous." The Court does not qualify that statement, nor does it require record evidence of such reasons. If the Court did, it would not be able to strike California's Schedule B requirement down in all its applications, because the only evidence in the record of donors with any reason to remain anonymous is that of petitioners'.

At best, then, a subjective preference for privacy, which previously did not confer standing, now subjects disclosure requirements to close scrutiny. Of course, all disclosure requires some loss of anonymity, and courts can always imagine that someone might, for some reason, prefer to keep their donations undisclosed. If such speculation is enough (and apparently it is), then all disclosure requirements *ipso facto* impose cognizable First Amendment burdens.

Indeed, the Court makes obvious its presumption that all disclosure requirements are burdensome by beginning its analysis of "burden" with an evaluation of means-end fit instead. "[A] reasonable assessment of the burdens imposed by disclosure," the Court explains, "should begin with an understanding of the extent to which the burdens are unnecessary, and that requires narrow tailoring."

I disagree. A reasonable assessment of the burdens imposed by disclosure should begin by determining whether those burdens even exist. If a disclosure requirement imposes no burdens at all, then of course there are no "unnecessary" burdens. Likewise, if a disclosure requirement imposes no burden for the Court to remedy, there is no need for it to be closely scrutinized. By forgoing the requirement that plaintiffs adduce evidence of tangible burdens, such as increased vulnerability to harassment or reprisals, the Court gives itself license to substitute its own policy preferences for those of politically accountable actors.

All this would be less troubling if the Court still required means-end tailoring commensurate to the actual burden imposed. It does not. Instead, it adopts a new rule that every reporting or disclosure requirement be narrowly tailored.

The Court now departs from this nuanced approach in favor of a "one size fits all" test. Regardless of whether there is any risk of public disclosure, and no matter if the burdens on associational rights are slight, heavy, or nonexistent, disclosure regimes must always be narrowly tailored.

Under a First Amendment analysis that is faithful to this Court's precedents, California's Schedule B requirement is constitutional. Begin with the burden it imposes on associational rights. Petitioners have unquestionably provided evidence that their donors face a reasonable probability of threats, harassment, and reprisals if their affiliations are made public. California's Schedule B regulation, however, is a nonpublic reporting requirement, and California has implemented security measures to ensure that Schedule B information remains confidential.

Nor have petitioners shown that their donors, or any organization's donors, will face threats, harassment, or reprisals if their names remain in the hands of a few California state officials. [T]he Court in no way suggests that California officials will use Schedule B information to retaliate against any organization's donors. If California's reporting requirement

Given the modesty of the First Amendment burden, California may justify its Schedule B requirement with a correspondingly modest showing that the means achieve its ends. See California easily meets this standard.

California collects Schedule Bs to facilitate supervision of charities that operate in the State. As the Court acknowledges, this is undoubtedly a significant governmental interest. In the United States, responsibility for overseeing charities has historically been vested in States' attorneys general, who are tasked with prosecuting charitable fraud, self-dealing, and misappropriation of charitable funds. Effective policing is critical to maintaining public confidence in, and continued giving to, charitable organizations. California's interest in exercising such oversight is especially compelling given the size of its charitable sector. Nearly a quarter of the country's charitable assets are held by charities registered in California.

The Schedule B reporting requirement is properly tailored to further California's efforts to police charitable fraud. The IRS Schedule B form requires organizations to disclose the names and addresses of their major donors, the total amount of their contributions, and whether the donation was cash or in-kind.

In sum, the evidence shows that California's confidential reporting requirement imposes trivial burdens on petitioners' associational rights and plays a meaningful role in Section attorneys' ability to identify and prosecute charities engaged in malfeasance. That is more than enough to satisfy the First Amendment here.

How, then, can their facial challenge succeed? Only because the Court has decided, in a radical departure from precedent, that there no longer need be any evidence that a disclosure requirement is likely to cause an objective burden on First Amendment rights before it can be struck down.

Today's decision discards decades of First Amendment jurisprudence recognizing that reporting and disclosure requirements do not directly burden associational rights. There is no other explanation for the Court's conclusion that, first, plaintiffs do not need to show they are actually burdened by a disclosure requirement; second, every disclosure requirement demands narrow tailoring; and third, a facial challenge can succeed in the absence of any evidence a state law burdens the associational rights of a substantial proportion of affected individuals.

Chapter 10

First Amendment: Religion

B. The Free Exercise Clause

3. The Current Test (casebook p. 1681)

As explained in the casebook, the current test for the Free Exercise Clause was announced in *Employment Division v. Smith* (1990): the Free Exercise Clause cannot be used to challenge a neutral law of general applicability. In *Fulton v. City of Philadelphia*, the Court clarified this test and held that a law is not of general applicability if it gives government officials discretion to grant exeptions. Three justices Alito, Thomas, and Gorsuch – urged the overruling of the *Smith* test. Two Others—Barrett and Kavanaugh—questioned it, but did not join in calling for it to be overruled.

FULTON v. CITY OF PHILADELPHIA
141 S. Ct. 1868 (2021)

Chief Justice ROBERTS delivered the opinion of the Court.

Catholic Social Services is a foster care agency in Philadelphia. The City stopped referring children to CSS upon discovering that the agency would not certify same-sex couples to be foster parents due to its religious beliefs about marriage. The City will renew its foster care contract with CSS only if the agency agrees to certify same-sex couples. The question presented is whether the actions of Philadelphia violate the First Amendment.

I

The Catholic Church has served the needy children of Philadelphia for over two centuries. In 1798, a priest in the City organized an association to care for orphans whose parents had died in a yellow fever epidemic. During the 19th century, nuns ran asylums for orphaned and destitute youth. When criticism of asylums mounted in the Progressive Era, see *id.*, at 37–40, the Church established the Catholic Children's Bureau to place children in foster homes. Petitioner CSS continues that mission today.

The Philadelphia foster care system depends on cooperation between the City and private foster agencies like CSS. When children cannot remain in their homes, the City's Department of Human Services assumes custody of them. The Department enters standard annual contracts with private foster agencies to place some of those children with foster families.

The placement process begins with review of prospective foster families. Pennsylvania law gives the authority to certify foster families to state-licensed foster agencies like CSS. Before certifying a family, an agency must conduct a home study during which it considers statutory criteria including the family's "ability to provide care, nurturing and supervision to children," "[e]xisting family relationships," and ability "to work in partnership" with a foster agency. The agency must decide whether to "approve, disapprove or provisionally approve the foster family."

When the Department seeks to place a child with a foster family, it sends its contracted agencies a request, known as a referral. The agencies report whether any of their certified families are available, and the Department places the child with what it regards as the most suitable family. The agency continues to support the family throughout the placement.

The religious views of CSS inform its work in this system. CSS believes that "marriage is a sacred bond between a man and a woman." Because the agency understands the certification of prospective foster families to be an endorsement of their relationships, it will not certify unmarried couples—regardless of their sexual orientation—or same-sex married couples. CSS does not object to certifying gay or lesbian individuals as single foster parents or to placing gay and lesbian children. No same-sex couple has ever sought certification from CSS. If one did, CSS would direct the couple to one of the more than 20 other agencies in the City, all of which currently certify same-sex couples. For over 50 years, CSS successfully contracted with the City to provide foster care services while holding to these beliefs.

But things changed in 2018. After receiving a complaint about a different agency, a newspaper ran a story in which a spokesman for the Archdiocese of Philadelphia stated that CSS would not be able to consider prospective foster parents in same-sex marriages. The City Council called for an investigation, saying that the City had "laws in place to protect its people from discrimination that occurs under the guise of religious freedom." The Philadelphia Commission on Human Relations launched an inquiry. And the Commissioner of the Department of Human Services held a meeting with the leadership of CSS. She remarked that "things have changed since 100 years ago," and "it would be great if we followed the teachings of Pope Francis, the voice of the Catholic Church." Immediately after the meeting, the Department informed CSS that it would no longer refer children to the agency. The City later explained that the refusal of CSS to certify same-sex couples violated a non-discrimination provision in its contract with the City as well as the non-discrimination requirements of the citywide Fair Practices Ordinance. The City stated that it would not enter a full foster care contract with CSS in the future unless the agency agreed to certify same-sex couples.

CSS and three foster parents affiliated with the agency filed suit against the City, the Department, and the Commission. As relevant here, CSS alleged that the referral freeze violated the Free Exercise and Free Speech Clauses of the First Amendment.

II

The Free Exercise Clause of the First Amendment, applicable to the States under the Fourteenth Amendment, provides that "Congress shall make no law . . . prohibiting the free exercise" of religion. As an initial matter, it is plain that the City's actions have burdened CSS's religious exercise by putting it to the choice of curtailing its mission or approving relationships inconsistent with its beliefs. The City disagrees. In its view, certification reflects only that foster parents satisfy the statutory criteria, not that the agency endorses their relationships. But CSS believes that certification is tantamount to endorsement. And "religious beliefs need not be acceptable, logical, consistent, or comprehensible to others in order to merit First Amendment protection." *Thomas v. Review Bd. of Ind. Employment Security Div.* (1981). Our task is to decide whether the burden the City has placed on the religious exercise of CSS is constitutionally permissible.

[Employment Division v.] Smith held that laws incidentally burdening religion are ordinarily not subject to strict scrutiny under the Free Exercise Clause so long as they are neutral and generally applicable. CSS urges us to overrule *Smith*, and the concurrences in the judgment argue in favor of doing so. But we need not revisit that decision here. This case falls outside *Smith* because the City has burdened the religious exercise of CSS through policies that do not meet the requirement of being neutral and generally applicable. See *Church of Lukumi Babalu Aye, Inc. v. Hialeah* (1993).

Government fails to act neutrally when it proceeds in a manner intolerant of religious beliefs or restricts practices because of their religious nature. CSS points to evidence in the record that it believes demonstrates that the

City has transgressed this neutrality standard, but we find it more straight-forward to resolve this case under the rubric of general applicability.

A law is not generally applicable if it "invite[s]" the government to con-sider the particular reasons for a person's conduct by providing " 'a mech-anism for individualized exemptions.'" For example, in *Sherbert v. Verner* (1963), a Seventh-day Adventist was fired because she would not work on Saturdays. Unable to find a job that would allow her to keep the Sabbath as her faith required, she applied for unemployment benefits. The State denied her application under a law prohibiting eligibility to claimants who had "failed, without good cause . . . to accept available suitable work." We held that the denial infringed her free exercise rights and could be justified only by a compelling interest.

Smith later explained that the unemployment benefits law in *Sherbert* was not generally applicable because the "good cause" standard permitted the government to grant exemptions based on the circumstances underly-ing each application. *Smith* went on to hold that "where the State has in place a system of individual exemptions, it may not refuse to extend that system to cases of 'religious hardship' without compelling reason."

A law also lacks general applicability if it prohibits religious conduct while permitting secular conduct that undermines the government's asserted interests in a similar way. In *Church of Lukumi Babalu Aye, Inc. v. Hialeah*, for instance, the City of Hialeah adopted several ordinances prohibiting animal sacrifice, a practice of the Santeria faith. The City claimed that the ordinances were necessary in part to protect public health, which was "threatened by the disposal of animal carcasses in open public places." But the ordinances did not regulate hunters' disposal of their kills or improper garbage disposal by restaurants, both of which posed a similar hazard. The Court concluded that this and other forms of underinclusive-ness meant that the ordinances were not generally applicable.

The City initially argued that CSS's practice violated section 3.21 of its standard foster care contract. We conclude, however, that this provision is not generally applicable as required by *Smith*. The current version of section 3.21 specifies in pertinent part:

> **"Rejection of Referral**. Provider shall not reject a child or family including, but not limited to, . . . prospective foster or adoptive parents, for Services based upon . . . their . . . sexual orientation . . . unless an exception is granted by the Commissioner or the Commissioner's designee, in his/her sole discretion."

Like the good cause provision in *Sherbert*, section 3.21 incorporates a system of individual exemptions, made available in this case at the "sole discretion" of the Commissioner. The City has made clear that the Commissioner "has no intention of granting an exception" to CSS. But the City "may not refuse to extend that [exemption] system to cases of 'religious hardship' without compelling reason."

The City and intervenor-respondents resist this conclusion on several grounds. They first argue that governments should enjoy greater leeway under the Free Exercise Clause when setting rules for contractors than when regulating the general public. The government, they observe, commands heightened powers when managing its internal operations.

These considerations cannot save the City here. As Philadelphia rightly acknowledges, "principles of neutrality and general applicability still constrain the government in its capacity as manager." We have never suggested that the government may discriminate against religion when acting in its managerial role. No matter the level of deference we extend to the City, the inclusion of a formal system of entirely discretionary exceptions in section 3.21 renders the contractual non-discrimination requirement not generally applicable.

Finally, the City and intervenor-respondents contend that the availability of exceptions under section 3.21 is irrelevant because the Commissioner has never granted one. That misapprehends the issue. The creation of a formal mechanism for granting exceptions renders a policy not generally applicable, regardless whether any exceptions have been given, because it "invite[s]" the government to decide which reasons for not complying with the policy are worthy of solicitude, — here, at the Commissioner's "sole discretion."

III

CSS has demonstrated that the City's actions are subject to "the most rigorous of scrutiny" under those precedents. Because the City's actions are therefore examined under the strictest scrutiny regardless of *Smith*, we have no occasion to reconsider that decision here.

A government policy can survive strict scrutiny only if it advances "interests of the highest order" and is narrowly tailored to achieve those interests. Put another way, so long as the government can achieve its interests in a manner that does not burden religion, it must do so.

The City asserts that its non-discrimination policies serve three compelling interests: maximizing the number of foster parents, protecting the City from liability, and ensuring equal treatment of prospective foster parents and foster children. The City states these objectives at a high level of generality, but the First Amendment demands a more precise analysis.

Rather than rely on "broadly formulated interests," courts must "scrutinize[ ] the asserted harm of granting specific exemptions to particular religious claimants." The question, then, is not whether the City has a compelling interest in enforcing its non-discrimination policies generally, but whether it has such an interest in denying an exception to CSS.

Once properly narrowed, the City's asserted interests are insufficient. Maximizing the number of foster families and minimizing liability are important goals, but the City fails to show that granting CSS an exception will put those goals at risk. If anything, including CSS in the program seems likely to increase, not reduce, the number of available foster parents. As for liability, the City offers only speculation that it might be sued over CSS's certification practices. Such speculation is insufficient to satisfy strict scrutiny, particularly because the authority to certify foster families is delegated to agencies by the State, not the City.

That leaves the interest of the City in the equal treatment of prospective foster parents and foster children. We do not doubt that this interest is a weighty one, for "[o]ur society has come to the recognition that gay persons and gay couples cannot be treated as social outcasts or as inferior in dignity and worth." On the facts of this case, however, this interest cannot justify denying CSS an exception for its religious exercise. The creation of a system of exceptions under the contract undermines the City's contention that its non-discrimination policies can brook no departures. The City offers no compelling reason why it has a particular interest in denying an exception to CSS while making them available to others.

As Philadelphia acknowledges, CSS has "long been a point of light in the City's foster-care system." CSS seeks only an accommodation that will allow it to continue serving the children of Philadelphia in a manner consistent with its religious beliefs; it does not seek to impose those beliefs on anyone else. The refusal of Philadelphia to contract with CSS for the provision of foster care services unless it agrees to certify same-sex couples as foster parents cannot survive strict scrutiny, and violates the First Amendment.

Justice BARRETT, with whom Justice KAVANAUGH joins, and with whom Justice BREYER joins as to all but the first paragraph, concurring.

In *Employment Div., Dept. of Human Resources of Ore. v. Smith* (1990), this Court held that a neutral and generally applicable law typically does not violate the Free Exercise Clause—no matter how severely that law burdens religious exercise. Petitioners, their *amici*, scholars, and Justices of this Court have made serious arguments that *Smith* ought to be overruled. While history looms large in this debate, I find the historical record

more silent than supportive on the question whether the founding generation understood the First Amendment to require religious exemptions from
generally applicable laws in at least some circumstances. In my view, the
textual and structural arguments against *Smith* are more compelling. As
a matter of text and structure, it is difficult to see why the Free Exercise
Clause—lone among the First Amendment freedoms—offers nothing
more than protection from discrimination.

Yet what should replace *Smith*? The prevailing assumption seems to be
that strict scrutiny would apply whenever a neutral and generally applicable law burdens religious exercise. But I am skeptical about swapping
Smith's categorical antidiscrimination approach for an equally categorical strict scrutiny regime, particularly when this Court's resolution of
conflicts between generally applicable laws and other First Amendment
rights—like speech and assembly—has been much more nuanced. There
would be a number of issues to work through if *Smith* were overruled.
To name a few: Should entities like Catholic Social Services—which is
an arm of the Catholic Church—be treated differently than individuals?
Should there be a distinction between indirect and direct burdens on religious exercise? What forms of scrutiny should apply? And if the answer is
strict scrutiny, would pre-*Smith* cases rejecting free exercise challenges to
garden-variety laws come out the same way?

We need not wrestle with these questions in this case, though, because
the same standard applies regardless whether *Smith* stays or goes. A longstanding tenet of our free exercise jurisprudence—one that both pre-dates
and survives *Smith*—is that a law burdening religious exercise must
satisfy strict scrutiny if it gives government officials discretion to grant
individualized exemptions. As the Court's opinion today explains, the
government contract at issue provides for individualized exemptions from
its nondiscrimination rule, thus triggering strict scrutiny. And all nine
Justices agree that the City cannot satisfy strict scrutiny. I therefore see no
reason to decide in this case whether *Smith* should be overruled, much less
what should replace it.

Justice ALITO, with whom Justice THOMAS and Justice GORSUCH join,
concurring in the judgment.

This case presents an important constitutional question that urgently
calls out for review: whether this Court's governing interpretation of a
bedrock constitutional right, the right to the free exercise of religion, is
fundamentally wrong and should be corrected.

In *Employment Div., Dept. of Human Resources of Ore. v. Smith* (1990),
the Court abruptly pushed aside nearly 40 years of precedent and held

that the First Amendment's Free Exercise Clause tolerates any rule that categorically prohibits or commands specified conduct so long as it does not target religious practice. Even if a rule serves no important purpose and has a devastating effect on religious freedom, the Constitution, according to *Smith*, provides no protection. This severe holding is ripe for reexamination.

I

There is no question that *Smith*'s interpretation can have startling consequences. Here are a few examples. Suppose that the Volstead Act, which implemented the Prohibition Amendment, had not contained an exception for sacramental wine. The Act would have been consistent with *Smith* even though it would have prevented the celebration of a Catholic Mass anywhere in the United States. Or suppose that a State, following the example of several European countries, made it unlawful to slaughter an animal that had not first been rendered unconscious. That law would be fine under *Smith* even though it would outlaw kosher and halal slaughter. Or suppose that a jurisdiction in this country, following the recommendations of medical associations in Europe, banned the circumcision of infants. A San Francisco ballot initiative in 2010 proposed just that. A categorical ban would be allowed by *Smith* even though it would prohibit an ancient and important Jewish and Muslim practice. Or suppose that this Court or some other court enforced a rigid rule prohibiting attorneys from wearing any form of head covering in court. The rule would satisfy *Smith* even though it would prevent Orthodox Jewish men, Sikh men, and many Muslim women from appearing. Many other examples could be added.

We may hope that legislators and others with rulemaking authority will not go as far as *Smith* allows, but the present case shows that the dangers posed by *Smith* are not hypothetical. The city of Philadelphia (City) has issued an ultimatum to an arm of the Catholic Church: Either engage in conduct that the Church views as contrary to the traditional Christian understanding of marriage or abandon a mission that dates back to the earliest days of the Church—providing for the care of orphaned and abandoned children.

Many people believe they have a religious obligation to assist such children. Jews and Christians regard this as a scriptural command, and it is a mission that the Catholic Church has undertaken since ancient times.

One of the questions that we accepted for review is "[w]hether *Employment Division v. Smith* should be revisited." We should confront that question. Regrettably, the Court declines to do so. Instead, it reverses based on what appears to be a superfluous (and likely to be short-lived) feature of the City's standard annual contract with foster care agencies. *Smith*'s holding about categorical rules does not apply if a rule permits individualized exemptions, and the majority seizes on the presence in the City's standard contract of language giving a City official the power to grant exemptions. The City tells us that it has never granted such an exemption and has no intention of handing one to CSS, but the majority reverses the decision below because the contract supposedly confers that never-used power.

This decision might as well be written on the dissolving paper sold in magic shops. The City has been adamant about pressuring CSS to give in, and if the City wants to get around today's decision, it can simply eliminate the never-used exemption power. If it does that, then, voilà, today's decision will vanish—and the parties will be back where they started. The City will claim that it is protected by *Smith*; CSS will argue that *Smith* should be overruled; the lower courts, bound by *Smith*, will reject that argument; and CSS will file a new petition in this Court challenging *Smith*. What is the point of going around in this circle?

We should reconsider *Smith* without further delay. The correct interpretation of the Free Exercise Clause is a question of great importance, and *Smith*'s interpretation is hard to defend. It can't be squared with the ordinary meaning of the text of the Free Exercise Clause or with the prevalent understanding of the scope of the free-exercise right at the time of the First Amendment's adoption. It swept aside decades of established precedent, and it has not aged well. Its interpretation has been undermined by subsequent scholarship on the original meaning of the Free Exercise Clause. Contrary to what many initially expected, *Smith* has not provided a clear-cut rule that is easy to apply, and experience has disproved the *Smith* majority's fear that retention of the Court's prior free-exercise jurisprudence would lead to "anarchy." It is high time for us to take a fresh look at what the Free Exercise Clause demands.

[II]

That project must begin with the constitutional text. *Smith*, however, paid shockingly little attention to the text of the Free Exercise Clause. Instead of examining what readers would have understood its words to mean when adopted, the opinion merely asked whether it was "permissible" to read the text to have the meaning that the majority fav This strange treatment of the constitutional text cannot be justified—and is especially surprising since it clashes so sharply with the way in which *Smith*'s author, Justice

Scalia, generally treated the text of the Constitution (and, indeed, with his entire theory of legal interpretation).

[W]e should begin by considering the "normal and ordinary" meaning of the text of the Free Exercise Clause: "Congress shall make no law . . . prohibiting the free exercise [of religion]." Most of these terms and phrases — "Congress," "shall make," "no law," and "religion" — do not require discussion for present purposes, and we can therefore focus on what remains: the term "prohibiting" and the phrase "the free exercise of religion."

Those words had essentially the same meaning in 1791 as they do today. "To prohibit" meant either "[t]o forbid" or "to hinder." 2 S. Johnson, A Dictionary of the English Language (1755) (Johnson (1755)). The term "exercise" had both a broad primary definition ("[p]ractice" or "outward performance") and a narrower secondary one (an "[a]ct of divine worship whether publick or private"). If we put these definitions together, the ordinary meaning of "prohibiting the free exercise of religion" was (and still is) forbidding or hindering unrestrained religious practices or worship. That straightforward understanding is a far cry from the interpretation adopted in *Smith*. It certainly does not suggest a distinction between laws that are generally applicable and laws that are targeted.

As interpreted in *Smith*, the Clause is essentially an anti-discrimination provision: It means that the Federal Government and the States cannot restrict conduct that constitutes a religious practice for some people unless it imposes the same restriction on everyone else who engages in the same conduct. *Smith* made no real attempt to square that equal-treatment interpretation with the ordinary meaning of the Free Exercise Clause's language, and it is hard to see how that could be done.

The key point for present purposes is that the text of the Free Exercise Clause gives a specific group of people (those who wish to engage in the "exercise of religion") the right to do so without hindrance. The language of the Clause does not tie this right to the treatment of persons not in this group.

The oddity of *Smith*'s interpretation can be illustrated by considering what the same sort of interpretation would mean if applied to other provisions of the Bill of Rights. Take the Sixth Amendment, which gives a specified group of people (the "accused" in criminal cases) a particular right (the right to the "Assistance of Counsel for [their] defence"). Suppose that Congress or a state legislature adopted a law banning counsel in *all litigation*, civil and criminal. Would anyone doubt that this law would violate the Sixth Amendment rights of criminal defendants?

Or consider the Seventh Amendment, which gives a specified group of people (parties in most civil "Suits at common law") "the right of trial by jury." Would there be any question that a law abolishing juries in *all* civil cases would violate the rights of parties in cases that fall within the Seventh Amendment's scope?

It is not necessary to belabor this point further. What all these examples show is that *Smith*'s interpretation conflicts with the ordinary meaning of the First Amendment's terms.

[III]

While we presume that the words of the Constitution carry their ordinary and normal meaning, we cannot disregard the possibility that some of the terms in the Free Exercise Clause had a special meaning that was well understood at the time. What was the free-exercise right understood to mean when the Bill of Rights was ratified? And in particular, was it clearly understood that the right simply required equal treatment for religious and secular conduct? [Justice Alito reviewed the history of religious freedom as of the time the First Amendment was ratified and concluded that it included protection from neutral laws of general applicability.]

Smith was wrongly decided. As long as it remains on the books, it threatens a fundamental freedom. And while precedent should not lightly be cast aside, the Court's error in *Smith* should now be corrected.

[IV]

If *Smith* is overruled, what legal standard should be applied in this case? The answer that comes most readily to mind is the standard that *Smith* replaced: A law that imposes a substantial burden on religious exercise can be sustained only if it is narrowly tailored to serve a compelling government interest.

Whether this test should be rephrased or supplemented with specific rules is a question that need not be resolved here because Philadelphia's ouster of CSS from foster care work simply does not further any interest that can properly be protected in this case. As noted, CSS's policy has not hindered any same-sex couples from becoming foster parents, and there is no threat that it will do so in the future.

CSS's policy has only one effect: It expresses the idea that same-sex couples should not be foster parents because only a man and a woman should marry. Many people today find this idea not only objectionable but hurtful. Nevertheless, protecting against this form of harm is not an interest that can justify the abridgment of First Amendment rights.

We have covered this ground repeatedly in free speech cases. In an open, pluralistic, self-governing society, the expression of an idea cannot be suppressed simply because some find it offensive, insulting, or even wounding. The same fundamental principle applies to religious practices that give offense. The preservation of religious freedom depends on that principle. Many core religious beliefs are perceived as hateful by members of other religions or nonbelievers. Proclaiming that there is only one God is offensive to polytheists, and saying that there are many gods is anathema to Jews, Christians, and Muslims. Declaring that Jesus was the Son of God is offensive to Judaism and Islam, and stating that Jesus was not the Son of God is insulting to Christian belief. Expressing a belief in God is nonsense to atheists, but denying the existence of God or proclaiming that religion has been a plague is infuriating to those for whom religion is all-important.

Suppressing speech — or religious practice — simply because it expresses an idea that some find hurtful is a zero-sum game. While CSS's ideas about marriage are likely to be objectionable to same-sex couples, lumping those who hold traditional beliefs about marriage together with racial bigots is insulting to those who retain such beliefs.

For all these reasons, I would overrule *Smith* and reverse the decision below. Philadelphia's exclusion of CSS from foster care work violates the Free Exercise Clause, and CSS is therefore entitled to an injunction barring Philadelphia from taking such action.

After receiving more than 2,500 pages of briefing and after more than a half-year of post-argument cogitation, the Court has emitted a wisp of a decision that leaves religious liberty in a confused and vulnerable state. Those who count on this Court to stand up for the First Amendment have every right to be disappointed — as am I.

4.   Supreme Court Decisions Since Employment Division v. Smith

b.   *Interfering with Choices as to Clergy* (casebook p. 1700)

In *Hosanna-Tabor Evangelical Lutheran Church and School v. EEOC* (2012) (casebook p. 1700), the Court held that it violated free exercise of religion to hold a religious school liable for the choices it makes as to teachers who are commissioned as ministers. In *Our Lady of Guadalupe*

School v. Morrissey-Berru, the Court went further and said that religious schools cannot be liable under employment discrimination law as to the choices it makes for its teachers.

OUR LADY OF GUADALUPE SCHOOL v. MORRISSEY-BERRU
140 S. Ct. 2049 (2020)

Justice ALITO delivered the opinion of the Court.

These cases require us to decide whether the First Amendment permits courts to intervene in employment disputes involving teachers at religious schools who are entrusted with the responsibility of instructing their students in the faith. The First Amendment protects the right of religious institutions "to decide for themselves, free from state interference, matters of church government as well as those of faith and doctrine."

Applying this principle, we held in *Hosanna-Tabor Evangelical Lutheran Church and School v. EEOC* (2012), that the First Amendment barred a court from entertaining an employment discrimination claim brought by an elementary school teacher, Cheryl Perich, against the religious school where she taught. Our decision built on a line of lower court cases adopting what was dubbed the "ministerial exception" to laws governing the employment relationship between a religious institution and certain key employees. We did not announce "a rigid formula" for determining whether an employee falls within this exception, but we identified circumstances that we found relevant in that case, including Perich's title as a "Minister of Religion, Commissioned," her educational training, and her responsibility to teach religion and participate with students in religious activities.

In the cases now before us, we consider employment discrimination claims brought by two elementary school teachers at Catholic schools whose teaching responsibilities are similar to Perich's. Although these teachers were not given the title of "minister" and have less religious training than Perich, we hold that their cases fall within the same rule that dictated our decision in *Hosanna-Tabor*. The religious education and formation of students is the very reason for the existence of most private religious schools, and therefore the selection and supervision of the teachers upon whom the schools rely to do this work lie at the core of their mission. Judicial review of the way in which religious schools discharge those responsibilities would undermine the independence of religious institutions in a way that the First Amendment does not tolerate.

I

The first of the two cases we now decide involves Agnes Morrissey-Berru, who was employed at Our Lady of Guadalupe School (OLG), a Roman Catholic primary school in the Archdiocese of Los Angeles. For many years, Morrissey-Berru was employed at OLG as a lay fifth or sixth grade teacher. Like most elementary school teachers, she taught all subjects, and since OLG is a Catholic school, the curriculum included religion. As a result, she was her students' religion teacher.

Morrissey-Berru earned a B.A. in English Language Arts, with a minor in secondary education, and she holds a California teaching credential. While on the faculty at OLG, she took religious education courses at the school's request, and was expected to attend faculty prayer services.

Each year, Morrissey-Berru and OLG entered into an employment agreement that set out the school's "mission" and Morrissey-Berru's duties. The agreement stated that the school's mission was "to develop and promote a Catholic School Faith Community," and it informed Morrissey-Berru that "[a]ll [her] duties and responsibilities as a Teache[r were to] be performed within this overriding commitment." The agreement explained that the school's hiring and retention decisions would be guided by its Catholic mission, and the agreement made clear that teachers were expected to "model and promote" Catholic "faith and morals." Under the agreement, Morrissey-Berru was required to participate in "[s]chool liturgical activities, as requested," and the agreement specified that she could be terminated "for 'cause'" for failing to carry out these duties or for "conduct that brings discredit upon the School or the Roman Catholic Church." The agreement required compliance with the faculty handbook, which sets out similar expectations. The pastor of the parish, a Catholic priest, had to approve Morrissey-Berru's hiring each year.

Like all teachers in the Archdiocese of Los Angeles, Morrissey-Berru was "considered a catechist," *i.e.*, "a teacher of religio[n]." Catechists are "responsible for the faith formation of the students in their charge each day." Morrissey-Berru provided religious instruction every day using a textbook designed for use in teaching religion to young Catholic students. Under the prescribed curriculum, she was expected to teach students, among other things, "to learn and express belief that Jesus is the son of God and the Word made flesh"; to "identify the ways" the church "carries on the mission of Jesus"; to "locate, read and understand stories from the Bible"; to "know the names, meanings, signs and symbols of each of the seven sacraments"; and to be able to "explain the communion of saints."

She tested her students on that curriculum in a yearly exam. *Id.*, at 87a. She also directed and produced an annual passion play.

Morrissey-Berru prepared her students for participation in the Mass and for communion and confession. She also occasionally selected and prepared students to read at Mass. And she was expected to take her students to Mass once a week and on certain feast days, and to take them to confession and to pray the Stations of the Cross. Each year, she brought them to the Catholic Cathedral in Los Angeles, where they participated as altar servers.

Morrissey-Berru also prayed with her students. Her class began or ended every day with a Hail Mary. She led the students in prayer at other times, such as when a family member was ill. And she taught them to recite the Apostle's Creed and the Nicene Creed, as well as prayers for specific purposes, such as in connection with the sacrament of confession. The school reviewed Morrissey-Berru's performance under religious standards. The "Classroom Observation Report" evaluated whether Catholic values were "infused through all subject areas" and whether there were religious signs and displays in the classroom.

In 2014, OLG asked Morrissey-Berru to move from a full-time to a part-time position, and the next year, the school declined to renew her contract. She filed a claim with the Equal Employment Opportunity Commission (EEOC), received a right-to-sue letter, and then filed suit under the Age Discrimination in Employment Act of 1967, claiming that the school had demoted her and had failed to renew her contract so that it could replace her with a younger teacher. The school maintains that it based its decisions on classroom performance — specifically, Morrissey-Berru's difficulty in administering a new reading and writing program, which had been introduced by the school's new principal as part of an effort to maintain accreditation and improve the school's academic program.

The second case concerns the late Kristen Biel, who worked for about a year and a half as a lay teacher at St. James School, another Catholic primary school in Los Angeles. For part of one academic year, Biel served as a long-term substitute teacher for a first grade class, and for one full year she was a full-time fifth grade teacher. Like Morrissey-Berru, she taught all subjects, including religion.

During her time at St. James, she attended a religious conference that imparted "[d]ifferent techniques on teaching and incorporating God" into the classroom. Biel was Catholic. Biel's employment agreement was in pertinent part nearly identical to Morrissey-Berru's.

St. James declined to renew Biel's contract after one full year at the school. She filed charges with the EEOC, and after receiving a right-to-sue

letter, brought this suit, alleging that she was discharged because she
had requested a leave of absence to obtain treatment for breast cancer. The school maintains that the decision was based on poor performance — namely, a failure to observe the planned curriculum and keep an
orderly classroom.

II

The First Amendment provides that "Congress shall make no law respecting an establishment of religion, or prohibiting the free exercise thereof."
Among other things, the Religion Clauses protect the right of churches and
other religious institutions to decide matters "of faith and doctrine" without government intrusion. State interference in that sphere would obvi-
ously violate the free exercise of religion, and any attempt by government
to dictate or even to influence such matters would constitute one of the
central attributes of an establishment of religion. The First Amendment
outlaws such intrusion.

The independence of religious institutions in matters of "faith and doctrine" is closely linked to independence in what we have termed "'matters
of church government.'" This does not mean that religious institutions
enjoy a general immunity from secular laws, but it does protect their
autonomy with respect to internal management decisions that are essential
to the institution's central mission. And a component of this autonomy is
the selection of the individuals who play certain key roles.

The "ministerial exception" was based on this insight. Under this rule,
courts are bound to stay out of employment disputes involving those holding certain important positions with churches and other religious institutions. The rule appears to have acquired the label "ministerial exception"
because the individuals involved in pioneering cases were described as
"ministers." But it is instructive to consider why a church's independence
on matters "of faith and doctrine" requires the authority to select, supervise, and if necessary, remove a minister without interference by secular
authorities. Without that power, a wayward minister's preaching, teaching, and counseling could contradict the church's tenets and lead the congregation away from the faith. The ministerial exception was recognized
to preserve a church's independent authority in such matters.

When the so-called ministerial exception finally reached this Court in
Hosanna-Tabor, we unanimously recognized that the Religion Clauses
foreclose certain employment discrimination claims brought against religious organizations. The constitutional foundation for our holding was the
general principle of church autonomy to which we have already referred:

independence in matters of faith and doctrine and in closely linked matters of internal government. Because Cheryl Perich, the teacher in *Hosanna-Tabor*, had a title that included the word "minister," we naturally concentrated on historical events involving clerical offices, but the abuses we identified were not limited to the control of appointments.

In determining whether a particular position falls within the *Hosanna-Tabor* exception, a variety of factors may be important. The circumstances that informed our decision in *Hosanna-Tabor* were relevant because of their relationship to Perich's "role in conveying the Church's message and carrying out its mission," but the other noted circumstances also shed light on that connection. In a denomination that uses the term "minister," conferring that title naturally suggests that the recipient has been given an important position of trust. In Perich's case, the title that she was awarded and used demanded satisfaction of significant academic requirements and was conferred only after a formal approval process, and those circumstances also evidenced the importance attached to her role. But our recognition of the significance of those factors in Perich's case did not mean that they must be met—or even that they are necessarily important—in all other cases.

Take the question of the title "minister." Simply giving an employee the title of "minister" is not enough to justify the exception. And by the same token, since many religious traditions do not use the title "minister," it cannot be a necessary requirement. Requiring the use of the title would constitute impermissible discrimination, and this problem cannot be solved simply by including positions that are thought to be the counterparts of a "minister," such as priests, nuns, rabbis, and imams. Nuns are not the same as Protestant ministers. A brief submitted by Jewish organizations makes the point that "Judaism has many 'ministers,'" that is, "the term 'minister' encompasses an extensive breadth of religious functionaries in Judaism." For Muslims, "an inquiry into whether imams or other leaders bear a title equivalent to 'minister' can present a troubling choice between denying a central pillar of Islam—*i.e.*, the equality of all believers—and risking loss of ministerial exception protections."

If titles were all-important, courts would have to decide which titles count and which do not, and it is hard to see how that could be done without looking behind the titles to what the positions actually entail. Moreover, attaching too much significance to titles would risk privileging religious traditions with formal organizational structures over those that are less formal.

For related reasons, the academic requirements of a position may show that the church in question regards the position as having an important responsibility in elucidating or teaching the tenets of the faith. Presumably the purpose of such requirements is to make sure that the person holding the position understands the faith and can explain it accurately and effectively. But insisting in every case on rigid academic requirements could have a distorting effect. This is certainly true with respect to teachers. Teaching children in an elementary school does not demand the same formal religious education as teaching theology to divinity students. Elementary school teachers often teach secular subjects in which they have little if any special training. In addition, religious traditions may differ in the degree of formal religious training thought to be needed in order to teach. In short, these circumstances, while instructive in *Hosanna-Tabor*, are not inflexible requirements and may have far less significance in some cases.

What matters, at bottom, is what an employee does. And implicit in our decision in *Hosanna-Tabor* was a recognition that educating young people in their faith, inculcating its teachings, and training them to live their faith are responsibilities that lie at the very core of the mission of a private religious school. As we put it, Perich had been entrusted with the responsibility of "transmitting the Lutheran faith to the next generation."

When we apply this understanding of the Religion Clauses to the cases now before us, it is apparent that Morrissey-Berru and Biel qualify for the exemption we recognized in *Hosanna-Tabor*. There is abundant record evidence that they both performed vital religious duties. Educating and forming students in the Catholic faith lay at the core of the mission of the schools where they taught, and their employment agreements and faculty handbooks specified in no uncertain terms that they were expected to help the schools carry out this mission and that their work would be evaluated to ensure that they were fulfilling that responsibility. As elementary school teachers responsible for providing instruction in all subjects, including religion, they were the members of the school staff who were entrusted most directly with the responsibility of educating their students in the faith. And not only were they obligated to provide instruction about the Catholic faith, but they were also expected to guide their students, by word and deed, toward the goal of living their lives in accordance with the faith. They prayed with their students, attended Mass with the students, and prepared the children for their participation in other religious activities. Their positions did not have all the attributes of Perich's. Their titles did not include the term "minister," and they had less formal religious training, but their core responsibilities as teachers of religion were essentially the same. And both their schools expressly saw them as playing a vital part in carrying out the mission of the church, and the schools' definition and explanation of their roles is important. In a country with the religious diversity of the United States, judges cannot be expected to have a complete understanding and appreciation of the role played by every person who performs a particular role in every religious tradition. A religious institution's explanation of the role of such employees in the life of the religion in question is important.

Respondents argue that the *Hosanna-Tabor* exception is not workable unless it is given a rigid structure, but we declined to adopt a "rigid formula" in *Hosanna-Tabor*, and the lower courts have been applying the exception for many years without such a formula. Here, as in *Hosanna-Tabor*, it is sufficient to decide the cases before us. When a school with a religious mission entrusts a teacher with the responsibility of educating and forming students in the faith, judicial intervention into disputes between the school and the teacher threatens the school's independence in a way that the First Amendment does not allow.

Justice THOMAS, with whom Justice GORSUCH joins, concurring.

I agree with the Court that Morrissey-Berru's and Biel's positions fall within the "ministerial exception," because, as Catholic school teachers, they are charged with "carry[ing] out [the religious] mission" of the parish schools. The Court properly notes that "judges have no warrant to second-guess [the schools'] judgment" of who should hold such a position "or to impose their own credentialing requirements." Accordingly, I join the Court's opinion in full. I write separately, however, to reiterate my view that the Religion Clauses require civil courts to defer to religious organizations' good-faith claims that a certain employee's position is "ministerial."

This deference is necessary because, as the Court rightly observes, judges lack the requisite "understanding and appreciation of the role played by every person who performs a particular role in every religious tradition." What qualifies as "ministerial" is an inherently theological question, and thus one that cannot be resolved by civil courts through legal analysis. Contrary to the dissent's claim, judges do not shirk their judicial duty or provide a mere "rubber stamp" when they defer to a religious organization's sincere beliefs. Rather, they heed the First Amendment, which "commands civil courts to decide [legal] disputes without resolving underlying controversies over religious doctrine."

Justice SOTOMAYOR, with whom Justice GINSBURG joins, dissenting.

Two employers fired their employees allegedly because one had breast cancer and the other was elderly. Purporting to rely on this Court's decision in *Hosanna-Tabor Evangelical Lutheran Church and School v. EEOC* (2012), the majority shields those employers from disability and age-discrimination claims. In the Court's view, because the employees taught short religion modules at Catholic elementary schools, they were "ministers" of the Catholic faith and thus could be fired for any reason, whether religious or nonreligious, benign or bigoted, without legal recourse. The Court reaches this result even though the teachers taught primarily secular subjects, lacked substantial religious titles and training, and were not even required to be Catholic. In foreclosing the teachers' claims, the Court skews the facts, ignores the applicable standard of review, and collapses *Hosanna-Tabor* 's careful analysis into a single consideration: whether a church thinks its employees play an important religious role. Because that simplistic approach has no basis in law and strips thousands of schoolteachers of their legal protections, I respectfully dissent.

I

Our pluralistic society requires religious entities to abide by generally applicable laws. *E.g.*, *Employment Div., Dept. of Human Resources of Ore. v. Smith* (1990). Consistent with the First Amendment (and over sincerely held religious objections), the Government may compel religious institutions to pay Social Security taxes for their employees, deny nonprofit status to entities that discriminate because of race, require applicants for certain public benefits to register with Social Security numbers, enforce child-labor protections, and impose minimum-wage laws.

Congress, however, has crafted exceptions to protect religious autonomy. Some antidiscrimination laws, like the Americans with Disabilities Act, permit a religious institution to consider religion when making employment decisions. Under that Act, a religious organization may also "require that all applicants and employees conform" to the entity's "religious tenets." Title VII further permits a school to prefer "hir[ing] and employ[ing]" people "of a particular religion" if its curriculum "propagat[es]" that religion. These statutory exceptions protect a religious entity's ability to make employment decisions—hiring or firing—for religious reasons.

The "ministerial exception," by contrast, is a judge-made doctrine. This Court first recognized it eight years ago in *Hosanna-Tabor*, concluding that the First Amendment categorically bars certain antidiscrimination suits by religious leaders against their religious employers. When it applies, the exception is extraordinarily potent: It gives an employer free rein to discriminate because of race, sex, pregnancy, age, disability, or other traits protected by law when selecting or firing their "ministers," even when the discrimination is wholly unrelated to the employer's religious beliefs or practices. That is, an employer need not cite or possess a religious reason at all; the ministerial exception even condones animus.

This analysis is context-specific. It necessarily turns on, among other things, the structure of the religious organization at issue. Put another way (and as the Court repeats throughout today's opinion), *Hosanna-Tabor* declined to adopt a "rigid formula for deciding when an employee qualifies as a minister." Rather, *Hosanna-Tabor* focused on four "circumstances" to determine whether a fourth-grade teacher, Cheryl Perich, was employed at a Lutheran school as a "minister": (1) "the formal title given [her] by the Church," (2) "the substance reflected in that title," (3) "her own use of that title," and (4) "the important religious functions she performed for the Church." Confirming that the ministerial exception applies to a circumscribed sub-category of faith leaders, the Court analyzed those four "factors," to situate Perich as a minister within the Lutheran Church's structure. Those considerations showed that Perich had a unique leadership role within her church.

II

Until today, no court had held that the ministerial exception applies with disputed facts like these and lay teachers like respondents, let alone at the summary-judgment stage.

Only by rewriting *Hosanna-Tabor* does the Court reach a different result. oday's Court yields to the concurrence's view with identical rhetoric. "What matters," the Court echoes, "is what an employee does."

But this vague statement is no easier to comprehend today than it was when the Court declined to adopt it eight years ago. It certainly does not sound like a legal framework. Rather, the Court insists that a "religious institution's explanation of the role of [its] employees in the life of the religion in question is important." But because the Court's new standard prizes a functional importance that it appears to deem churches in the best position to explain, one cannot help but conclude that the Court has just traded legal analysis for a rubber stamp.

Indeed, the Court reasons that "judges cannot be expected to have a complete understanding and appreciation" of the law and facts in ministerial-exception cases, and all but abandons judicial review. Although today's decision is limited to certain "teachers of religion," its reasoning risks rendering almost every Catholic parishioner and parent in the Archdiocese of Los Angeles a Catholic minister. That is, the Court's apparent deference here threatens to make nearly anyone whom the schools might hire "ministers" unprotected from discrimination in the hiring process. That cannot be right. Although certain religious functions may be important to a church, a person's performance of some of those functions does not mechanically trigger a categorical exemption from generally applicable antidiscrimination laws.

Today's decision thus invites the "potential for abuse" against which circuit courts have long warned. Nevermind that the Court renders almost all of the Court's opinion in *Hosanna-Tabor* irrelevant. It risks allowing employers to decide for themselves whether discrimination is actionable. Indeed, today's decision reframes the ministerial exception as broadly as it can, without regard to the statutory exceptions tailored to protect religious practice. As a result, the Court absolves religious institutions of any animus completely irrelevant to their religious beliefs or practices and all but forbids courts to inquire further about whether the employee is in fact a leader of the religion. Nothing in *Hosanna-Tabor* (or at least its majority opinion) condones such judicial abdication.

III

The Court's conclusion portends grave consequences. As the Government (arguing for Biel at the time) explained to the Ninth Circuit, "thousands of Catholic teachers" may lose employment-law protections because of today's outcome. Other sources tally over a hundred thousand secular teachers whose rights are at risk. And that says nothing of the rights of countless coaches, camp counselors, nurses, social-service workers, in-house lawyers, media-relations personnel, and many others who work for religious institutions. All these employees could be subject to discrimination for reasons completely irrelevant to their employers' religious tenets.

In expanding the ministerial exception far beyond its historic narrowness, the Court overrides Congress' carefully tailored exceptions for religious employers. Little if nothing appears left of the statutory exemptions after today's constitutional broadside. So long as the employer determines that an employee's "duties" are "vital" to "carrying out the mission of the church," then today's laissez-faire analysis appears to allow that employer to make employment decisions because of a person's skin color, age, disability, sex, or any other protected trait for reasons having nothing to do with religion.

This sweeping result is profoundly unfair. The Court is not only wrong on the facts, but its error also risks upending antidiscrimination protections for many employees of religious entities. Recently, this Court has lamented a perceived "discrimination against religion." Yet here it swings the pendulum in the extreme opposite direction, permitting religious entities to discriminate widely and with impunity for reasons wholly divorced from religious beliefs. The inherent injustice in the Court's conclusion will be impossible to ignore for long, particularly in a pluralistic society like ours. One must hope that a decision deft enough to remold *Hosanna-Tabor* to fit the result reached today reflects the Court's capacity to cabin the consequences tomorrow.

c. Denial of Funding to Religious Entities (casebook p. 1700)

In *Trinity Lutheran Church of Columbia, Inc. v. Comer* (casebook p. 1703), the Court held that it violated the Free Exercise Clause for a state to deny religious schools funding for playgrounds that was provided to secular schools. In *Espinoza v. Montana Department of Revenue*, the Court went even further and held that it violated free exercise when the Montana Supreme Court struck down a Montana tax credit program as violating the state constitution because it would have provided benefits to those sending their children to religious schools. The 5-4 decision implies that the government *must* provide benefits to religious schools when it gives them to secular schools, unless doing so would violate the Establishment Clause of the First Amendment.

ESPINOZA v. MONTANA DEPARTMENT OF REVENUE
140 S. Ct. 2246 (2020)

Chief Justice ROBERTS delivered the opinion of the Court.

The Montana Legislature established a program to provide tuition assistance to parents who send their children to private schools. The program grants a tax credit to anyone who donates to certain organizations that in turn award scholarships to selected students attending such schools. When petitioners sought to use the scholarships at a religious school, the Montana Supreme Court struck down the program. The Court relied on the "no-aid" provision of the State Constitution, which prohibits any aid to a school controlled by a "church, sect, or denomination." The question presented is whether the Free Exercise Clause of the United States Constitution barred that application of the no-aid provision.

I

In 2015, the Montana Legislature sought "to provide parental and student choice in education" by enacting a scholarship program for students attending private schools. The program grants a tax credit of up to $150 to any taxpayer who donates to a participating "student scholarship organization." The scholarship organizations then use the donations to award scholarships to children for tuition at a private school.

A family whose child is awarded a scholarship under the program may use it at any "qualified education provider"—that is, any private school that meets certain accreditation, testing, and safety requirements. Virtually every private school in Montana qualifies. Upon receiving a scholarship, the family designates its school of choice, and the scholarship organization sends the scholarship funds directly to the school. Neither the scholarship organization nor its donors can restrict awards to particular types of schools.

The Montana Legislature allotted $3 million annually to fund the tax credits, beginning in 2016. If the annual allotment is exhausted, it increases by 10% the following year. The program is slated to expire in 2023.

The Montana Legislature also directed that the program be administered in accordance with Article X, section 6, of the Montana Constitution, which contains a "no-aid" provision barring government aid to sectarian schools.

This suit was brought by three mothers whose children attend Stillwater Christian School in northwestern Montana. Stillwater is a private Christian school that meets the statutory criteria for "qualified education providers." It serves students in prekindergarten through 12th grade, and petitioners chose the school in large part because it "teaches the same Christian values that [they] teach at home." The child of one petitioner has already received scholarships from Big Sky, and the other petitioners' children are eligible for scholarships and planned to apply. While in effect, however, Rule 1 blocked petitioners from using scholarship funds for tuition at Stillwater. To overcome that obstacle, petitioners sued the Department of Revenue in Montana state court.

In December 2018, the Montana Supreme Court [held] that the program aided religious schools in violation of the no-aid provision of the Montana Constitution. In the Court's view, the no-aid provision "broadly and strictly prohibits aid to sectarian schools." The scholarship program provided such aid by using tax credits to "subsidize tuition payments" at private schools that are "religiously affiliated" or "controlled in whole or in part by churches." In that way, the scholarship program flouted the

State Constitution's "guarantee to all Montanans that their government will not use state funds to aid religious schools."

The Montana Supreme Court went on to hold that the violation of the no-aid provision required invalidating the entire scholarship program. The Court explained that the program provided "no mechanism" for preventing aid from flowing to religious schools, and therefore the scholarship program could not "under *any* circumstance" be construed as consistent with the no-aid provision. As a result, the tax credit is no longer available to support scholarships at either religious or secular private schools.

II

A

The Religion Clauses of the First Amendment provide that "Congress shall make no law respecting an establishment of religion, or prohibiting the free exercise thereof." Here, the parties do not dispute that the scholarship program is permissible under the Establishment Clause. Nor could they. We have repeatedly held that the Establishment Clause is not offended when religious observers and organizations benefit from neutral government programs. Any Establishment Clause objection to the scholarship program here is particularly unavailing because the government support makes its way to religious schools only as a result of Montanans independently choosing to spend their scholarships at such schools. The Montana Supreme Court, however, held as a matter of state law that even such indirect government support qualified as "aid" prohibited under the Montana Constitution.

The question for this Court is whether the Free Exercise Clause precluded the Montana Supreme Court from applying Montana's no-aid provision to bar religious schools from the scholarship program.

The Free Exercise Clause, which applies to the States under the Fourteenth Amendment, "protects religious observers against unequal treatment" and against "laws that impose special disabilities on the basis of religious status." Those "basic principle[s]" have long guided this Court.

Most recently, *Trinity Lutheran* [*of Columbia, Missouri v. Comer* (2017)], distilled these and other decisions to the same effect into the "unremarkable" conclusion that disqualifying otherwise eligible recipients from a public benefit "solely because of their religious character" imposes "a penalty on the free exercise of religion that triggers the most exacting scrutiny."

Here too Montana's no-aid provision bars religious schools from public benefits solely because of the religious character of the schools. The provision also bars parents who wish to send their children to a religious school from those same benefits, again solely because of the religious character of the school. This is apparent from the plain text. The provision bars aid to any school "controlled in whole or in part by any church, sect, or denomination." The provision's title — "Aid prohibited to sectarian schools" — confirms that the provision singles out schools based on their religious character. And the Montana Supreme Court explained that the provision forbids aid to any school that is "sectarian," "religiously affiliated," or "controlled in whole or in part by churches." The provision plainly excludes schools from government aid solely because of religious status.

To be eligible for government aid under the Montana Constitution, a school must divorce itself from any religious control or affiliation. Placing such a condition on benefits or privileges "inevitably deters or discourages the exercise of First Amendment rights." The Free Exercise Clause protects against even "indirect coercion," and a State "punishe[s] the free exercise of religion" by disqualifying the religious from government aid as Montana did here. Such status-based discrimination is subject to "the strictest scrutiny." It is enough in this case to conclude that strict scrutiny applies under *Trinity Lutheran* because Montana's no-aid provision discriminates based on religious status.

B

Seeking to avoid *Trinity Lutheran*, the Department contends that this case is instead governed by *Locke v. Davey* (2004). *Locke* also involved a scholarship program. The State of Washington provided scholarships paid out of the State's general fund to help students pursuing postsecondary education. The scholarships could be used at accredited religious and nonreligious schools alike, but Washington prohibited students from using the scholarships to pursue devotional theology degrees, which prepared students for a calling as clergy. This prohibition prevented Davey from using his scholarship to obtain a degree that would have enabled him to become a pastor. We held that Washington had not violated the Free Exercise Clause.

Locke differs from this case in two critical ways. First, *Locke* explained that Washington had "merely chosen not to fund a distinct category of instruction": the "essentially religious endeavor" of training a minister "to lead a congregation." Thus, Davey "was denied a scholarship because of what he proposed *to do* — use the funds to prepare for the ministry." Apart from that narrow restriction, Washington's program allowed scholarships to be used at "pervasively religious schools" that incorporated religious instruction throughout their classes. By contrast, Montana's Constitution does not zero in on any particular "essentially religious" course of instruction at a religious school. Rather, as we have explained, the no-aid provision bars all aid to a religious school "simply because of what it is," putting the school to a choice between being religious or receiving government benefits. At the same time, the provision puts families to a choice between sending their children to a religious school or receiving such benefits.

Second, *Locke* invoked a "historic and substantial" state interest in not funding the training of clergy, explaining that "opposition to . . . funding 'to support church leaders' lay at the historic core of the Religion Clauses." As evidence of that tradition, the Court in *Locke* emphasized that the propriety of state-supported clergy was a central subject of founding-era debates, and that most state constitutions from that era prohibited the expenditure of tax dollars to support the clergy.

But no comparable "historic and substantial" tradition supports Montana's decision to disqualify religious schools from government aid. In the founding era and the early 19th century, governments provided financial support to private schools, including denominational ones. "Far from prohibiting such support, the early state constitutions and statutes actively encouraged this policy." Local governments provided grants to private schools, including religious ones, for the education of the poor. Even States with bans on government-supported clergy, such as New Jersey, Pennsylvania, and Georgia, provided various forms of aid to religious schools. Early federal aid (often land grants) went to religious schools. Congress provided support to denominational schools in the District of Columbia until 1848, and Congress paid churches to run schools for American Indians through the end of the 19th century. After the Civil War, Congress spent large sums on education for emancipated freedmen, often by supporting denominational schools in the South through the Freedmen's Bureau.

The Department argues that a tradition *against* state support for religious schools arose in the second half of the 19th century, as more than 30 States — including Montana — adopted no-aid provisions. Such a development, of course, cannot by itself establish an early American tradition. In addition, many of the no-aid provisions belong to a more checkered tradition shared with the Blaine Amendment of the 1870s. That proposal — which Congress nearly passed — would have added to the Federal Constitution a provision similar to the state no-aid provisions, prohibiting

States from aiding "sectarian" schools. "[I]t was an open secret that 'sectarian' was code for 'Catholic.'" The Blaine Amendment was "born of bigotry" and "arose at a time of pervasive hostility to the Catholic Church and to Catholics in general"; many of its state counterparts have a similarly "shameful pedigree." The no-aid provisions of the 19th century hardly evince a tradition that should inform our understanding of the Free Exercise Clause.

C

Two dissenters would chart new courses. Justice Sotomayor would grant the government "some room" to "single . . . out" religious entities "for exclusion," based on what she views as "the interests embodied in the Religion Clauses." Justice Breyer, building on his solo opinion in *Trinity Lutheran*, would adopt a "flexible, context-specific approach" that "may well vary" from case to case. As best we can tell, courts applying this approach would contemplate the particular benefit and restriction at issue and discern their relationship to religion and society, taking into account "context and consequences measured in light of [the] purposes" of the Religion Clauses. What is clear is that Justice Breyer would afford much freer rein to judges than our current regime, arguing that "there is 'no test-related substitute for the exercise of legal judgment.'"

The simplest response is that these dissents follow from prior separate writings, not from the Court's decision in *Trinity Lutheran* or the decades of precedent on which it relied. These precedents have "repeatedly confirmed" the straightforward rule that we apply today: When otherwise eligible recipients are disqualified from a public benefit "solely because of their religious character," we must apply strict scrutiny. This rule against express religious discrimination is no "doctrinal innovation." Far from it. As *Trinity Lutheran* explained, the rule is "unremarkable in light of our prior decisions."

For innovation, one must look to the dissents. Their "room[y]" or "flexible" approaches to discrimination against religious organizations and observers would mark a significant departure from our free exercise precedents. The protections of the Free Exercise Clause do not depend on a "judgment-by-judgment analysis" regarding whether discrimination against religious adherents would somehow serve ill-defined interests.

D

Because the Montana Supreme Court applied the no-aid provision to discriminate against schools and parents based on the religious character of the school, the "strictest scrutiny" is required. That "stringent standard" is not "watered down but really means what it says," To satisfy it, government action "must advance 'interests of the highest order' and must be narrowly tailored in pursuit of those interests."

The Montana Supreme Court asserted that the no-aid provision serves Montana's interest in separating church and State "more fiercely" than the Federal Constitution. But "that interest cannot qualify as compelling" in the face of the infringement of free exercise here. A State's interest "in achieving greater separation of church and State than is already ensured under the Establishment Clause . . . is limited by the Free Exercise Clause."

The Department also suggests that the no-aid provision advances Montana's interests in public education. According to the Department, the no-aid provision safeguards the public school system by ensuring that government support is not diverted to private schools. But, under that framing, the no-aid provision is fatally underinclusive because its "proffered objectives are not pursued with respect to analogous nonreligious conduct." On the Department's view, an interest in public education is undermined by diverting government support to *any* private school, yet the no-aid provision bars aid only to *religious* ones. A law does not advance "an interest of the highest order when it leaves appreciable damage to that supposedly vital interest unprohibited."

State need not subsidize private education. But once a State decides to do so, it cannot disqualify some private schools solely because they are religious.

III

The Department argues that, at the end of the day, there is no free exercise violation here because the Montana Supreme Court ultimately eliminated the scholarship program altogether. According to the Department, now that there is no program, religious schools and adherents cannot complain that they are excluded from any generally available benefit. Two dissenters agree.

The descriptions are not accurate. The Montana Legislature created the scholarship program; the Legislature never chose to end it, for policy or other reasons. The program was eliminated by a court, and not based on some innocuous principle of state law. Rather, the Montana Supreme Court invalidated the program pursuant to a state law provision that expressly discriminates on the basis of religious status. The Court applied that provision to hold that religious schools were barred from participating in the program. Then, seeing no other "mechanism" to make absolutely sure that religious schools received no aid, the court chose to invalidate the entire program. The final step in this line of reasoning eliminated the program, to the detriment of religious and non-religious schools alike. But the Court's error of federal law occurred at the beginning. When the Court was called upon to apply a state law no-aid provision to exclude religious schools from the program, it was obligated by the Federal Constitution to reject the invitation. Had the Court recognized that this was, indeed, "one of those cases" in which application of the no-aid provision "would violate the Free Exercise Clause," the Court would not have proceeded to find a violation of that provision. And, in the absence of such a state law violation, the Court would have had no basis for terminating the program. Because the elimination of the program flowed directly from the Montana Supreme Court's failure to follow the dictates of federal law, it cannot be defended as a neutral policy decision, or as resting on adequate and independent state law grounds.

Justice THOMAS, with whom Justice GORSUCH joins, concurring.

The Court correctly concludes that Montana's no-aid provision expressly discriminates against religion in violation of the Free Exercise Clause. And it properly provides relief to Montana religious schools and the petitioners who wish to use Montana's scholarship program to send their children to such schools. I write separately to explain how this Court's interpretation of the Establishment Clause continues to hamper free exercise rights. Until we correct course on that interpretation, individuals will continue to face needless obstacles in their attempts to vindicate their religious freedom.

I

This case involves the Free Exercise Clause, not the Establishment Clause. But as in all cases involving a state actor, the modern understanding of the Establishment Clause is a "brooding omnipresence," ever ready to be used to justify the government's infringement on religious freedom. Under the modern, but erroneous, view of the Establishment Clause, the government must treat all religions equally and treat religion equally to nonreligion. As this Court stated in its first case applying the Establishment Clause to the States, the government cannot "pass laws which aid one religion, aid all religions, or prefer one religion over another." This "equality principle," the theory goes, prohibits the government from expressing any preference for religion — or even permitting any signs of religion in the governmental realm. Thus, when a plaintiff brings a free exercise claim, the government may defend its law, as Montana did here, on the ground that the law's restrictions are *required* to prevent it from "establishing" religion.

This understanding of the Establishment Clause is unmoored from the original meaning of the First Amendment. As I have explained in previous cases, at the founding, the Clause served only to "protec[t] States, and by extension their citizens, from the imposition of an established religion by the *Federal* Government." Under this view, the Clause resists incorporation against the States.

II

The Court's current understanding of the Establishment Clause actually thwarts, rather than promotes, equal treatment of religion. Under a proper understanding of the Establishment Clause, robust and lively debate about the role of religion in government is permitted, even encouraged, at the state and local level. The Court's distorted view of the Establishment Clause, however, removes the entire subject of religion from the realm of permissible governmental activity, instead mandating strict separation.

This interpretation of the Establishment Clause operates as a type of content-based restriction on the government. The Court has interpreted the Free Speech Clause to prohibit content-based restrictions because they "value some forms of speech over others," thus tending to "tilt public debate in a preferred direction". The content-based restriction imposed by this Court's Establishment Clause jurisprudence operates no differently. It communicates a message that religion is dangerous and in need of policing, which in turn has the effect of tilting society in favor of devaluing religion.

Historical evidence suggests that many advocates for this separationist view were originally motivated by hostility toward certain disfavored religions. And this Court's adoption of a separationist interpretation has itself sometimes bordered on religious hostility.

As I have recently explained, this Court has an unfortunate tendency to prefer certain constitutional rights over others. The Free Exercise Clause, although enshrined explicitly in the Constitution, rests on the lowest rung of the Court's ladder of rights, and precariously so at that. Returning the Establishment Clause to its proper scope will not completely rectify the Court's disparate treatment of constitutional rights, but it will go a long way toward allowing free exercise of religion to flourish as the Framers intended. I look forward to the day when the Court takes up this task in earnest.

Justice ALITO, concurring.

I join the opinion of the Court in full. The basis of the decision below was a Montana constitutional provision that, according to the Montana Supreme Court, forbids parents from participating in a publicly funded scholarship program simply because they send their children to religious schools. Regardless of the motivation for this provision or its predecessor, its application here violates the Free Exercise Clause.

Nevertheless, the provision's origin is relevant under the decision we issued earlier this Term in *Ramos v. Louisiana* (2020). The question in *Ramos* was whether Louisiana and Oregon laws allowing non-unanimous jury verdicts in criminal trials violated the Sixth Amendment. The Court held that they did, emphasizing that the States originally adopted those laws for racially discriminatory reasons. The role of the Ku Klux Klan was highlighted.

I argued in dissent that this original motivation, though deplorable, had no bearing on the laws' constitutionality because such laws can be adopted for non-discriminatory reasons, and "both States readopted their rules under different circumstances in later years." But I lost, and *Ramos* is now precedent. If the original motivation for the laws mattered there, it certainly matters here.

The origin of Montana's "no-aid" provision, is emphasized in petitioners' brief and in the briefs of numerous supporting *amici*. These briefs, most of which were not filed by organizations affiliated with the Catholic Church, point out that Montana's provision was modeled on the failed Blaine Amendment to the Constitution of the United States. Named after House Speaker James Blaine, the Congressman who introduced it in 1875, the amendment was prompted by virulent prejudice against immigrants, particularly Catholic immigrants. In effect, the amendment would have "bar[red] any aid" to Catholic and other "sectarian" schools. As noted in a publication from the United States Commission on Civil Rights, a prominent supporter of this ban was the Ku Klux Klan.

The Blaine Amendment was narrowly defeated, passing in the House but falling just short of the two-thirds majority needed in the Senate to refer the amendment to the States. fterwards, most States adopted provisions like Montana's to achieve the same objective at the state level, often as a condition of entering the Union. Thirty-eight States still have these "little Blaine Amendments" today.

The resulting wave of state laws withholding public aid from "sectarian" schools cannot be understood outside this context. Indeed, there are stronger reasons for considering original motivations here than in *Ramos* because, unlike the neutral language of Louisiana's and Oregon's nonunanimity rules, Montana's no-aid provision retains the bigoted code language used throughout state Blaine Amendments.

The tax-credit program adopted by the Montana Legislature but overturned by the Montana Supreme Court provided necessary aid for parents who pay taxes to support the public schools but who disagree with the teaching there. The program helped parents of modest means do what more affluent parents can do: send their children to a school of their choice. The argument that the decision below treats everyone the same is reminiscent of Anatole France's sardonic remark that "'[t]he law, in its majestic equality, forbids the rich as well as the poor to sleep under bridges, to beg in the streets, and to steal bread.'"

Justice GINSBURG, with whom Justice KAGAN joins, dissenting.

The Montana Legislature enacted a scholarship program to fund tuition for students attending private secondary schools. In the decision below, the Montana Supreme Court struck down that program in its entirety. The program, the state court ruled, conflicted with the State Constitution's no-aid provision, which forbids government appropriations to religious schools. Parents who sought to use the program's scholarships to fund their children's religious education challenged the state court's ruling. They argue in this Court that the Montana court's application of the no-aid provision violated the Free Exercise Clause of the Federal Constitution. Importantly, the parents, petitioners here, disclaim any challenge to the no-aid provision on its face. They instead argue — and this Court's majority accepts — that the provision is unconstitutional as applied because the First Amendment prohibits discrimination in tuition-benefit programs based on a school's religious status. Because the state court's decision does not so discriminate, I would reject petitioners' free exercise claim.

Petitioners argue that the Montana Supreme Court's decision fails when measured against *Trinity Lutheran*. I do not see how. Past decisions in this area have entailed *differential treatment* occasioning a burden on a plaintiff's religious exercise. This case is missing that essential component. Recall that the Montana court remedied the state constitutional violation by striking the scholarship program in its entirety. Under that decree, secular and sectarian schools alike are ineligible for benefits, so the decision cannot be said to entail differential treatment based on petitioners' religion. Put somewhat differently, petitioners argue that the Free Exercise Clause requires a State to treat institutions and people neutrally when doling out a benefit — and neutrally is how Montana treats them in the wake of the state court's decision.

Accordingly, the Montana Supreme Court's decision does not place a burden on petitioners' religious exercise. Petitioners may still send their children to a religious school. And the Montana Supreme Court's decision does not pressure them to do otherwise. Unlike the law in *Trinity Lutheran*, the decision below puts petitioners to no "choice": Neither giving up their faith, nor declining to send their children to sectarian schools, would affect their entitlement to scholarship funding. There simply are no scholarship funds to be had.

Nearing the end of its opinion, the Court writes: "A State need not subsidize private education. But once a State decides to do so, it cannot disqualify some private schools solely because they are religious." Because Montana's Supreme Court did not make such a decision—its judgment put all private school parents in the same boat—this Court had no occasion to address the matter. On that sole ground, and reaching no other issue, I dissent from the Court's judgment.

Justice BREYER, with whom Justice KAGAN joins as to Part I, dissenting.

The majority holds that the Free Exercise Clause forbids a State to draw any distinction between secular and religious uses of government aid to private schools that is not required by the Establishment Clause. The majority's approach and its conclusion in this case, I fear, risk the kind of entanglement and conflict that the Religion Clauses are intended to prevent. I consequently dissent.

I

We all recognize that the First Amendment prohibits discrimination against religion. At the same time, our history and federal constitutional precedent reflect a deep concern that state funding for religious teaching, by stirring fears of preference or in other ways, might fuel religious discord and division and thereby threaten religious freedom itself. The Court has consequently made it clear that the Constitution commits the government to a "position of neutrality" in respect to religion.

The inherent tension between the Establishment and Free Exercise Clauses means, however, that the "course of constitutional neutrality in this area cannot be an absolutely straight line." Indeed, "rigidity could well defeat the basic purpose of these provisions, which is to insure that no religion be sponsored or favored, none commanded, and none inhibited."

That, in significant part, is why the Court has held that "there is room for play in the joints" between the Clauses' express prohibitions that is "productive of a benevolent neutrality," allowing "religious exercise to exist without sponsorship and without interference." It has held that there "are some state actions permitted by the Establishment Clause but not required by the Free Exercise Clause." And that "play in the joints" should, in my view, play a determinative role here.

It may be that, under our precedents, the Establishment Clause does not *forbid* Montana to subsidize the education of petitioners' children. But, the question here is whether the Free Exercise Clause *requires* it to do so. The majority believes that the answer to that question is "yes." It writes that "once a State decides" to support nonpublic education, "it cannot disqualify some private schools solely because they are religious." I shall explain why I disagree.

The majority finds that the school-playground case, *Trinity Lutheran*, and not the religious-studies case, *Locke*, controls here. I disagree. In my view, the program at issue here is strikingly similar to the program we upheld in *Locke* and importantly different from the program we found unconstitutional in *Trinity Lutheran*. Like the State of Washington in *Locke*, Montana has chosen not to fund (at a distance) "an essentially religious endeavor"—an education designed to " 'induce religious faith.'" That kind of program simply cannot be likened to Missouri's decision to exclude a church school from applying for a grant to resurface its playground.

The Court in *Locke* recognized that the study of devotional theology can be "akin to a religious calling as well as an academic pursuit." Indeed, "the shaping, through primary education, of the next generation's minds and spirits" may be as critical as training for the ministry, which itself, after all, is but one of the activities necessary to help assure a religion's survival. That is why many faith leaders emphasize the central role of schools in their religious missions. It is why at least some teachers at religious schools see their work as a form of ministry. And petitioners have testified that it is a "major reason" why they chose religious schools for their children.

Nothing in the Constitution discourages this type of instruction. To the contrary, the Free Exercise Clause draws upon a history that places great value upon the freedom of parents to teach their children the tenets of their faith.

What, then, is the difference between *Locke* and the present case? And what is it that leads the majority to conclude that funding the study of religion is more like paying to fix up a playground (*Trinity Lutheran*) than paying for a degree in theology (*Locke*)? The majority's principal argument appears to be that, as in *Trinity Lutheran*, Montana has excluded religious schools from its program "solely because of the religious character of the schools." The majority seeks to contrast this *status*-based discrimination with the program at issue in *Locke*, which it says denied scholarships to divinity students based on the religious *use* to which they put the funds — *i.e.*, training for the ministry, as opposed to secular professions.

It is true that Montana's no-aid provision broadly bars state aid to schools based on their religious affiliation. But this case does not involve a claim of status-based discrimination. The schools do not apply or compete for scholarships, they are not parties to this litigation, and no one here purports to represent their interests. We are instead faced with a suit by *parents* who assert that *their* free exercise rights are violated by the application of the no-aid provision to prevent them from *using* taxpayer-supported scholarships to attend the schools of their choosing. In other words, the problem, as in *Locke*, is what petitioners "'propos[e] *to do*—use the funds to'" obtain a religious education.

Even if the schools' status were relevant, I do not see what bearing the majority's distinction could have here. There is no dispute that religious schools seek generally to inspire religious faith and values in their students. How else could petitioners claim that barring them from using state aid to attend these schools violates their free exercise rights? Thus, the question in this case—unlike in *Trinity Lutheran*—boils down to what the schools would *do* with state support. And the upshot is that here, as in *Locke*, we confront a State's decision not to fund the inculcation of religious truths.

If, for 250 years, we have drawn a line at forcing taxpayers to pay the salaries of those who teach their faith from the pulpit, I do not see how we can today require Montana to adopt a different view respecting those who teach it in the classroom.

II

In reaching its conclusion that the Free Exercise Clause requires Montana to allow petitioners to use taxpayer-supported scholarships to pay for their children's religious education, the majority makes several doctrinal innovations that, in my view, are misguided and threaten adverse consequences. I disagree, then, with what I see as the majority's doctrinal omission, its misplaced application of a legal presumption, and its suggestion that this presumption is appropriate in many, if not all, cases involving government benefits. As I see the matter, our differences run deeper than a simple disagreement about the application of prior case law.

For one thing, government benefits come in many shapes and sizes. The appropriate way to approach a State's benefit-related decision may well vary depending upon the relation between the Religion Clauses and the specific benefit and restriction at issue. For another, disagreements that concern religion and its relation to a particular benefit may prove unusually difficult to resolve. They may involve small but important details of a particular benefit program. Does one detail affect one religion negatively and another positively? What about a religion that objects to the particular way in which the government seeks to enforce mandatory (say, qualification-related) provisions of a particular benefit program? Or the religious group that for religious reasons cannot accept government support? And what happens when qualification requirements mean that government money flows to one religion rather than another? Courts are ill equipped to deal with such conflicts. Yet, in a Nation with scores of different religions, many such disagreements are possible. And I have only scratched the surface.

The majority claims that giving weight to these considerations would be a departure from our precedent and give courts too much discretion to interpret the Religion Clauses. But we have long understood that the "application" of the First Amendment's mandate of neutrality "requires interpretation of a delicate sort." "Each value judgment under the Religion Clauses," we have explained, must "turn on whether particular acts in question are intended to establish or interfere with religious beliefs and practices or have the effect of doing so."

Nor does the majority's approach avoid judicial entanglement in difficult and sensitive questions. To the contrary, as I have just explained, it burdens courts with the still more complex task of untangling disputes between religious organizations and state governments, instead of giving deference to state legislators' choices to avoid such issues altogether. At the same time, it puts States in a legislative dilemma, caught between the demands of the Free Exercise and Establishment Clauses, without "breathing room" to help ameliorate the problem.

And what are the limits of the Court's holding? The majority asserts that States "need not subsidize private education." But it does not explain why that is so. If making scholarships available to only secular nonpublic schools exerts "coercive" pressure on parents whose faith impels them to enroll their children in religious schools, then how is a State's decision to fund only secular *public* schools any less coercive? Under the majority's reasoning, the parents in both cases are put to a choice between their beliefs and a taxpayer-sponsored education.

Accepting the majority's distinction between public and nonpublic schools does little to address the uncertainty that its holding introduces. What about charter schools? States vary widely in how they permit charter schools to be structured, funded, and controlled. How would the majority's rule distinguish between those States in which support for charter schools is akin to public school funding and those in which it triggers a constitutional obligation to fund private religious schools? The majority's rule provides no guidance, even as it sharply limits the ability of courts and legislatures to balance the potentially competing interests that underlie the Free Exercise and Antiestablishment Clauses.

Justice SOTOMAYOR, dissenting.

The majority holds that a Montana scholarship program unlawfully discriminated against religious schools by excluding them from a tax benefit. The threshold problem, however, is that such tax benefits no longer exist for anyone in the State. The Montana Supreme Court invalidated the program on state-law grounds, thereby foreclosing the as-applied challenge petitioners raise here. Indeed, nothing required the state court to uphold the program or the state legislature to maintain it. The Court nevertheless reframes the case and appears to ask whether a longstanding Montana constitutional provision is facially invalid under the Free Exercise Clause, even though petitioners disavowed bringing such a claim. But by resolving a constitutional question not presented, the Court fails to heed Article III principles older than the Religion Clause it expounds.

Not only is the Court wrong to decide this case at all, it decides it wrongly. In *Trinity Lutheran Church of Columbia, Inc. v. Comer* (2017), this Court held, "for the first time, that the Constitution requires the government to provide public funds directly to a church." Here, the Court invokes that precedent to require a State to subsidize religious schools if it enacts an education tax credit. Because this decision further "slights both our precedents and our history" and "weakens this country's longstanding commitment to a separation of church and state beneficial to both," I respectfully dissent.

I

The Montana Supreme Court invalidated a state tax-credit program because it was inconsistent with the Montana Constitution's "no-aid provision," which forbids government appropriations for sectarian purposes, including funding religious schools. In so doing, the court expressly declined to resolve federal constitutional issues. The court also remedied the only potential harm of discriminatory treatment by striking down the program altogether. After the state court's decision, neither secular nor sectarian schools receive the program's tax benefits.

Petitioners' free exercise claim is not cognizable. The Free Exercise Clause, the Court has said, protects against "indirect coercion or penalties on the free exercise of religion." Accordingly, this Court's cases have required not only differential treatment, but also a resulting burden on religious exercise.

Neither differential treatment nor coercion exists here because the Montana Supreme Court invalidated the tax-credit program entirely. Because no secondary school (secular or sectarian) is eligible for benefits, the state court's ruling neither treats petitioners differently based on religion nor burdens their religious exercise. Petitioners remain free to send their children to the religious school of their choosing and to exercise their faith.

To be sure, petitioners may want to apply for scholarships and would prefer that Montana subsidize their children's religious education. But this Court had never before held unconstitutional government action that merely failed to benefit religious exercise.

II

The Court's analysis of Montana's defunct tax program reprises the error in *Trinity Lutheran*. Contra the Court's current approach, our free exercise precedents had long granted the government "some room to recognize the unique status of religious entities and to single them out on that basis for exclusion from otherwise generally applicable laws."

Until *Trinity Lutheran*, the right to exercise one's religion did not include a right to have the State pay for that religious practice. That is because a contrary rule risks reading the Establishment Clause out of the Constitution. Although the Establishment Clause "permit[s] some government funding of secular functions performed by sectarian organizations," the Court's decisions "provide[d] no precedent for the use of public funds to finance religious activities." After all, the government must avoid "an unlawful fostering of religion."

Here, a State may refuse to extend certain aid programs to religious entities when doing so avoids "historic and substantial" antiestablishment concerns. Properly understood, this case is no different from *Locke* because petitioners seek to procure what the plaintiffs in *Locke* could not: taxpayer funds to support religious schooling.

The Court further suggests that by abstaining from funding religious activity, the State is "'suppress[ing]" and "penaliz[ing]" religious activity. But a State's decision not to fund religious activity does not "disfavor religion; rather, it represents a valid choice to remain secular in the face of serious establishment and free exercise concerns." That is, a "legislature's decision not to subsidize the exercise of a fundamental right does not infringe the right." Finally, it is no answer to say that this case involves "discrimination." A "decision to treat entities differently based on distinctions that the Religion Clauses make relevant does not amount to discrimination."

Today's ruling is perverse. Without any need or power to do so, the Court appears to require a State to reinstate a tax-credit program that the Constitution did not demand in the first place. We once recognized that "[w]hile the Free Exercise Clause clearly prohibits the use of state action to deny the rights of free exercise to anyone, it has never meant that a majority could use the machinery of the State to practice its beliefs." Today's Court, by contrast, rejects the Religion Clauses' balanced values in favor of a new theory of free exercise, and it does so only by setting aside well-established judicial constraints.

d. *Exceptions for Religion to Closure Orders to Stop the Spread of COVID-19 (new)*

Many governors imposed closure orders to stop the spread of COVID-19 that included restrictions on religious worship. The matters came to the Supreme Court as requests for injunctions. The first two cases came in May and July 2020 and the Court denied the requests for injunctions. *South Bay Pentecostal Church v. Newsom,* 140 S.Ct. 1613 (2020); *Calvary Chapel Dayton Valley v. Sisolak*, 140 S.Ct. 2803 (2020). Both were 5-4 rulings, with the majority comprised on Chief Justice Roberts and Justices Ginsburg, Breyer, Sotomayor, and Kagan.

But in two later rulings, in November 2020 and April 2021, the Court, 5-4 ruled in favor of religious challenges to the closure orders. In both, the majority was the four dissenters from the earlier cases, Justices Thomas, Alito, Gorsuch, and Kavanaugh, together with Justice Barrett. The opinions in the cases are important in the Court stressing how religion must be treated relative to secular activities under the Free Exercise Clause.

ROMAN CATHOLIC DIOCESE OF BROOKLYN v. CUOMO
141 S. Ct. 63 (2020)

PER CURIAM.

This emergency application and another, Agudath Israel of America, et al. v. Cuomo, present the same issue, and this opinion addresses both cases. Both applications seek relief from an Executive Order issued by the Governor of New York that imposes very severe restrictions on attendance at religious services in areas classified as "red" or "orange" zones. In red zones, no more than 10 persons may attend each religious service, and in orange zones, attendance is capped at 25. The two applications, one filed by the Roman Catholic Diocese of Brooklyn and the other by Agudath Israel of America and affiliated entities, contend that these restrictions violate the Free Exercise Clause of the First Amendment, and they ask us to enjoin enforcement of the restrictions while they pursue appellate review.

Citing a variety of remarks made by the Governor, Agudath Israel argues that the Governor specifically targeted the Orthodox Jewish community and gerrymandered the boundaries of red and orange zones to ensure that heavily Orthodox areas were included. Both the Diocese and Agudath Israel maintain that the regulations treat houses of worship much more harshly than comparable secular facilities. And they tell us without contradiction that they have complied with all public health guidance, have implemented additional precautionary measures, and have operated at 25% or 33% capacity for months without a single outbreak.

The applicants have clearly established their entitlement to relief pending appellate review. They have shown that their First Amendment claims are likely to prevail, that denying them relief would lead to irreparable injury, and that granting relief would not harm the public interest. Because of the need to issue an order promptly, we provide only a brief summary of the reasons why immediate relief is essential.

Likelihood of success on the merits. The applicants have made a strong showing that the challenged restrictions violate "the minimum requirement of neutrality" to religion. As noted by the dissent in the court below, statements made in connection with the challenged rules can be viewed as targeting the " 'ultra-Orthodox [Jewish] community.'" But even if we put those comments aside, the regulations cannot be viewed as neutral because they single out houses of worship for especially harsh treatment.

In a red zone, while a synagogue or church may not admit more than 10 persons, businesses categorized as "essential" may admit as many people as they wish. And the list of "essential" businesses includes things such as acupuncture facilities, camp grounds, garages, as well as many whose services are not limited to those that can be regarded as essential, such as all plants manufacturing chemicals and microelectronics and all transportation facilities. The disparate treatment is even more striking in an orange zone. While attendance at houses of worship is limited to 25 persons, even non-essential businesses may decide for themselves how many persons to admit.

These categorizations lead to troubling results. At the hearing in the District Court, a health department official testified about a large store in Brooklyn that could "literally have hundreds of people shopping there on any given day." Yet a nearby church or synagogue would be prohibited from allowing more than 10 or 25 people inside for a worship service. And the Governor has stated that factories and schools have contributed to the spread of COVID–19, but they are treated less harshly than the Diocese's churches and Agudath Israel's synagogues, which have admirable safety records.

Because the challenged restrictions are not "neutral" and of "general applicability," they must satisfy "strict scrutiny," and this means that they must be "narrowly tailored" to serve a "compelling" state interest. Stemming the spread of COVID–19 is unquestionably a compelling interest, but it is hard to see how the challenged regulations can be regarded as "narrowly tailored." They are far more restrictive than any COVID–related regulations that have previously come before the Court, much tighter than those adopted by many other jurisdictions hard-hit by the pandemic, and far more severe than has been shown to be required to prevent the spread of the virus at the applicants' services. The District Court noted that "there ha[d] not been any COVID–19 outbreak in any of the Diocese's churches since they reopened," and it praised the Diocese's record in combatting the spread of the disease. It found that the Diocese had been constantly "ahead of the curve, enforcing stricter safety protocols than the State required." Similarly, Agudath Israel notes that "[t]he Governor does not dispute that [it] ha[s] rigorously implemented and adhered to all health protocols and that there has been no outbreak of COVID–19 in [its] congregations."

Not only is there no evidence that the applicants have contributed to the spread of COVID–19 but there are many other less restrictive rules that could be adopted to minimize the risk to those attending religious services. Among other things, the maximum attendance at a religious service could be tied to the size of the church or synagogue. Almost all of the 26 Diocese churches immediately affected by the Executive Order can seat at least 500 people, about 14 can accommodate at least 700, and 2 can seat over 1,000. Similarly, Agudath Israel of Kew Garden Hills can seat up to 400. It is hard to believe that admitting more than 10 people to a 1,000–seat church or 400–seat synagogue would create a more serious health risk than the many other activities that the State allows.

Irreparable harm. There can be no question that the challenged restrictions, if enforced, will cause irreparable harm. "The loss of First Amendment freedoms, for even minimal periods of time, unquestionably constitutes irreparable injury." If only 10 people are admitted to each service, the great majority of those who wish to attend Mass on Sunday or services in a synagogue on Shabbat will be barred. And while those who are shut out may in some instances be able to watch services on television, such remote viewing is not the same as personal attendance. Catholics who watch a Mass at home cannot receive communion, and there are important religious traditions in the Orthodox Jewish faith that require personal attendance.

Public interest. Finally, it has not been shown that granting the applications will harm the public. As noted, the State has not claimed that attendance at the applicants' services has resulted in the spread of the disease. And the State has not shown that public health would be imperiled if less restrictive measures were imposed.

Members of this Court are not public health experts, and we should respect the judgment of those with special expertise and responsibility in this area. But even in a pandemic, the Constitution cannot be put away and forgotten. The restrictions at issue here, by effectively barring many from attending religious services, strike at the very heart of the First Amendment's guarantee of religious liberty. Before allowing this to occur, we have a duty to conduct a serious examination of the need for such a drastic measure.

For these reasons, we hold that enforcement of the Governor's severe restrictions on the applicants' religious services must be enjoined.

Justice GORSUCH concurring.

Government is not free to disregard the First Amendment in times of crisis. At a minimum, that Amendment prohibits government officials from treating religious exercises worse than comparable secular activities, unless they are pursuing a compelling interest and using the least restrictive means available. Yet recently, during the COVID pandemic, certain States seem to have ignored these long-settled principles.

Today's case supplies just the latest example. New York's Governor has asserted the power to assign different color codes to different parts of the State and govern each by executive decree. In "red zones," houses of worship are all but closed—limited to a maximum of 10 people. In the Orthodox Jewish community that limit might operate to exclude all women, considering 10 men are necessary to establish a *minyan*, or a quorum. In "orange zones," it's not much different. Churches and synagogues are limited to a maximum of 25 people. These restrictions apply even to the largest cathedrals and synagogues, which ordinarily hold hundreds. And the restrictions apply no matter the precautions taken, including social distancing, wearing masks, leaving doors and windows open, forgoing singing, and disinfecting spaces between services.

At the same time, the Governor has chosen to impose *no* capacity restrictions on certain businesses he considers "essential." And it turns out the businesses the Governor considers essential include hardware stores, acupuncturists, and liquor stores. Bicycle repair shops, certain signage companies, accountants, lawyers, and insurance agents are all essential too. So, at least according to the Governor, it may be unsafe to go to church, but it is always fine to pick up another bottle of wine, shop for a new bike, or spend the afternoon exploring your distal points and meridians. Who knew public health would so perfectly align with secular convenience?

As almost everyone on the Court today recognizes, squaring the Governor's edicts with our traditional First Amendment rules is no easy task. People may gather inside for extended periods in bus stations and airports, in laundromats and banks, in hardware stores and liquor shops. No apparent reason exists why people may not gather, subject to identical restrictions, in churches or synagogues, especially when religious institutions have made plain that they stand ready, able, and willing to follow all the safety precautions required of "essential" businesses and perhaps more besides. The only explanation for treating religious places differently seems to be a judgment that what happens there just isn't as "essential" as what happens in secular spaces. Indeed, the Governor is remarkably frank about this: In his judgment laundry and liquor, travel and tools, are all "essential" while traditional religious exercises are not. *That* is exactly the kind of discrimination the First Amendment forbids.

It is time—past time—to make plain that, while the pandemic poses many grave challenges, there is no world in which the Constitution tolerates color-coded executive edicts that reopen liquor stores and bike shops but shutter churches, synagogues, and mosques.

Chief Justice ROBERTS dissenting.

I would not grant injunctive relief under the present circumstances. There is simply no need to do so. After the Diocese and Agudath Israel filed their applications, the Governor revised the designations of the affected areas.

None of the houses of worship identified in the applications is now subject to any fixed numerical restrictions. At these locations, the applicants can hold services with up to 50% of capacity, which is at least as favorable as the relief they currently seek.

Numerical capacity limits of 10 and 25 people, depending on the applicable zone, do seem unduly restrictive. And it may well be that such restrictions violate the Free Exercise Clause. It is not necessary, however, for us to rule on that serious and difficult question at this time. The Governor might reinstate the restrictions. But he also might not. And it is a significant matter to override determinations made by public health officials concerning what is necessary for public safety in the midst of a deadly pandemic. If the Governor does reinstate the numerical restrictions the applicants can return to this Court, and we could act quickly on their renewed applications. As things now stand, however, the applicants have not demonstrated their entitlement to "the extraordinary remedy of injunction." An order telling the Governor not to do what he's not doing fails to meet that stringent standard.

Justice BREYER, with whom Justice SOTOMAYOR and Justice KAGAN join, dissenting.

New York regulations designed to fight the rapidly spreading — and, in many cases, fatal — COVID–19 virus permit the Governor to identify hot spots where infection rates have spiked and to designate those hot spots as red zones, the immediately surrounding areas as orange zones, and the outlying areas as yellow zones. The regulations impose restrictions within these zones (with the strictest restrictions in the red zones and the least strict restrictions in the yellow zones) to curb transmission of the virus and prevent spread into nearby areas.

For one thing, there is no need now to issue any such injunction. Those parts of Brooklyn and Queens where the Diocese's churches and the two applicant synagogues are located are no longer within red or orange zones. Thus, none of the applicants are now subject to the fixed-capacity restrictions that they challenge in their applications. The specific applicant houses of worship are now in yellow zones where they can hold services up to 50% of maximum capacity. And the applicants do not challenge any yellow zone restrictions, as the conditions in the yellow zone provide them with more than the relief they asked for in their applications.

Instead, the applicants point out that the State might reimpose the red or orange zone restrictions in the future. But, were that to occur, they could refile their applications here, by letter brief if necessary. And this Court, if necessary, could then decide the matter in a day or two, perhaps even in a few hours. Why should this Court act now without argument or full consideration in the ordinary course (and prior to the Court of Appeals' consideration of the matter) when there is no legal or practical need for it to do so? I have found no convincing answer to that question.

COVID–19 has infected more than 12 million Americans and caused more than 250,000 deaths nationwide. At least 26,000 of those deaths have occurred in the State of New York, with 16,000 in New York City alone. And the number of COVID–19 cases is many times the number of deaths. The Nation is now experiencing a second surge of infections. In New York, for example, the 7-day average of new confirmed cases per day has risen from around 700 at the end of the summer to over 4,800 last week. Nationwide, the number of new confirmed cases per day is now higher than it has ever been.

At the same time, members of the scientific and medical communities tell us that the virus is transmitted from person to person through respiratory droplets produced when a person or group of people talk, sing, cough, or breathe near each other. Thus, according to experts, the risk of transmission is higher when people are in close contact with one another for prolonged periods of time, particularly indoors or in other enclosed spaces. The nature of the epidemic, the spikes, the uncertainties, and the need for quick action, taken together, mean that the State has countervailing arguments based upon health, safety, and administrative considerations that must be balanced against the applicants' First Amendment challenges.

We have previously recognized that courts must grant elected officials "broad" discretion when they "undertake to act in areas fraught with medical and scientific uncertainties." That is because the "Constitution principally entrusts the safety and the health of the people to the politically accountable officials of the States." The elected branches of state and national governments can marshal scientific expertise and craft specific policies in response to "changing facts on the ground." And they can do so more quickly than can courts. That is particularly true of a court, such as this Court, which does not conduct evidentiary hearings. It is true even more so where, as here, the need for action is immediate, the information likely limited, the making of exceptions difficult, and the disease-related circumstances rapidly changing.

Justice SOTOMAYOR with whom Justice KAGAN joins, dissenting.

Amidst a pandemic that has already claimed over a quarter million American lives, the Court today enjoins one of New York's public health measures aimed at containing the spread of COVID–19 in areas facing the most severe outbreaks. Earlier this year, this Court twice stayed its hand when asked to issue similar extraordinary relief. I see no justification for the Court's change of heart, and I fear that granting applications such as the one filed by the Roman Catholic Diocese of Brooklyn (Diocese) will only exacerbate the Nation's suffering.

New York applies "[s]imilar or more severe restrictions . . . to comparable secular gatherings, including lectures, concerts, movie showings, spectator sports, and theatrical performances, where large groups of people gather in close proximity for extended periods of time." Likewise, New York "treats more leniently only dissimilar activities, such as operating grocery stores, banks, and laundromats, in which people neither congregate in large groups nor remain in close proximity for extended periods." That should be enough to decide this case.

The Diocese suggests that, because New York's regulation singles out houses of worship by name, it cannot be neutral with respect to the practice of religion. Application 22. Thus, the argument goes, the regulation must, *ipso facto*, be subject to strict scrutiny. It is true that New York's policy refers to religion on its face. But as I have just explained, that is because the policy singles out religious institutions for preferential treatment in comparison to secular gatherings, not because it discriminates against them. Surely the Diocese cannot demand laxer restrictions by pointing out that it is already being treated better than comparable secular institutions.

Free religious exercise is one of our most treasured and jealously guarded constitutional rights. States may not discriminate against religious institutions, even when faced with a crisis as deadly as this one. But those principles are not at stake today. The Constitution does not forbid States from responding to public health crises through regulations that treat religious institutions equally or more favorably than comparable secular institutions, particularly when those regulations save lives. Because New York's COVID–19 restrictions do just that, I respectfully dissent.

***

TANDON v. NEWSOM
141 S. Ct. 1294 (2021)

PER CURIAM.

The Ninth Circuit's failure to grant an injunction pending appeal was erroneous. This Court's decisions have made the following points clear.

First, government regulations are not neutral and generally applicable, and therefore trigger strict scrutiny under the Free Exercise Clause, whenever they treat *any* comparable secular activity more favorably than religious exercise. *Roman Catholic Diocese of Brooklyn v. Cuomo* (2020) (*per curiam*). It is no answer that a State treats some comparable secular businesses or other activities as poorly as or even less favorably than the religious exercise at issue.

Second, whether two activities are comparable for purposes of the Free Exercise Clause must be judged against the asserted government interest that justifies the regulation at issue. Comparability is concerned with the risks various activities pose, not the reasons why people gather.

Third, the government has the burden to establish that the challenged law satisfies strict scrutiny. To do so in this context, it must do more than assert that certain risk factors "are always present in worship, or always absent from the other secular activities" the government may allow. Instead, narrow tailoring requires the government to show that measures less restrictive of the First Amendment activity could not address its interest in reducing the spread of COVID. Where the government permits other activities to proceed with precautions, it must show that the religious exercise at issue is more dangerous than those activities even when the same precautions are applied. Otherwise, precautions that suffice for other activities suffice for religious exercise too.

Fourth, even if the government withdraws or modifies a COVID restriction in the course of litigation, that does not necessarily moot the case. And so long as a case is not moot, litigants otherwise entitled to emergency injunctive relief remain entitled to such relief where the applicants "remain under a constant threat" that government officials will use their power to reinstate the challenged restrictions.

These principles dictated the outcome in this case. First, California treats some comparable secular activities more favorably than at-home religious exercise, permitting hair salons, retail stores, personal care services, movie theaters, private suites at sporting events and concerts, and indoor restaurants to bring together more than three households at a time. Second, the Ninth Circuit did not conclude that those activities pose a lesser risk of transmission than *applicants'* proposed religious exercise at home. Third, instead of requiring the State to explain why it could not safely permit at-home worshipers to gather in larger numbers while using precautions used in secular activities, the Ninth Circuit erroneously declared that such measures might not "translate readily" to the home. The State cannot "assume the worst when people go to worship but assume the best when people go to work." And fourth, although California officials changed the challenged policy shortly after this application was filed, the previous restrictions remain in place until April 15th, and officials with a track record of "moving the goalposts" retain authority to reinstate those heightened restrictions at any time.

Applicants are likely to succeed on the merits of their free exercise claim; they are irreparably harmed by the loss of free exercise rights "for even minimal periods of time"; and the State has not shown that "public health would be imperiled" by employing less restrictive measures. Accordingly, applicants are entitled to an injunction pending appeal.

The CHIEF JUSTICE would deny the application.

Justice KAGAN, with whom Justice BREYER and Justice SOTOMAYOR join, dissenting.

I would deny the application. The First Amendment requires that a State treat religious conduct as well as the State treats comparable secular conduct. Sometimes finding the right secular analogue may raise hard questions. But not today. California limits religious gatherings in homes to three households. If the State also limits all secular gatherings in homes to three households, it has complied with the First Amendment. And the State does exactly that: It has adopted a blanket restriction on at-home gatherings of all kinds, religious and secular alike. California need not, as the *per curiam* insists, treat at-home religious gatherings the same as hardware stores and hair salons — and thus unlike at-home secular gatherings, the obvious comparator here. As the *per curiam*'s reliance on separate opinions and unreasoned orders signals, the law does not require that the State equally treat apples and watermelons.

And even supposing a court should cast so expansive a comparative net, the *per curiam*'s analysis of this case defies the factual record. According to the *per curiam*, "the Ninth Circuit did not conclude that" activities like frequenting stores or salons "pose a lesser risk of transmission" than applicants' at-home religious activities. But Judges Milan Smith and Bade explained for the court that those activities do pose lesser risks for at least three reasons. First, "when people gather in social settings, their interactions are likely to be longer than they would be in a commercial setting," with participants "more likely to be involved in prolonged conversations." Second, "private houses are typically smaller and less ventilated than commercial establishments." And third, "social distancing and mask-wearing are less likely in private settings and enforcement is more difficult." These are not the mere musings of two appellate judges: The district court found each of these facts based on the uncontested testimony of California's public-health experts. No doubt this evidence is inconvenient for the *per curiam*'s preferred result. But the Court has no warrant to ignore the record in a case that (on its own view) turns on risk assessments.

In ordering California to weaken its restrictions on at-home gatherings, the majority yet again "insists on treating unlike cases, not like ones, equivalently." And it once more commands California "to ignore its experts' scientific findings," thus impairing "the State's effort to address a public health emergency." Because the majority continues to disregard law and facts alike, I respectfully dissent from this latest *per curiam* decision.